NATIVE LIFE IN SOUTH AFRICA

Solomon Tshekisho Plaatje

PRESENTED BY BRITAIN

Longman

Longman Group UK Limited,
Longman House, Burnt Mill, Harlow, Essex, CM20 2JE, England
and Associated Companies throughout the World

First published by P.S. King and Co., London 1916
First published in Longman African Classics 1987
Introduction © Brian Willan 1987

Set in Baskerville

Produced by Longman Group (FE) Ltd
Printed in Hong Kong

ISBN 0-582-78589-8

Contents

Introduction
Editor's note
Glossary
Prologue
1 A retrospect
2 The grim struggle between right and wrong
3 The Natives' Land Act
4 One night with the fugitives
5 Another night with the sufferers
6 Our indebtedness to white women
7 Persecution of coloured women in the
    Orange 'Free' State
8 At Thaba Ncho: a secretarial fiasco
9 The fateful thirteen
10 The Natives' Land Act in Cape Colony
11 The passing of Cape ideals
12 Tengo Jabavu, the pioneer native pressman
13 The Native Congress and the
    Union Government
14 The Kimberley Congress
15 The appeal for imperial protection
16 The London Press and the Natives' Land Act
17 The P.S.A. and Brotherhoods
18 Armed natives in the South African War
19 The South African races and the European War
20 Coloured people's help rejected
21 Epilogue
22 Report of the Lands Commission: an analysis

Introduction

Native Life in South Africa is one of South Africa's great political books and one of the most eloquent African political statements ever to have been written. First published in 1916, it was first and foremost a response to the Natives' Land Act of 1913, one of the most important and far-reaching pieces of legislation in South African history and a foundation-stone of today's *apartheid* state. *Native Life in South Africa* provides an account of the origins of this legislation, and a devastating description of some of its immediate effects. But it goes beyond this to explore the wider political and historical context that produced the policies embodied in the Land Act, and documents meticulously the steps taken by South Africa's rulers to exclude black South Africans from the exercise of political power up to the time of the First World War. It traces, too, the development of African opposition to this process, and contains an invaluable account of the early years of the South African Native National Congress, forerunner of today's African National Congress. The first book of its kind to have been written by a black South African, it has a unique importance as a political statement and testimony: not to its author alone, but to a generation of African political leaders and the early struggle for black political rights in South Africa.

Native Life in South Africa was written in a period when most politically active black South Africans placed great confidence in the due processes of law, in the patient representation of grievances through reasoned statement and debate, appeal and petition. These were methods that had yielded rewards in the past, and at the time there seemed every reason to believe that they would continue to do so. Africans living in the Cape Colony had long been accustomed to enjoying voting rights, and at the time of the Anglo-Boer war of 1899-1902 many had hoped that these rights would be extended to the Transvaal and Orange Free State. It was not to be. British imperial policy for Southern Africa after the war was directed towards reconciling Boer and Briton, and the price of this was the subordination of black political aspirations: in the new structures that took shape after the Peace of Vereeniging in 1902 the essential function of the black population, it became increasingly clear, was to be the provision of their labour.

At the same time, among South Africa's white rulers, a consensus of how best to resolve the contradiction between the aspirations of black South Africans and the role thus assigned to them began to emerge. It can be summed up in one word: segregation. In contrast to the Cape Colony's traditional policy of seeking to involve black South Africans in its affairs on a basis of class rather than race or colour, during the first decade of the twentieth century the predominant ruling-class policy for dealing with 'the native problem', as it was called, was the notion of restricting African land ownership to a very small part of South Africa's land surface, and within these areas erecting a local political and administrative structure within which black South African political aspirations were to be limited and contained.

With the creation of the Union of South Africa in 1910 the transformation of these ideas into a coherent programme of legislation was brought a step closer. For a while there was a period of inactivity, of consolidation, as blacks and whites alike came to terms with the new conditions created by the Act of Union. But during the second year of Union the government's intentions became clearer, and in 1913 the first stage of this grand legislative programme was laid before the South African House of Assembly: the Natives' Land Bill (reproduced in Chapter 3). It proposed to confine African land holding to less than ten per cent of the land surface of the Union of South Africa, and it contained a variety of other provisions that sought, in essence, to meet the insistent demands of white farmers for more cheap labour. In particular, it responded to the demands of white farmers in the Transvaal and Orange Free State to have sharecroppers living on their land transformed into farm labourers or servants. It was with the effects of these clauses of the Land Act (as it became in June 1913) that Plaatje was to be particularly concerned in *Native Life in South Africa*, and he spent many weeks travelling in the countryside investigating the effects of their implementation: his descriptions of what he saw provide perhaps the most moving chapters of the book.

The Natives' Land Act provoked an unprecedented level of political activity and protest among black South Africans. The South African Native National Congress had been formed in January 1912, but the effect of the promulgation of this piece of legislation was to galvanise it into action across the country: nothing contributed more to securing its acceptance as a national movement, or of overcoming the geographical and social divisions that had hitherto proved such a stumbling block to the emergence of a united African political movement. Under the leadership of John Dube, its President, and Plaatje himself as Secretary, Congress brought its protests before the South African authorities, pleading that the act be suspended. When their requests were ignored they decided to take the one constitutional option that remained open to them: to appeal to the British imperial government in London, which still possessed the right, constitutionally speaking, to disallow any legislation passed by the South African parliament. In May 1914 the deputation that had been elected—consisting of John Dube, Walter Rubusana, Saul Msane, T.M. Mapikela, and Solomon Plaatje—departed for England.

Plaatje began writing what became *Native Life in South Africa* on board the ship that took the delegates to England: 'I am compiling this little book on the Natives' Land Act and its operation', he wrote, 'which I hope to get through the press immediately after landing in England'. His intention was that the book should help in their campaign to bring their case before the British public—for they had few illusions that the British Colonial Secretary, Lord Harcourt, was likely to accede to their requests. From the beginning *Native Life in South Africa* was conceived as part of a political campaign, and formulated primarily as an appeal to the British people.

2

Such were the circumstances in which *Native Life in South Africa* was conceived and the political context from which it arose: they are themselves covered in far more detail in the book itself. But what of the author, Solomon Plaatje? Despite his Dutch-sounding surname, Plaatje was of Barolong origin, and had been born in the Boshop district of the Orange Free State in 1876. He was brought up on a German mission station at Pniel, close to Barkly West, had only a primary education, and moved to Kimberley in 1894 to take up a job as a letter-carrier with the post office. Studying assiduously in his spare time he mastered six African languages (he also spoke English, Dutch, and German), and four years later moved to Mafeking to become clerk and interpreter at the local magistrate's court. During the famous siege, which he survived unscathed, he gave valuable help to the British military authorities—'so satisfactory', he wrote later, that Charles Bell, the magistrate for whom he worked, 'was created a C.M.G. at the end of the siege'. He gained an important insight, too, into the world of journalism through his contact with the war correspondents in Mafeking, several of whom he worked for as well.

Shortly afterwards, Plaatje left the Cape Civil Service to become editor of an English/Tswana newspaper, *Koranta ea Becoana* ('The Bechuana Gazette'), started with the assistance of a local Barolong chief, Silas Molema. It provided Plaatje with the opportunity to utilise his talents in a way that the Cape Civil Service could no longer accommodate, and the means too of giving expression to the sense of responsibility for the leadership of his people that he believed his knowledge and abilities fitted him for. Over the next few years Plaatje built up a reputation as a spokesman for his people, bringing grievances to the attention of the authorities, succeeding very often in securing at least some degree of redress. But by the end of the first decade of the twentieth century *Koranta ea Becoana* was finally overcome by financial difficulties and Plaatje himself spent an unhappy period seeking to make a living through recruiting labour for the mines on the Witwatersrand: so pressing were his financial difficulties, indeed, that he was prevented from taking any part in the upsurge of political activity among Africans in response to the creation of the Union of South Africa in 1910.

Later that year, though, Plaatje moved to Kimberley once again to become the editor of a new newspaper — *Tsala ea Becoana* ('The Friend of the Bechuana'), later renamed *Tsala ea Batho* ('The Friend of the People'). He was one of the founders of the South African Native National Congress, was elected its first General Secretary, and it was he more than anybody else who led the mounting opposition to the Natives' Land Act in 1913 and 1914. Once it was decided to send a deputation to England it was natural that Plaatje should have been elected a member of it—recognition both of his talents for organisation and leadership, and of the special efforts he had made to investigate the drastic effects of the Natives' Land Act, reported first in the columns of his newspaper, later in the pages of *Native Life in South Africa*. It can have come as little surprise to his fellow delegates that he planned to develop the results of these investigations into book form. Thus it was that Plaatje busied himself with this task on the voyage to England.

3

Plaatje did not succeed, however, in his plan to get the book published immediately after landing in England: in fact, it did not appear until nearly two years later, a delay which was to have an important bearing upon the shape and content of the book as a whole. Above all it was influenced by the outbreak of the First World War at the beginning of August 1914, and by Plaatje's consequent perception of the need to link the presentation of his case to the British public with the war against Germany. His account of the Natives' Land Act and its effects thus became subsumed within a wider and very much more comprehensive political and historical commentary upon South African affairs, his overriding aim being to demonstrate the loyalty of the African people to the cause of the imperial government—past and present—in the hope that this would ultimately move the authorities to due recognition of their political rights and redress of their grievances; and to secure, above all, the repeal of the Natives' Land Act.

At the same time as Plaatje worked on *Native Life in South Africa* in late 1914 and early 1915 he was also conducting a one-man campaign, addressing meetings throughout the United Kingdom: again, the best account of this is to be found in the book itself. Plaatje's fellow delegates on the Congress delegation had returned home to South Africa shortly after the war broke out, leaving him to continue with his work and to see his book through to publication. It was Plaatje's own decision to stay on in England, and it was a courageous thing to do: he was almost penniless, he risked jeopardising the future of his newspaper business in Kimberley by staying away, and he now faced the problem of interesting the British public in the cause of his people in what must have seemed a remote part of the empire, at a time when their overwhelming preoccupation was with the war against Germany.

In the circumstances the completion and publication of *Native Life in South Africa* in May 1916 was a remarkable achievement, accomplished in the face of difficulties that would have defeated all but the most determined and resourceful of men. The greatest problem he faced was raising the money to finance the printing of the book. Plaatje had hoped that the Barolong chief, Lekoko, would send the money he needed for this, but Lekoko died in June 1915 before sending anything, and so Plaatje was left to try to raise what was required in England himself. His task was not made any easier by the fierce opposition he encountered from John Harris, Organising Secretary of the influential Anti-Slavery and Aborigines' Protection Society, the one organisation that might have been expected to be sympathetic to his cause. Harris could have raised the money to see *Native Life* through to publication had he so wished, but his view was that the principle of segregation—which he believed to be embodied in the Natives' Land Act—should be supported in the best interests of the African people, and he therefore actively discouraged potential contributors from giving Plaatje any money for this purpose: small wonder that several years later Plaatje was to comment bitterly upon the eleven months he had spent 'fighting Harris who was battling to suppress *Native Life* in the press'.

4

The sacrifices that Plaatje had made in the course of his long struggle to get *Native Life in South Africa* published were more than justified by the response to it, although in England this was inevitably muted by the continuing public preoccupation with the war against Germany. Apart from John Harris, who sought to discredit both the book and its author, *Native Life* was on the whole favourably reviewed, and nearly all the reviews acknowledged that Plaatje had presented a powerful case which at the very least needed answering. Most were agreed, however, that nothing could or should be done until the successful conclusion of the war: General Botha, the South African Prime Minister, was, after all, a valued wartime ally of the British government and had problems enough of his own in South Africa without these being added to them. Consideration of Plaatje's case, in effect, was to be suspended for the duration of the war.

In South Africa, reactions to *Native Life in South Africa* were rather stronger. The book was a sustained attack upon the ideas justifying policies of segregation, and Plaatje's predictions of what was likely to be added to the areas set aside for African occupation seemed only to be confirmed by the Report of the Lands Commission in 1916. This had been set up in terms of the legislation of 1913 to try to find more land for African occupation, but as Plaatje had predicted in *Native Life*, its offerings were meagre in the extreme. Even he was staggered at the manner in which the Report contrived to do this: 'Until this Report reached me', he wrote, 'I never would have believed my white fellow countrymen capable of conceiving the all but diabolical schemes propounded between the covers of Volume I of the Report of the South African Lands Commission, 1916, and clothing them in such plausible forms as to mislead even sincere and well-informed friends of the natives.'*

Native Life in South Africa brought Plaatje both fame and

notoriety. It was a measure of the impact the book made (it was reprinted several times between 1917 and 1919) that it was on several occasions discussed in the South African House of Assembly. On one of these occasions the Minister of Lands described it as a 'scurrilous attack upon the Boers': on another, Plaatje was accused of 'endeavouring to spread the belief that the Boer was the oppressor of the natives'. General Botha's view of the book was somewhat more restrained, but hostile nevertheless. 'Mr Plaatje', he wrote,

> is a special pleader, and consciously or unconsciously he has, in my opinion, been somewhat biased in his strictures against the Government in regard to the Natives' Land Act: he has exaggerated incidents which tell in his favour, and suppressed facts that should be within his knowledge which show the honest attempts made by the Government to avoid the infliction of hardships in carrying out a principle which, you must remember, was sanctioned by the legislature.

Plaatje's point, of course, was that only when that legislature was fully representative of the people of South Africa could its deliberations and enactments be justified in claiming authority.

Among Plaatje's own people *Native Life in South Africa* was received rather differently. If the comments made upon the book in the South African House of Assembly were a measure of the predominant white view of the book, then the decision of the South African Native National Congress to offer Plaatje the presidency of the organisation in 1917 (several months after he had returned home from England) was a measure of his reputation among the African people. Plaatje turned down the offer because, he wrote, 'the deterioration of my business during my enforced absence made the idea utterly impossible'. The struggle to get *Native Life* published had indeed had dire personal consequences: Plaatje had fallen heavily into debt during the two and a half years he had spent in England; his newspaper *Tsala ea Batho*, had been forced

---

*Plaatje's analysis of the Report of the Lands Commission was included in second and subsequent editions of *Native Life in South Africa*, and forms the final chapter of the present edition.

to cease publication (it never resumed); and his family, too, had been forced to borrow heavily during this absence. Plaatje was simply not in a position to contemplate taking on the onerous position of the presidency of Congress with these difficulties still to be resolved. His colleague, S.M. Makgotho, assumed the leadership of Congress instead, although Plaatje did agree to become Vice-President.

Two years later, in 1919, Plaatje returned to England, this time as the leader of a second Congress delegation. Believing that the outbreak of war in 1914 had prevented the first Congress delegation from fulfilling its mission, Plaatje and his colleagues hoped now to capitalise upon the impact that he had made in England with his book and the campaign of which it was part. Ultimately, they met with no more success than the first delegation, but on this occasion they did at least secure an interview with David Lloyd George, the British Prime Minister. He listened sympathetically, wrote to General Smuts (by now the South African Prime Minister) about the matter, but could do no more. South Africa was a self-governing dominion of the empire, and the British authorities had no desire to intervene in its affairs, least of all in order to change policies for which they had so large a measure of responsibility. Plaatje nevertheless continued with his campaign to enlighten the British public about the conditions faced by his people in South Africa, and produced a pamphlet entitled *Some of the Legal Disabilities Suffered by the Native Population of the Union of South Africa and Imperial Responsibility*, and then wrote another book which he described as a 'companion volume' to *Native Life in South Africa*, his intention being to provide a political commentary upon South African affairs from the point where *Native Life* leaves off in 1916. Sadly, this volume was never published, and all trace of it has disappeared: *Native Life in South Africa*, rather than being the first of two volumes, thus stands alone.

Thereafter, Plaatje took his campaign to Canada and the United States of America, finally returning home to South Africa late in 1923, accepting at last that there was no longer any prospect of securing any form of outside intervention on behalf of his people. During the remaining nine years of his life he continued to fight for the political rights of his people from a variety of platforms, he was heavily involved in the temperance movement, and he devoted much time and energy to writing in his native language of Setswana. In 1930 he succeeded at last in finding a publisher for his historical epic, *Mhudi*, written (in English) in London ten years earlier.

In his many contributions to the press Plaatje nevertheless returned time and time again to the effects of the Natives' Land Act. Whereas *Native Life in South Africa* had been his response to the immediate effects of the legislation, he continued—in the 1920s and early 1930s—to attribute much of what he saw around him, in both town and countryside, to the longer-term consequences of the act: the poverty, the landlessness, the overcrowding, the despair that he so often encountered on his travels. For all of this he continued to believe that the Natives' Land Act carried a heavy burden of responsibility.

5

Native Life in South Africa stands today as very much more than the product of a forgotten phase in the African political struggle. Since the passage of the Natives' Land Act in 1913 the South African state has continued to exclude the majority of its population from the exercise of political power, substituting instead a succession of segregated institutions based on the geographical areas delineated for African occupation in the Land Act. After the Land Act itself came the Native Affairs Act in 1920, the Natives (Urban Areas) Act in 1923, the Native Administration Act in 1927, and in 1936 a package of legislative measures (the so-called Hertzog bills) which added marginally to the areas set aside for African occupation by the original Natives' Land Act, established new forms of segregated consultative machinery, and removed Africans from the common voters' roll in the Cape Colony. Throughout the 1930s Plaatje and his colleagues had fought consistently against the introduction of this legislation: in some ways it was perhaps as well that he did not live long enough to experience his own disfranchisement, for this he would have regarded as the ultimate betrayal of the political ideals for which he stood.

Since the 1920s and 1930s the terminology used by successive South African governments for these policies has changed over the years: 'segregation' gave way to 'separate development', then to 'multinational development', while the 'reserves' of Plaatje's day became 'homelands', 'Bantustans' and more recently have assumed the trappings of 'independent states', although their 'independence' is recognised by no other country except South Africa. In essence the policy has remained the same: one only has to compare what the Natives' Land Act defined as 'reserves' and 'scheduled areas' in 1913 with the areas of land occupied by today's 'independent states' (see map on p. xix) to see how little has really changed, or to appreciate how significant the Land Act has been in laying the legislative and territorial foundations of present-day South Africa. The origins of today's apartheid state, as *Native Life in South Africa* so clearly reveals, are to be found well before the accession to power of the ruling Afrikaner Nationalist government in 1948.

Plaatje had little doubt about the eventual outcome of the policies he condemned in *Native Life in South Africa*. A man of great vision, he warned—here and elsewhere—of the ultimate consequences for his country if the policies embodied in the Natives' Land Act were pursued to their logical conclusion. As if it were too painful to spell it out himself, Plaatje used the words of another writer and poet—quoted in the final chapter of the book—to warn of what lay ahead if South Africa's rulers did not change course.

Since Plaatje's day the nature of black political protest in South Africa has changed. Exhausting all hope of persuading South Africa's rulers to change their policies by force of argument and appeal to a common humanity, the African nationalist movement moved slowly, often very hesitantly, towards more forceful methods of protest. After the Second World War the African National Congress adopted a strategy of passive resistance, and launched its famous Defiance Campaign in 1952. Failing to influence the South African government through such means, the ANC resorted eventually to the policy of armed struggle to which it is today committed. Such methods are very different from those advocated by Plaatje in *Native Life in South Africa*, but it was necessary that these should have been tried and found wanting before new forms of protest could develop. *Native Life in South Africa* remains the classic statement and account of the early stages of a struggle which continues today.

BRIAN WILLAN

Editor's note

This edition of *Native Life in South Africa* has been slightly abridged so as to make it more accessible for the modern reader. A number of passages from other books, documents, newspaper reports and parliamentary debates from which Plaatje quotes at length have been abbreviated, and in some cases omitted, where this could be done without affecting the thrust of his argument.

In addition, four chapters from the original edition have been omitted entirely. These are:

1. The chapter entitled 'Dr Abdurahman, President of the APO', which fell between 'The Fateful Thirteen' (Chapter 9) and 'The Land Act in Cape Colony' (Chapter 10), consisting almost exclusively of a long speech by Dr Abdurahman against the policies of the Union government in 1913.

2. Two chapters which came after Chapter 20, entitled 'The South African Boers and the European War' and 'The Boer Rebellion', tracing Boer reactions to the outbreak of the First World War and the subsequent rebellion (late in 1914) against the South African government. Plaatje had originally intended to include these in his book in order to contrast the behaviour of the Boers with that of the African population, whom he portrayed as loyal supporters of the South African and imperial governments in the war against Germany, and hence entitled to justice in their political claims.

3. A chapter entitled 'Piet Grobler' which Plaatje included immediately before his 'Epilogue' (now numbered Chapter 21), consisting of an attack upon one of the most vehemently 'anti-British' South African members of parliament, and originally written as a lecture in his campaign in England.

Editor's Note

Chapter 22, 'Report of the Lands Commission: an analysis', did not appear in the first edition of *Native Life in South Africa*, but Plaatje added it to the second and subsequent editions of the book once he had had the opportunity to read and comment upon the report, and it has been included in the present edition in view of its centrality to the Natives' Land Act, Plaatje's main concern in the book. Finally, my own introduction and the earlier biographical sketch replace the two-page section Plaatje included about himself in the original edition, most of which consisted of a short account of his life (up to 1910), written by Vere Stent, editor of the *Pretoria News*.

B.W.

Glossary of Dutch (Afrikaans) words and phrases

backvelder	person from the countryside
'Dag Jong'	Good day (young fellow)
dorp	small town or village
haakdoorns	acacia trees
karosses	sheepskin rugs
kleintjies	little ones
kopje	small hill
morgen	unit of land measurement, equivalent to just over two acres
predikant	minister
rondloper	vagabond
schepsels	creatures
taal	local dialect of Dutch (Afrikaans)
velbroeks	skin trousers
veldschoens	shoes
voortrekker	one of the Boer pioneers who left the Cape Colony in the 1830s to escape British rule
vrouw	woman, housewife
vuilgoed	rubbish

Prologue

We have often read books, written by well-known scholars, who disavow, on behalf of their works, any claim to literary perfection. How much more necessary, then, that a South African native working man, who has never received any secondary training, should in attempting authorship disclaim, on behalf of this work, any title to literary merit. Mine is but a sincere narrative of a melancholy situation, in which, with all its shortcomings, I have endeavoured to describe the difficulties of the South African natives under a very strange law, so as most readily to be understood by the sympathetic reader.

The information contained in the following chapters is the result of personal observations made by the author in certain districts of the Transvaal, Orange 'Free' State and the Province of the Cape of Good Hope. In pursuance of this private inquiry, I reached Ladybrand early in September 1913, when, my financial resources being exhausted, I decided to drop the inquiry and return home. But my friend, Mr W.Z. Fenyang, of the farm Rietfontein, in the 'Free' State, offered to convey me to the south of Moroka district, where I saw much of the trouble, and further, he paid my railway fare from Thaba Ncho back to Kimberley.

In the following November, it was felt that as Mr Saul Msane, the organiser for the South African Native National Congress, was touring the eastern districts of the Transvaal, and Mr Dube, the President, was touring the northern districts and Natal, and as the finances of the Congress did not permit an additional traveller, no information would be forthcoming in regard to the operation of the mischievous Act in the Cape Province. So Mr J.M. Nyokong, of the farm Maseru, offered to bear part of the expenses if I would undertake a visit to the Cape. I must add that beyond spending six weeks on the tour to the Cape, the visit did not cost me much, for Mr W.D. Soga, of King Williamstown, very generously supplemented Mr Nyokong's offer and accompanied me on a part of the journey.

Besides the information received and the hospitality enjoyed from these and other friends, the author is indebted, for further information, to Mr Attorney Msimang, of Johannesburg. Mr Msimang toured some of the districts, compiled a list of some of the sufferers from the Natives' Land Act, and learnt the circumstances of their eviction. His list, however, is not full, its compilation having been undertaken in May 1914, when the main exodus of the evicted tenants to the cities and Protectorates had already taken place, and when eyewitnesses of the evils of the Act had already fled the country. But it is useful in showing that the persecution is still continuing, for, according to this list, a good many families were evicted a year after the Act was enforced, and many more were at that time under notice to quit. Mr Msimang modestly states, in an explanatory note, that his pamphlet contains 'comparatively few instances of actual cases of hardship under the Natives' Land Act, 1913, to vindicate the leaders of the South African Native National Congress from the gross imputation, by the Native Affairs Department, that they make general allegations of hardships without producing any specific cases that can bear examination'. Mr Msimang, who took a number of sworn statements from the sufferers, adds that 'in Natal, for example, all of these instances have been reported to the magistrates and the Chief Native Commissioner. Every time they are told to find themselves other places, or remain where they are under labour conditions. At Peters and Colworth, seventy-nine and a hundred families respectively are being ejected by the Government itself without providing land for them.'

Some readers may perhaps think that I have taken the colonial Parliament rather severely to task. But to any reader who holds with Bacon, that 'the pencil hath laboured more in describing the afflictions of Job than the felicities of Solomon', I would say: 'Do, if we dare make the request, and place yourself in our shoes.' If, after a proper declaration of war, you found your kinsmen driven from pillar to post in the manner that the South African Natives have been harried and scurried by Act No.27 of 1913, you would, though aware that it is part of the fortunes of war, find it difficult to suppress your hatred of the enemy. Similarly, if you see your countrymen and countrywomen driven from home, their homes broken up, with no hopes of redress, on the mandate of a Government to which they had loyally paid taxation without representation—driven from their homes, because they do not want to become servants; and when you know that half of these homeless ones have perforce submitted to the conditions and accepted service on terms that are unprofitable to themselves; if you remember that more would have submitted but for the fact that no master has any use of a servant with forty head of cattle, or a hundred or more sheep; and if you further bear in mind that many landowners are anxious to live at peace with, and to keep your people as tenants, but that they are debarred from doing so by your Government which threatens them with a fine of £100 or six months' imprisonment, you would, I think, likewise find it very difficult to maintain a level head or wield a temperate pen.

For instance, let us say, the London County Council decrees that no man shall rent a room, or hire a house, in the City of London unless he be a servant in the employ of the landlord, adding that there shall be a fine of one hundred pounds on anyone who attempts to sell a house to a non-householder; imagine such a thing and its effects, then you have some approach to an accurate picture of the operation of the South African Natives' Land Act of 1913. In conclusion, let me ask the reader's support in our campaign for the repeal of such a law, and in making this request I pray that none of my readers may live to find themselves in a position so intolerable.

This appeal is not on behalf of the naked hordes of cannibals who are represented in fantastic pictures displayed in the shop-windows in Europe, most of them imaginary; but it is on behalf of five million loyal British subjects who shoulder 'the black man's burden' every day, doing so without looking forward to any decoration or thanks. 'The black man's burden' includes the faithful performance of all the unskilled and least-paying labour in South Africa, the payment of direct taxation to the various municipalities, at the rate of from 1s to 5s per mensem per capita (to develop and beautify the white quarters of the towns while the black quarters remain unattended) besides taxes to the provincial and central Government, varying from 12s to £3 12s per annum, for the maintenance of Government schools from which native children are excluded. In addition to these native duties and taxes, it is also part of 'the black man's burden' to pay all duties levied from the favoured race. With the increasing difficulty of finding openings to earn the money for paying these multifarious taxes, the dumb pack-ox, being inarticulate in the councils of state, has no means of making known to its keeper that the burden is straining its back to breaking-point.

When Sir John French appealed to the British people for more shells during Easter week, the Governor-General of South Africa, addressing a fashionable crowd at the City Hall, Johannesburg, most of whom had never seen the mouth of a mine, congratulated them on the fact that 'under the strain of war and rebellion the gold industry had been maintained at full pitch', and he added that 'every ounce of gold was worth many shells to the allies'. But His Excellency had not a word of encouragement for the 200,000 subterranean heroes who by day and night, for a mere pittance, lay down their limbs and their lives to the familiar 'fall of rock' and who, at deep levels ranging from 1,000 feet to 1,000 yards in the bowels of the earth, sacrifice their lungs to the rock dust which develops miners' phthisis and pneumonia—poor reward, but a sacrifice that enables the world's richest gold mines, in the Johannesburg area alone, to maintain the credit of the empire with a weekly output of £750,000 worth of raw gold. Surely the appeal of chattels who render service of such great value deserves the attention of the British people.

Finally, I would say as Professor Du Bois says in his book *The Souls of Black Folk,* on the relations between the sons of master and man, 'I have not glossed over matters for policy's sake, for I fear we have already gone too far in that sort of

4

thing. On the other hand I have sincerely sought to let no unfair exaggerations creep in. I do not doubt that in some communities conditions are better than those I have indicated; while I am no less certain that in other communities they are far worse.'

1   A retrospect

Awaking on Friday morning, June 20, 1913, the South African native found himself, not actually a slave, but a pariah in the land of his birth.

The 4,500,000 black South Africans are domiciled as follows: one and three-quarter millions in locations and reserves, over half a million within municipalities or in urban areas, and nearly a million as squatters on farms owned by Europeans. The remainder are employed either on the public roads or railway lines, or as servants by European farmers, qualifying, that is, by hard work and saving to start farming on their own account.

A squatter in South Africa is a native who owns some live-stock and, having no land of his own, hires a farm or grazing and ploughing rights from a landowner to raise grain for his own use and feed his stock. Hence, these squatters are hit very hard by an Act which passed both Houses of Parliament during the session of 1913, received the signature of the Governor-General on June 16, was gazetted on June 19, and forthwith came into operation. It may here be mentioned that on that day Lord Gladstone signed no fewer than sixteen new acts of Parliament—some of them being rather voluminous—while three days earlier, His Excellency signed another batch of eight, of which the bulk was beyond the capability of any mortal to read and digest in four days.

But the great revolutionary change thus wrought by a single stroke of the pen, in the condition of the native, was not realized by him until about the end of June. As a rule many farm tenancies expire at the end of the half-year, so that in June 1913, not knowing that it was impracticable to make fresh contracts, some natives unwittingly went to search for new places of abode, which some farmers, ignorant of the law, quite as unwittingly accorded to them. It was only when they went to register the new tenancies that the law officers of the Crown laid bare the cruel fact that to provide a landless native with accommodation was forbidden under a penalty of £100, or six months imprisonment. Then only was the situation realized.

Other natives who had taken up fresh places on European farms under verbal contracts, which needed no registration, actually founded new homes in spite of the law, neither the white farmer nor the native tenant being aware of the serious penalties they were exposed to by their verbal contracts.

In justice to the Government, it must be stated that no police officers scoured the country in search of law-breakers, to prosecute them under this law. Had this been done, many £100 cheques would have passed into the Government coffers during that black July, the first month after Lord Gladstone affixed his signature to the Natives' Land Act, No.27 of 1913.

The complication of this cruel law is made manifest by the fact that it was found necessary for a high officer of the Government to tour the provinces soon after the Act came into force, with the object of 'teaching' magistrates how to administer it. A congress of magistrates—a most unusual thing—was also called in Pretoria to find a way for carrying out the King's writ in the face of the difficulties arising from this tangle of the Act. We may add that nearly all white lawyers in South Africa, to whom we spoke about this measure, had either not seen the Act at all, or had not read it carefully, so that in both cases they could not tell exactly for whose benefit it had been passed. The study of this law required a much longer time than the lawyers, unless specially briefed, could devote to it, so that they hardly knew what all the trouble was about. It was the native in the four provinces who knew all about it, for he had not read it in books but had himself been through its mill, which like an automatic machine ground him relentlessly since the end of the month of June. Not the least but one of the cruellest and most ironical phases—and nearly every clause of this Act teems with irony—is the Schedule or appendix giving the so-called Scheduled Native Areas; and what are these 'Scheduled Native Areas'?

7

They are the native locations which were reserved for the exclusive use of certain native clans. They are inalienable and cannot be bought or sold, yet the Act says that in these 'Scheduled Native Areas' natives only may buy land. The areas being inalienable, not even members of the clans, for whose benefit the locations are held in trust, can buy land therein. The areas could only be sold if the whole clan rebelled; in that case the location would be confiscated. But as long as the clans of the location remain loyal to the Government, nobody can buy any land within these areas. Under the respective charters of these areas, not even a member of the clan can get a separate title as owner in an area—let alone a native outsider who had grown up among white people and done all his farming on white man's land.

If we exclude the arid tracts of Bechuanaland, these locations appear to have been granted on such a small scale that each of them got so overcrowded that much of the population had to go out and settle on the farms of white farmers through lack of space in the locations. Yet a majority of the legislators, although well aware of all these limitations, and without remedying any of them, legislate shall we say, 'with its tongue in its cheek' that only natives may buy land in native locations.

Again, the locations form but one-eighteenth of the total area of the Union, leaving the remaining seventeen parts for the one million whites. It is moreover true that, numerically, the Act was passed by the consent of a majority of both Houses of Parliament, but it is equally true that it was steam-rolled into the statute book against the bitterest opposition of the best brains of both Houses. A most curious aspect of this singular law is that even the Minister, since deceased, who introduced it, subsequently declared himself against it, adding that he only forced it through in order to stave off something worse. Indeed, it is correct to say that Mr Sauer, who introduced the Bill, spoke against it repeatedly in the House; he deleted the milder provisions, inserted more drastic amendments, then in conclusion he would combat his own arguments by calling the ministerial steamroller to support the Government and vote for the drastic amendments. The only explanation of the puzzle constituted as such by these 'hot-and-cold' methods is that Mr Sauer was legislating for an electorate, at the expense of another section of the population which was without direct representation in Parliament. None of the non-European races in the provinces of Natal, Transvaal and the 'Free' State can exercise the franchise. They have no say in the selection of members for the Union Parliament. That right is only limited to white men, so that a large number of the members of Parliament who voted for this measure have no responsibility towards the black races.

Before reproducing this tyrannical enactment it would perhaps be well to recapitulate briefly the influences that led up to it. When the Union of the South African colonies became an accomplished fact, a dread was expressed by ex-Republicans that the liberal native policy of the Cape would supersede the repressive policy of the old Republics, and they lost no time in taking definite steps to force down the throats of the Union legislature, as it were, laws which the Dutch Presidents of pre-war days, with the British suzerainty over their heads, did not dare enforce against the native people then under them. With the formation of the Union, the Imperial Government, for reasons which had never been satisfactorily explained, unreservedly handed over the natives to the colonists, and these colonists, as a rule, are dominated by the Dutch Republican spirit. Thus the suzerainty of Great Britain, which under the reign of Her late Majesty Victoria, of blessed memory, was the natives' only bulwark, has not apparently been withdrawn or relaxed and the Republicans, like a lot of bloodhounds long held in the leash, use the free hand given by the Imperial Government not only to guard against a possible supersession of Cape ideals of toleration, but to effectively extend throughout the Union the drastic native policy pursued by the province which is misnamed 'Free' State, and enforce it with the utmost rigour.

During the first year of the Union, it would seem that General Botha made an honest attempt to live up to his London promises, that are mentioned by Mr Merriman in his speech (reproduced elsewhere) on the second reading of the bill in Parliament. It would seem that General Botha endeavoured to allay British apprehensions and concern for the welfare of the native population. In pursuance of this policy General Botha won the approbation of all natives by appointing Hon. H. Burton, a Cape minister, to the portfolio of Native Affairs. That the appointment was a happy one, from the native point of view, became manifest when Mr Burton signalized the ushering in of Union, by releasing Chief Dinizulu-ka-Cetywayo, who at that time was undergoing a sentence of imprisonment imposed by the Natal Supreme Court, and by the restoration to Dinizulu of his pension of £500 a year. Also, in deference to the wishes of the Native Congress, Mr Burton abrogated two particularly obnoxious Natal measures, one legalizing the 'Sibalo' system of forced labour, the other prohibiting public meetings by natives without the consent of the Government. These abrogations placed the natives of Natal in almost the same position as the Cape natives though without giving them the franchise. So, too, when a drastic Squatters' Bill was gazetted early in 1912, and the recently formed Native National Congress sent a deputation to interview Mr Burton in Cape Town; after hearing the deputation, he graciously consented to withdraw the proposed measure, pending the allotment of new locations in which natives evicted by such a measure could find an asylum. In further deference to the representations of the Native Congress, in which they were supported by Senators the Hon. W.P. Schreiner, Colonel Stanford, and Mr Krogh, the Union Government gazetted another bill in January 1911, to amend an anomaly which, at that time, was peculiar to the 'Free' State: an anomaly under which a native can neither purchase nor lease land, and native landowners in the 'Free' State could only sell their land to the white people.

The gazetted bill proposed to legalize only in one district of the Orange 'Free' State the sale of landed property by a native to another native as well as to a white man, but it did not propose to enable natives to buy land from white men. The object of the bill was to remove a hardship, mentioned elsewhere in this sketch, by which a 'Free' State native was by law debarred from inheriting landed property left to him under his uncle's will. But against such small attempts at reform, proposed or carried out by the Union

Government in the interest of the natives, granted in small instalments of a teaspoonful at a time — reforms dictated solely by feelings of justice and equity — ex-Republicans were furious.

From platform, press, and pulpit it was suggested that General Botha's administration was too English and needed overhauling. The Dutch peasants along the countryside were inflamed by hearing that their gallant leader desired to anglicize the country. Nothing was more repellent to the ideas of the back-veld Dutch, and so at small meetings in the country districts resolutions were passed stating that the Botha administration had outlived its usefulness. These resolutions reaching the press from day to day had the effect of stirring up the Dutch voters against the ministry, and particularly against the head. At this time General Botha's sound policy began to weaken. He transferred Hon. H. Burton, first Minister of Natives, to the portfolio of Railways and Harbours, and appointed General Hertzog, of all people in the world, to the portfolio of Native Affairs.

The good-humoured indulgence of some Dutch and English farmers towards their native squatters, and the affectionate loyalty of some of these native squatters in return, will cause a keen observer, arriving at a South African farm, to be lost in admiration for this mutual good feeling. He will wonder as to the meaning of the fabled bugbear anent the alleged struggle between white and black, which in reality appears to exist only in the fertile brains of the politician. Thus let the new arrival go to one of the farms in Bethlehem or Harrismith districts for example, and see how willingly the native toils in the fields; see him gathering in his crops and handing over the white farmer's share of the crop to the owner of the land; watch the farmer receiving his tribute from the native tenants, and see him deliver the first prize to the native tenant who raised the largest crop during that season; let him also see both the natives, and the landowning white farmers following to perfection the give-and-take policy of 'live and let live', and he will conclude that it would be gross sacrilege to attempt to disturb such harmonious relations between these people of different races and colours. But with a ruthless hand the Natives' Land Act

11

has succeeded in remorselessly destroying those happy relations.

First of all, General Hertzog, the new Minister of Native Affairs, travelled up and down the country lecturing farmers on their folly in letting ground to the natives; the racial extremists of his party hailed him as the right man for the post, for, as his conduct showed them, he would soon 'fix up' the natives. At one or two places he was actually welcomed as the future Prime Minister of the Union. On the other hand, General Botha, who at that time seemed to have become visibly timid, endeavoured to ingratiate himself with his discontented supporters by joining his lieutenant in travelling to and fro, denouncing the Dutch farmers for not expelling the natives from their farms and replacing them with poor whites. This became a regular ministerial campaign against the natives, so that it seemed clear that if any native could still find a place in the land, it was not due to the action of the Government. In his campaign the Premier said other unhappy things which were diametrically opposed to his London speeches of two years before; and while the Dutch colonists railed at him for trying to anglicise the country, English speakers and writers justly accused him of speaking with two voices; cartoonists, too, caricatured him as having two heads—one, they said, for London, and the second one for South Africa.

The uncertain tenure by which Englishmen in the public service held their posts became the subject of debates in the Union Parliament, and the employment of Government servants of colour was decidedly precarious. They were swept out of the railway and postal service with a strong racial broom, in order to make room for poor whites, mainly of Dutch descent. Concession after concession was wrung from the Government by fanatically Dutch postulants for office, for Government doles and other favours, who, like the daughters of the horse-leech in the Proverbs of Solomon, continually cried, 'Give, give'. By these events we had clearly turned the corner and were pacing backwards to pre-Union days, going back, back, and still further backward, to the conditions which prevailed in the old Republics, and (if a check is not applied) we shall steadily drift back to the old days of the old Dutch East Indian administration.

The bill which proposed to ameliorate the 'Free' State cruelty, to which reference has been made above, was dropped like a hot potato. Ministers made some wild and undignified speeches, of which the following spicy extract, from a speech by the Rt. Hon. Abraham Fisher to his constituents at Bethlehem, is a typical sample:

'What is it you want?' he asked. 'We have passed all the collie[1] laws and we have passed all the Kaffir laws. The ''Free'' State has been safeguarded and all her colour laws have been adopted by Parliament. What more can the Government do for you?' And so the Union ship in this reactionary sea sailed on and on and on, until she struck an iceberg—the sudden dismissal of General Hertzog.

To the bitter sorrow of his admirers, General Hertzog, who is the fearless exponent of Dutch ideals, was relieved of his portfolios of Justice and Native Affairs—it was then the Dutch extremists, in consequence of their favourite's dismissal, gave vent to their anger in the most disagreeable manner. One could infer from their platform speeches that, from their point of view, scarcely anyone else had any rights in South Africa, and least of all the man with a black skin.

In the face of this, the Government's timidity was almost unendurable. They played up to the desires of the racial extremists, with the result that a deadlock overtook the administration. Violent laws like the Immigration Law (against British Indians and alien Asiatics) and the Natives' Land Act were indecently hurried through Parliament to allay the susceptibilities of 'Free' State Republicans. No Minister found time to undertake such useful legislation as the Coloured People's Occupation Bill, the Native Disputes Bill, the Marriage Bill, the University Bill, etc, etc. An apology was demanded from the High Commissioner in London for delivering himself of sentiments which were felt to be too British for the palates of his Dutch employers in South Africa, and the Prime Minister had almost to apologise for having at times so far forgotten himself as to act more like a Crown Minister than a simple Africander. 'Free' State

---

[1] A contemptuous South African term for British Indians.

13

demands became so persistent that Ministers seemed to have forgotten the assurances they gave His Majesty's Government in London regarding the safety of His Majesty's coloured subjects within the Union. They trampled underfoot their own election pledges, made during the first Union general election, guaranteeing justice and fair treatment to the law-abiding natives.

The campaign, to compass the elimination of the blacks from the farms, was not at all popular with landowners, who made huge profits out of the renting off their farms to natives. Platform speakers and newspaper writers coined an opprobrious phrase which designated this letting of farms to natives as 'Kafir-farming', and attempted to prove that it was almost as immoral as 'baby-farming'. But landowners pocketed the annual rents, and showed no inclination to substitute the less industrious 'poor whites' for the more industrious natives. Old Baas M—, a typical Dutch landowner of the 'Free' State, having collected his share of the crop of 1912, addressing a few words of encouragement to his native tenants, on the subject of expelling the blacks from the farms, said in the Taal: 'How dare any number of men, wearing tall hats and frock coats, living in Cape Town hotels at the expense of other men, order me to evict my natives. This is my ground; it cost my money, not Parliament's, and I will see them banged (barst) before I do it.'

It then became evident that the authority of Parliament would have to be sought to compel the obstinate landowners to get rid of their natives. And the compliance of Parliament with this demand was the greatest ministerial surrender to the Republican malcontents, resulting in the introduction and passage of the Natives' Land Act of 1913, inasmuch as the Act decreed, in the name of His Majesty the King, that pending the adoption of a report to be made by a commission, somewhere in the dim and unknown future, it shall be unlawful for natives to buy or lease land, except in scheduled native areas. And under severe pains and penalties they were to be deprived of the bare human rights of living on the land, except as servants in the employ of the whites—rights which were never seriously challenged under the Republican régime, no matter how politicians raved against the natives.

14

2　The grim struggle between right and wrong

On February 18, 1913, General L. Lemmer, member for Marico, Transvaal, asked the Minister of Lands (a) How many farms or portions of farms in the Transvaal Province have during the last three years been registered in the names of natives; (b) what is the extent of the land so registered; and (c) how much was paid for it?

The Minister of Lands replied: (a) 78 farms; (b) 144,416 morgen; and (c) £94,907.

Some very disturbing elements suggest themselves in this question and in its prompt answer. A question of the kind should have taken some time to reach Pretoria from the seat of Parliament; more time to search for and compile the necessary information, and further time to get the answer to the table of the House of Assembly in Capetown. For instance, on March 11 Mr T.L. Schreiner called for an explanation in connexion with the same return. He had to ask again on April 1, the answer in each instance being that the required 'information had been telegraphed for and would be laid on the table when it is available' (vide Union Hansard, pp.777 and 1,175). It was only on May 13—two months and two days after—that an answer to Mr Schreiner's question of March 11 could be furnished.

Again, on May 20 Mr Schreiner called for a similar return, embracing the four provinces of the Union.[1] If it were so easy for General Lemmer to get a reply in regard to the Transvaal, where most of the registration took place, it should have been relatively more easy to add the information from the Cape and Natal, since no registration could have taken place in the Orange 'Free' State, where natives cannot buy land. But strange to say, all that Mr. Schreiner could get

---

[1] It does not appear to have occurred to anyone to call for a return showing transfers of land from blacks to whites.

out of the Minister was a promise to furnish a reply when it is available, and it does not appear to be on record that it was ever furnished during that session. Therefore, a native cannot be blamed for suspecting that when General Lemmer asked his question, the return was 'cut and dried' and available to be laid on the table as soon as it was called for.

Another significant point is that the questioner did not want to know the extent of land bought by natives, but of the land 'registered in their names' during the period; and Mr Schreiner was able to show later in the session by an analysis of the return that it mainly comprised land awarded to native tribes by the Republican Government, some of it when they conquered the country. They include farms bought or awarded to natives as long ago as the early 60s and 70s, but the owners were not able to obtain titles as the late Republican Government did not allow natives to register land in their own names. They had been held in trust for them by European friends or missionaries, and it was only during the last three years that the owners claimed direct titles, which right was restored to them since the British occupation.

But the Lemmer return did its fell work. It scared every white man in the country. They got alarmed to hear that natives had during the past three(!) years 'bought' land to the extent of 50,000 morgen per annum.

Thanks to Mr Schreiner's questions, however, the misleading features of the statistical scarecrow were revealed—but, unfortunately too late.

ORIGIN OF THE TROUBLE

On February 29, 1913, Mr J.G. Keyter (a 'Free' State member) moved: That the Government be requested to submit to the House *during the present session* a general Pass and Squatters Bill to prohibit coloured people (1) from *wandering about without a proper pass;* (2) from *squatting on farms;* and (3) from *sowing on the share system.*

Mr T.P. Brain,[2] another 'Free' Stater, seconded the motion.

[2] This gentleman died during 1913.

Mr P.G.W. Grobler,[3] a Transvaaler, moved (as an amendment) to add at the end of the motion: 'and further *to take effective measures to restrict the purchase and lease of land by Natives*'.

Mr Schreiner strongly protested against both the motion and the amendment.

The Minister for Native Affairs[4] spoke somewhat against Mr Keyter's motion but promised to comply with Mr Grobler's amendment, which promise he redeemed by introducing a Natives' Land Bill.

Before the Bill was introduced, the Minister made the unprecedented announcement that the Governor-General had given his assurance that the royal assent would not be withheld from the Natives' Land Bill. Section 65 of the South African constitution provides that the King may disallow an Act of Parliament within twelve months after the Governor-General signed it. And the abrogation of the constitution, as far as this bill is concerned, literally gave licence to the political libertines of South Africa; as, being thus freed from all legislative restraint, they wasted no further time listening to such trifles as reason and argument.

The following are extracts from the debates on the Natives' Land Bill as reported in the Union Hansard of 1913.

The adjourned debate on the motion for the second reading of the Natives' Land Bill was resumed by **Mr J.X. Merriman** (Victoria West). It was with very great reluctance (the right hon. gentleman said) that he rose to speak on this measure. It would have been more convenient to have given a silent vote, but he felt, and he was afraid, that after many years of devoted attention to this question of the native policy of South Africa, he would not be doing his duty if he did not give this House—for what it was worth—the result of his experience through these years.

He should like to emphasise a brighter side of the question, and that was to point out that the natives,

---

[3] Mr Grobler forfeited his seat when he was convicted of complicity in the recent rebellion.
[4] Hon. J.W. Sauer, Minister of Native Affairs, died a month after the Bill became law.

if they were well managed, were an invaluable asset to the people of this country. (Hear, hear). Let them take our trade figures and compare them with the trade figures of the other large British dominions. Our figures were surprising when measured by the white population, but if they took the richest dominion that there was under the British Crown outside South Africa, and took the trade value of those figures per head of the white population, and multiply those figures by our European population, then they might very well apply any balance they had to our native population, and then they would see, strangely enough, that upon that basis it worked out that the actual trade of three natives was worth about that of one white man. That, of course, was a very imperfect way of looking at the value of these people because the trade value of some of these natives was far greater than the trade value of some of our white people. He had merely indicated these trade figures to show what an enormous asset we had in the natives in that respect. Let them think what the industry of the natives had done for us. Who had built our railways, who had dug our mines, and developed this country as far as it was developed? Who had been the actual manual worker who had done that? The native: the coloured races of this country. We must never forget that we owed them a debt in that respect—a debt not often acknowledged by what we did for them. Proceeding, he said that they ought to think what they owed to the docility of the natives, and the wonderfully easy way in which they had been governed when treated properly. He also paid a tribute to the honesty of the natives.

What must strike anyone was the fact that though this Bill was really, to a certain extent, a beginning, or was thought to be in certain quarters, of a revolution in their dealing with the native races, it was not even mentioned in the speech of the Governor-General. It fell upon them like a bolt from the blue. He remembered the afternoon. They had heard a very impassioned and very heated speech from the hon. member for Ficksburg on the enormous danger of squatting in the Free State, and that was the occasion for introducing a general statement of the policy of the Government towards the natives and the introduction of this Bill. He did not think that that was the way they like to see a thing of this magnitude approached. They often heard demands for what was called a general declaration of policy with regard to native affairs—a policy which should be applied to the highest civilised native, the owner of a farm, and the naked barbarian. They could not do it. People who demanded a general declaration of that kind had not had the experience which some of them had had. The hon. member who spoke before him said that he was in favour of the underlying principle of the Bill. What was the underlying principle? The underlying principle was what one read into the Bill. One hon. member read into it that it was the separation of the two races. That might have been done when the two races first came in contact at the Fish River, but it could not be done now. Since then they had been developing the country with the labour of these people. They had been advancing by our aid. They had mixed themselves up with these people in an inextricable fashion and then some said 'Haul your native policy out of the drawer and begin with a policy of separation'. He was sure that the hon. member who had brought in the Bill had no idea of that sort in his mind. Another person had the idea that they were going to set up a sort of pale—a sort of kraal in which they were going to drive these people. Then another side said that the policy towards the natives should be firm and just, while the other side said that it should be just and firm.

It seemed to him that they had not got sufficient information. Beyond the bald statistics which were given by the Minister in the course of his interesting and moderate speech, they had nothing. They were going into a thing that would stir South Africa from end to end, and which affected hundreds of thousands of both races. They had no information as to what were the ideas of the natives. It was unfortunate that, owing to this lack of information, wrong ideas had got about with regard to this Bill. It was difficult to find out what the native thought about these things; he doubted whether anybody could say that he had got at the mind of the native. The only way, and he must say that he did not take it as a real indication, was what they wrote in their newspapers. He was alarmed, but not surprised, at some of the articles in their newspapers, because they took their views from the heated speeches and writings in party newspapers all over the country, and they were very much alarmed. He thought that before a Bill of this sort was passed, there should be some attempt made to get their views. As far as one section was concerned, the Bill was going to set up a sort of pale—that there was going to be a sort of kraal in which all the natives were to be driven, and they were to be left to develop on their own lines. To allow them to go on their own lines was merely to drive them back into barbarism; their own lines meant barbarous lines; their own lines were cruel lines. All along they had been bringing them away from their own lines. It reminded him of what an English writer said about a similar policy in Ireland, because when the English went to Ireland they regarded the native Irish in the way some extreme people here regarded the natives of South Africa. They thought they would root them out. They treated them as dogs, and thought that they were dogs. They set up a pale. They set the Irish within that pale, to develop upon their own lines, but there were always Englishmen living in that pale, just as in the same way they found Europeans living among natives. Sir George Davis in describing this policy wrote that it was the intention of the Government to set up a separation between English and Irish, intending in time that the English should root out the Irish. If they changed the Irish for natives they would see how the illustration would apply. A policy more foredoomed to failure in South Africa could not be initiated. It was a policy that would keep South Africa back, perhaps for ever. (Hear, hear). What would be the effect of driving these civilised natives back into reserves? At the present time, every civilised man—if they treated him properly—every civilised man was becoming an owner of land outside native reserves, and therefore he was an asset of strength to the country. He was a loyalist. He was not going to risk losing his property. He was on the side of the European. If they drove these people back into reserves they became our bitterest enemies. Therefore, he viewed anything that tended that way with the gravest suspicion. Again, in this Bill there was not sufficient distinction between those natives who tried to educate themselves and the ordinary raw barbarian. They were all classed under the word 'native.'

He came now to what was the main object of the Bill, and that was: to do away with the squatting evil. Why was there a squatting evil? Was it the fault of the native? (An hon. member: No). Was it the fault of the law? (No). They had got the most stringent laws concerning natives of all the laws in the whole country, in the province of which his hon. friend (Mr Keyter) was a member. He did not think anything was more surprising than when they came to look at the increases in the native population in the Cape, and the increase during the census periods from 1904 to 1911—he wanted hon. members to pay some attention to this, because it showed the value of legislation—the increase in the Cape Province during that period was 8.33 per cent. In Natal, which had a huge—in fact, an overwhelming—native population, curiously enough, the increase was the same even to the actual decimal figure, viz., 8.33 per cent, but some allowance must be made, because a large number of natives were out at work in the mines. Now, in the Transvaal—and in the mines. In the Transvaal the natives increased by 30.1 per cent. Now, when they came to his friend's little State, where the most stringent laws were made to keep out the natives, how much did they suppose the natives increased in the Free State? By no less than 44 per cent. (Opposition cheers). Was that the fault of the natives? No, it was because having the most stringent laws—

the people found it best to evade those laws. (Hear, hear). He hoped his hon. friend would be a little tolerant. Do let him pick the mote out of his own eye before he tried to pick the beam out of other people's. (Hear, hear). In the Free State these laws were very severe; for instance, punishments—amazing punishments—were given, and yet the result was the increase in five years by 44 per cent of their native population. This was something that they should take a warning by. They were going to do away with the squatter in appearance, but he would still survive as a labour tenant. They might do away with the labour tenant and he would still be surviving as a labour servant. How was the Government to distinguish between these? They had in the Cape a law which stated how many labour tenants a man should have upon his farm.

What they wanted in this country was administration and not more legislation, and if they were to put the laws which they had into force in the Free State at the present time he had no doubt that there would be a rebellion. (Hear, hear). They would have platforms swarming with people who would say that they could not grow one bag of mealies without the natives. But they had the laws to do it. Now they went and tried in this Bill to make a uniform law. Turning towards the Minister, Mr Merriman said: 'My poor friend! that after all the years we had laboured together he of all people should be the author of a uniform law on native matters! (Laughter). I say this more in sorrow than in anger—(laughter)—because the conditions were totally different in the four Provinces.'

Mr H. Mentz (Zoutpansberg) said the right hon. gentleman had earned their gratitude for the high tone in which he had carried the debate. The speech which he had delivered was a most instructive one, and although the speaker was not in entire agreement with him on all points, he was in agreement with the point that the matter was one to be handled with prudence, but it was to be regretted that under the Bill a Commission was to be appointed. The Minister should not listen to the request for a postponement of the question, by referring it to a Select Committee. If they were to refer the Bill to a Select Committee, it would never be passed this year.

Mr G.L. Steytler (Rouxville) expressed his thanks to the Government for bringing forward the Bill. He said he felt that it was not a complete solution of the whole question, but it was certainly a step in the right direction.

Mr A. Fawcus (Umlazi) said that as the representative of 70,000 natives in Natal, not one of whom so far as he knew had a vote, he should like, on their behalf, to thank the right hon. member for Victoria West for the manner in which he handled the question. In the course of his speech the right hon. gentleman asked, what did the natives think about this Bill before the House? His (Mr Fawcus') opinion was that the natives did not think anything at all about it. He should not think there was one native in a thousand in South Africa who was aware that this matter, so vitally affecting their future, was at present at issue. The hon. member for Middelburg had referred to the natives as 'schepsels.' He believed the day was rapidly passing away when we should refer to natives as 'schepsels.' They were an easy-going folk, and they thought little about title deeds and land laws. So great was the native's attachment to the land on which he lived, in many instances, that they could not rackrent him off it. These were the people that the Bill wished to dispossess and drive off the land. The figures placed before them showed that the land held by the Europeans per head was fifty times the amount held per head by the natives. Surely there was no need at the present time for legislation which would prevent natives getting a little more land than they now had. He did not think it could be put down to the fault of the native if he was willing to buy and live on land rather than pay rent. The figures given in this connexion were very instructive. Eight acres per head were held by the natives in the Cape, six acres in Natal, about one and a half acres in the Transvaal, and about one-third of an acre in the Free State. He thought this Bill was perhaps coming on a little before there was any necessity for it.

Mr C.G. Fichardt (Ladybrand) said he felt very much that the Bill that was before the House did not carry out all that should be carried out, and that was equality of justice. If they were to deal fairly with the natives of this country, then according to population they should give them four-fifths of the country, or at least a half. How were they going to do that? As he said in the earlier part of his remarks, he was prepared to accept the Bill as something to go on with, but he hoped that in the future it would not constitute a stumbling-block. He would much rather have seen that the matter had been gone into more fully, and that some scheme had been laid before them so that they might have more readily been able to judge how the Bill would work. It was because of all these difficulties that he felt that they could only accept the Bill if it laid down that there was no intention of taking the country from the white people and handing it over to the blacks.

Mr J.G. Keyter (Ficksburg) said he wished to openly denounce, and most emphatically so, that the people or the Government of the Orange Free State had treated the coloured people unreasonably or unjustly, or in any way oppressively. On the contrary, the O.F.S. had always treated the coloured people with the greatest consideration and the utmost justice. The O.F.S had made what Mr Merriman called stringent laws. He (Mr Keyter) called them just laws. They told the coloured people plainly that the O.F.S was a white man's country, and that they intended to keep it so. (Hear, hear). They told the coloured people that they were not to be allowed to buy or hire land, and that they were not going to tolerate an equality of whites and blacks; and he said that they were not going to tolerate that in the future, and if an attempt were made to force that on them, they would resist it at any cost to the last,[5]

[5] By passing the Bill, the Government conceded all the extravagant demands of the 'Free' State; yet, a year later they took up arms against the Government.

for if they did tolerate it, they would very soon find that they would be a bastard nation. His experience was that the native should be treated firmly, kept in his place and treated honestly. They should not give him a gun one day and fight him for it the next day. They should tell him, as the Free State told him, that it was a white man's country, that he was not going to be allowed to buy land there or to hire land there, and that if he wanted to be there he must be in service.

THIRD READING DEBATE

Sir Lionel Phillips (Yeoville): But why should a Bill of this sort be brought before them now? The Government in the past had not been bashful in the appointing of Commissions, and one question he would ask was why, in this important matter, the Government had not appointed a Commission to take all the evidence and then come to the House with a measure which the House would have to approve of. Instead of that, they were cancelling the rights the natives had in South Africa, and creating a very awkward hiatus between the time the Commission would be appointed and the time the Commission could define the areas which would be regarded as white areas and the areas which would be regarded as native areas. That was the one serious blot upon this measure.

He could see no justification, except that the hon. Minister, yielding to pressure from a certain section on that side of the House, had hastily brought on this measure. He thought from the speeches made in the House it was the consensus of opinion that natives should not have farms in areas that were essentially white, just as it was desirable that white men should not be found in areas essentially native. And especially when they told the native population that they were taking away from them a right they had today, and they were going to substitute that right by appointing a Commission, they were giving them very little justification for being satisfied with this measure. He did not think they were going to gain anything by putting the cart before the horse. He did not know if Mr Schreiner was accurate, but he told them that, roughly, in the Transvaal, where the matter was most acute, the native population had brought something like 12,000 or 15,000 morgen of land in twelve years. That, he thought, showed there was no extreme urgency for the measure. To that extent he agreed entirely with the hon. member, and he believed the Minister would be well advised to send the Bill to a Select Committee, so that many of the details, which were extremely complicated and difficult, might be thrashed out in that atmosphere, rather than on the floor of the House. (Opposition cheers).

Mr E.N. Grobler (Edenburg) said: The present was one of the best measures that the Government had so far brought forward, and it appeared clear that they had a Government which truly represented the wishes of the public. It was impossible to delay the solution of the native problem, and legislation on the subject had for a long time past been asked for.[6] At the same time, he did not entirely agree with the methods, proposed to be applied, and he did not like the system of allocating reserves for natives. When once those reserves had been allocated, would it not result in injury to agriculture and cattle breeding? The farmers would suffer from lack of labour, and the deficiency would be a growing one. Neither could he agree to the principle of expropriation of land belonging to whites in order to increase the size of the native reserves. He considered the Bill was a complicated one. The matter should be settled by way of taxation, in the following way. All natives who were in the service of whites should be exempted from taxation, and treated as well as possible, and other natives should be encouraged to take similar service. There were enormous reserves where

---

[6] By a 'solution of the Native problem,' 'Free' State farmers generally mean the re-establishment of slavery.

natives could go and live,[7] and if they refused to go there they should be required to pay a stiff tax. Then they would go and work for white people. The hon. member for Tembuland had offered many objections to the Bill. They should make that hon. member king of Tembuland. In a country of the blind a man with one eye would be king.

Sir W.B. Berry (Queenstown) said that he would like to know why the Minister had run away from the Bill that had passed the second reading, and now tabled another Bill in the shape of many amendments. One would naturally complain that, seeing that they had in that House a Native Affairs Committee, a non- party committee, specially chosen to consider all matters relating to native affairs, that Bill, which was a most important matter and dealt with native affairs from A to Z, should have been referred to that committee. The same thing happened last session in reference to a Bill of the Minister of Native Affairs kept on the paper until nearly the end of the session, and the House had to take the very unusual step almost on the last day of moving that committee proceedings on that Bill be taken that day six months. He (Sir W.B. Berry) proposed to move a similar amendment to the motion now before the House. In the remarks he addressed when the Bill came up for second reading he had ventured to say that there was no call for a bill of that nature at all; there was no need for a Bill revolutionising the attitude of the Union with respect to the natives generally. The only clue that could get to the reason why the Bill was introduced was that a few die-hards on the other side of the House had given the Minister to understand that unless he brought in a Bill of that kind, or of a similarly drastic nature, the position of the Government was in danger. He hoped some of these

[7] It will be observed that these and similar mythological disquisitions subsequently formed General Botha's assurances to Mr Harcourt. See Chapter 15. But some light is thrown on the subject of these visionary Native Reserves by Mr Fawcus' speech based on official statistics (pp.23-4).

27

die-hards would come forward that evening and tell them plainly and bluntly why they wanted that Bill, why they were going to thrust it on the country without any notice, and why they were calling on the House to revolutionise the whole tenor and the whole order of things in regard to land matters as far as the natives were concerned. Proceeding, the hon. member said the only justification that had been offered for this Bill was that a large amount of land had been transferred from Europeans to natives. An analysis of the return, however, showed that only sixteen farms in the Transvaal had been so transferred during the last three years. Surely that was not any justification why the European people of the Union should get into a panic and why the administration of the day were seeking to place on the Statute Book this most drastic legislation. Another reason why he objected to this Bill was that it purported to appoint a Commission to investigate to what extent and in what parts and in what time land should be selected by the Commission for the purpose of being reserved as additional native areas within the Union. They were not given any guarantee that the Commission was going to be appointed nor any guarantee that it would ever report, but at the same time whilst these indefinite assurances were attempted to be given to the House there was no getting over this fact, that there was no time limit in the Bill by which the real enacting clause in the Bill was to have any cessation. When he spoke on this Bill before he supported it only on the understanding that a time limit was to be put in, or that it should be an annual Bill. He said unhesitatingly that the whole tendency of the Bill, as it stood at the second reading, and more especially as it stood with the amendments by the Minister on the notice paper, was to drive the native peasant off the land. The only refuge that that native had was the town.

The country had not been prepared in any way for a Bill of this kind. A cry had been heard throughout the land against the iniquities proposed in the Bill. If it had been found absolutely necessary that legislation of this kind should be introduced, the least that could be expected was that ample time should be given to the natives to thoroughly acquire a knowledge of the contents of the measure. That opportunity had not been given them, and in this respect there was a very serious grievance. For the good order and peace of the Union there was a very great danger ahead. He understood from those well versed in native affairs that one of the greatest dangers that could threaten us was to give the natives anything in the shape of a common grievance. Divide and rule had been a wise precaution in the government of the natives. When a common grievance was found by four or five million people one could understand how great that grievance must be. One amendment the Minister had put on the paper must give serious pause. The late Minister of Native Affairs issued to members last session a Squatters' Bill. The greatest objection to that measure, and one which he thought led to its withdrawal, was that it proposed to remove thousands upon thousands of natives from land which they had been in the occupation of for scores of years. It was in consequence of the disturbance which that Bill caused throughout the Union that it was withdrawn. In one of the amendments on the paper the present Minister of Native Affairs brought back in a somewhat clandestine manner the most objectionable feature of the Bill that was withdrawn.

Mr Speaker: The amendment is not yet before the House.

Sir W.B. Berry: What Bill is it then that is to go into Committee? (Hear, hear). Is it the Bill which was read a second time or the Bill comprised in the Minister's amendments? He moved that the house go into committee on the Bill this day six months.

Mr T.L. Schreiner (Tembuland), in seconding the amendment, said that sufficient notice had not been given of the provisions of the Bill, although the natives, thanks to the time which had elapsed since the second reading, were better acquainted with the measure than they were a little while ago.

Mr Schreiner proceeded to quote opinions from native newspapers on the Bill. The *Tsala ea Batho,* of Kimberley, said: 'We are standing on the brink of the precipice. We appealed to certain members of Parliament against the suspension clause in Mr Sauer's Land Bill, and the result of our appeal has been an agreement between Sir Thomas Smartt and the Minister to the effect that the first part of the Bill only be proceeded with. The effect of this agreement is infinitely worse than the whole Bill. In its entirety, there were certain saving clauses, one of them practically excluding the Cape Province from the operation of the Bill. Under the present agreement, all these clauses are dropped, and section 1 of the Bill, which prohibits the sale of land between Europeans and natives (pending the report of a future Commission) is applicable to all parts of the Union, including the Cape Province. Now, then, if this suspension clause becomes law, what is going to happen? It is simply this: That the whole land policy of the Union of South Africa is the land policy of the Orange Free State, and it will be as difficult to abrogate that suspension as it is difficult to recall a bullet, once fired through someone's head, and resuscitate the victim. Our object then should be to prevent the pistol being fired off, as prevention is infinitely better than cure.' One paper that he was quoting from was (Mr Schreiner went on to say) pleased, because it believed that this Bill was going to Select Committee. There was another native paper, published in Natal, which acknowledged the efforts which the missionaries had made on behalf of the natives in regard to this Bill. There was a native paper, published at Dundee, which said that, if the Bill were in the interests of the natives, and the Government were actuated by a sincere regard for them, they would not have hesitated to publish it broadcast, instead of being in such haste to push the matter through the House.[8]

[8] All efforts to induce the South African Government to circulate translations of the Natives' Land Act among the natives of the Union have proved fruitless.

Mr Schreiner (continuing) referred to the resolution passed by the Natal Missionary Conference, and the views expressed by the Chairman of the Transvaal Missionary Conference in opposition to the Bill. He mentioned that it had been decided in Johannesburg to call a meeting of missionary societies throughout the Union, to determine what action could be taken in case clause 1 was proceeded with. He had also received a telegram from the Witwatersrand Church Council, stating that a telegram had been sent to the Minister strongly protesting against section 1 being enacted before the proposed Commission had thoroughly investigated the whole question of alternative areas. Mr Schreiner urged that, if they proceeded with this Bill, and passed clause 1 of the old Bill, and appointed a Commission, these restrictions with regard to purchase and sale, which the natives had feared, and which the missionaries, on behalf of the natives, feared and protested against would become fact. For that reason, he said they should rather put off the Bill.

Everyone was feeling the pressure of their legislative duties. Was this the time, therefore, for passing a measure of such a far-reaching character and where every clause demanded the most careful consideration and scrutiny? Was it the right thing because he had a majority at this session? He held that this was not right. It was not fair to those who had the solution of the question at heart. (Cheers).

Sir E.H. Walton (Port Elizabeth, Central) said he entirely supported the amendment of the hon. member for Queenstown. He had a telegram from a mass meeting of natives held in Port Elizabeth, in which they hoped that the House would postpone decision on this question until the Commission had sat and reported. That seemed to him an entirely reasonable request and it seemed all the more necessary that this should be done on account of the very large alterations that it had been found necessary to make in the Bill.

They had native protests from all parts of South Africa against this measure, and when one saw what was proposed in this Act, they could not wonder at these protests. (Hear, hear). Therefore he put it that these protests should receive fair consideration from members on all sides of the House. Legislation of this kind was unfortunate from the point of view of the natives. The more intelligent of the natives in this country were asking for time. They said: 'You are putting this thing upon us, give us time to consider it. Allow this Commission to get to work, allow this Commission to put before us the provisions you are going to make for us, and when this is done we will submit to anything that is fair.' No man, and the native was just a man like the rest of us, liked the old arrangements to be disturbed, because it upset him, and the native might oppose it, because he was frightened. They must admit that they had not given the native leaders and chiefs an opportunity to come down to Cape Town and give their views. It was unfortunate that this measure had been more or less rushed. There was no mention of it in the Governor-General's speech, and therefore the natives were not prepared for the consideration of the question.

Mr M. Alexander (Cape Town, Castle) said he was still of opinion that a very dangerous principle was introduced in the Bill, especially so far as the Cape was concerned. In the speech delivered by the Governor at the opening of the session there was not the slightest reference to the present measure, which apparently had been brought in as an afterthought, and something must have occurred after the Governor-General's speech was delivered, otherwise one could not conceive of such an important Bill being omitted from the speech. As it was the Bill would simply hang things up until the Commission reported, and now the House would be legislating in the dark. The vast majority of natives had declared themselves to be against the Bill. He had had no desire whatever that party capital should be made out of the measure—(Hear, hear)—but he desired to see a measure which would bear the mark of statesmanship, and not of panic and hurry. Their Commission could report before next session, and then in the early stages of the session a Bill could be introduced and be adopted on its merits. In the interests of South Africa, in the interests of the natives, and in the interests of just legislation let the Government withdraw the Bill, and appoint a Commission, and then justice and no injustice would be done. (Hear, hear).

Dr A.H. Watkins (Barkly) said that there was a tacit understanding that the Minister would refer this Bill, if he were not prepared to accept a purely temporary measure, to a select committee. During the three years of the Union Parliament every matter practically dealing with natives had been brought before the Select Committee on Native Affairs and their opinion had been asked. For some reason, which it was difficult for him to understand, the Minister had not seen fit to carry out that course. Sixteen days had elapsed since the second reading of this Bill was taken on which the Select Committee could have sat morning after morning and dealt with the Bill.

The necessity of passing only a temporary measure instead of appearing to pass a measure which would permanently deal with this question, was more evident tonight than when they took the second reading.

The Bill was contested at every stage and numerous divisions were challenged. In each instance, the Speaker would put the question, and the 'steamroller' would go to work with the inevitable result. The division lists ranged from 17 against 71 to 32 against 60, the majority in each case being in favour of repression.

3   The Natives' Land Act

Up to now we have dealt with the history of the Land Act from its commencement, and all the speeches and official documents we have mentioned hitherto say nothing about restricting Europeans in their ownership of land. And no matter what other principles one might read into the Act, it would be found that the principles underlying it were those of extending the 'Free' State land laws throughout the Union—an extension by which natives would be prohibited from investing their earnings in land whereon they could end their days in peace.

There seems to be good reason for believing that the Government were advised, by the legal advisers of the Crown, that the Natives' Land Bill would be class legislation of a kind that would never be allowed by His Majesty's Government. The originators of the Bill, however, were determined so to circumvent the constitutional quibble raised by the legal advisers as to seal our doom; and by adroitly manipulating its legal phrases, it seems that it was recast in such a matter as to give it a semblance of a paper restriction on European encroachment on native rights. But class legislation the Act is, for whereas in his travels about South Africa, since the passing of this Act, the author has met many a native family with their stock, turned out by the Act upon the roads, he never met one white man so hounded by the same Act, and debarred from living where he pleased.

The squatters form a particular section of the community specifically affected by the Land Act; and there is no such person in South Africa as a white squatter. Although it is insistently affirmed that the law applies both to Europeans and natives, the conclusion cannot be avoided that it is directed exclusively against the native. This is the naked truth that turns all other explanations of the fact into mere shuffling and juggling. And the reader will find that in Section 11, at the end of the statute which is here reproduced (whether the omission of Europeans was a mistake of the Parliamentary draftsmen, or the printers, we know not), it is expressly stated that 'this Act may be cited for all purposes as the *Natives'* Land Act, 1913'. Who, then, will continue to argue that it was intended for Europeans as well?

[No. 27, 1913]

ACT
TO

Make further provision as to the purchase and leasing of Land by Natives and other Persons in the several parts of the Union and for other purposes in connection with the ownership and occupation of Land by Natives and other Persons.

BE IT ENACTED by the King's Most Excellent Majesty, the Senate and the House of Assembly of the Union of South Africa, as follows:

1. (1) From and after the commencement of this Act, land outside the scheduled native areas shall, until Parliament, acting upon the report of the commission appointed under this Act, shall have made other provision, be subjected to the following provisions, that is to say:

Except with the approval of the Governor-General—

(*a*) a native shall not enter into any agreement or transaction for the purchase, hire, or other acquisition from a person other than a native, of any such land or of any right thereto, interest therein, or servitude thereover; and

(*b*) a person other than a native shall not enter into any agreement or transaction for the purchase, hire, or other acquisition from a native of any such land or of any right thereto, interest therein, or servitude thereover.

(2) From and after the commencement of this Act,

no person other than a native shall purchase, hire or in any other manner whatever acquire any land in a scheduled native area or enter into any agreement or transaction for the purchase, hire or other acquisition, direct or indirect, of any such land or of any right thereto or interest therein or servitude thereover, except with the approval of the Governor-General.

(3) A statement showing the number of approvals granted by the Governor-General under sub-sections (1) and (2) of this section and giving the names and addresses of the persons to whom such approvals were granted, the reasons for granting the same, and the situation of the lands in respect of which they were granted, shall, within six weeks after the commencement of each ordinary session of Parliament, be laid upon the Tables by both Houses of Parliament.

(4) Every agreement or any other transaction whatever entered into in contravention of this section shall be null and void *ab initio*.

2. (1) As soon as may be after the commencement of this Act the Governor-General shall appoint a commission whose functions shall be to inquire and report

   (a) what areas should be set apart as areas within which natives shall not be permitted to acquire or hire land or interests in land;

   (b) what areas should be set apart as areas within which persons other than natives shall not be permitted to acquire or hire land or interests in land.

The commission shall submit with any such report—

   (i) descriptions of the boundaries of any area which it proposes should be so set apart; and

   (ii) a map or maps showing every such area.

(2) The commission shall proceed with and complete its inquiry and present its reports and recommendations to the Minister within two years after the commencement of this Act, and may present *interim* reports and recommendations. Provided that Parliament may by resolution extend (if necessary) the time

for the completion of the commission's inquiry. All such reports and recommendations shall be laid by the Minister, as soon as possible after the receipt thereof, upon the Tables of both Houses of Parliament.

3. (1) The commission shall consist of not less than five persons, and if any member of the commission die or resign or, owing to absence or any other reason, is unable to act, his place shall be filled by the Governor-General.

(2) The commission may delegate to any of its members the carrying out of any part of an inquiry which under this Act it is appointed to hold and may appoint persons to assist it or to act as assessors thereto or with any members thereof delegated as aforesaid, and may regulate its own procedure.

(3) The reports and recommendations of the majority of the commission shall be deemed to be the reports and recommendations of the commission. Provided that any recommendations of any member who dissents from the majority of the commission shall, if signed by him, be included in any such report aforesaid.

(4) The commission or any member thereof or any person acting as assistant, or assessor, or secretary thereto may enter upon any land for the purposes of its inquiries and obtain thereon the information necessary to prosecute the inquiries. The commission shall without fee or other charge have access to the records and register relating to land in any public office or in the office of any divisional council or other local authority.

4. (1) For the purposes of establishing any such area as is described in section *two*, the Governor-General may, out of moneys which Parliament may vote for the purpose, acquire any land or interest in land.

(2) In default of agreement with the owners of the land or the holders of interests therein the provisions of the law in force in the Province in which such land or interest in land is situate relating to the expropriation of land for public purposes shall apply and, if in any Province there be no such law, the provisions of

Proclamation No. 5 of 1902 of the Transvaal and any amendment thereof shall *mutatis mutandis* apply.

5. (1) Any person who is a party to any attempted purchase, sale, hire or lease, or to any agreement or transaction which is in contravention of this Act or any regulation made thereunder shall be guilty of an offence and liable on conviction to a fine not exceeding one hundred pounds or, in default of payment, to imprisonment with or without hard labour for a period not exceeding six months, and if the act constituting the offence be a continuing one, the offender shall be liable to a further fine not exceeding five pounds for every day which that act continues.

(2) In the event of such an offence being committed by a company, corporation, or other body of persons (not being a firm or partnership), every director, secretary, or manager of such company, corporation, or body who is within the Union shall be liable to prosecution and punishment and, in the event of any such offence being committed by a firm or partnership, every member of the firm or partnership who is within the Union shall be liable to prosecution and punishment.

6. In so far as the occupation by natives of land outside the scheduled native areas may be affected by this Act, the provisions thereof shall be construed as being in addition to and not in substitution for any law in force at the commencement thereof relating to such occupation; but in the event of a conflict between the provisions of this Act and the provisions of any such law, the provisions of this Act shall, save as is specially provided therein, prevail:

Provided that—

(*a*) nothing in any such law or in this Act shall be construed as restricting the number of natives who, as farm labourers, may reside on any farm in the Transvaal;

(*b*) in any proceedings for a contravention of this Act the burden of proving that a native is a farm labourer shall be upon the accused;

(*c*) until Parliament, acting upon the report of the

said commission, has made other provision, no native resident on any farm in the Transvaal or Natal shall be liable to penalties or to be removed from such farm under any law, if at the commencement of this Act he or the head of his family is registered for taxation or other purposes in the department of Native Affairs as being resident on such farm, nor shall the owner of any such farm be liable to the penalties imposed by section *five* in respect of the occupation of the land by such native; but nothing herein contained shall affect any right possessed by law by an owner or lessee of a farm to remove any native therefrom.

7. (1) Chapter XXXIV of the Orange Free State Law Book and Law No. 4 of 1895 of the Orange Free State shall remain of full force and effect, subject to the modifications and interpretations in this section provided, and sub-section (1) (*a*) of the next succeeding section shall not apply to the Orange Free State.

(2) Those heads of families, with their families, who are described in article *twenty* of Law No. 4 of 1895 of the Orange Free State shall in the circumstances described in that article be deemed to fall under the provisions of Ordinance No. 7 of 1904 of that Province or of any other law hereafter enacted amending or substituted for that Ordinance.

(3) Whenever in Chapter XXXIV of the Orange Free State Law Book the expressions 'lease' and 'leasing' are used, those expressions shall be construed as including or referring to an agreement or arrangement whereby a person, in consideration of his being permitted to occupy land, renders or promises to render to any person a share of the produce thereof, or any valuable consideration of any kind whatever other than his own labour or services or the labour or services of any of his family.

8. (1) Nothing in this Act contained shall be construed as,

(*a*) preventing the continuation or renewal (until

Parliament acting upon the report of the said commission has made other provision) of any agreement or arrangement lawfully entered into and in existence at the commencement of this Act which is a hiring or leasing of land as defined in this Act; or

(b) invalidating or affecting in any manner whatever any agreement or any other transaction for the purchase of land lawfully entered into prior to the commencement of this Act, or as prohibiting any person from purchasing at any sale held by order of a competent court any land which was hypothecated by a mortgage bond passed before the commencement of this Act; or

(c) prohibiting the acquisition at any time of land or interests in land by devolution or succession on death, whether under a will or on intestacy; or

(d) preventing the due registration in the proper deeds office (whenever registration is necessary) of documents giving effect to any such agreement, transaction, devolution or succession as is in this section mentioned; or

(e) prohibiting any person from claiming, acquiring, or holding any such servitude as under Chapter VII, of the Irrigation and Conservation of Waters Act, 1912, he is specially entitled to claim, acquire, or hold; or

(f) in any way altering the law in force at the commencement of this Act relating to the acquisition of rights to minerals, precious or base metals or precious stones; or

(g) applying to land within the limits in which a municipal council, town council, town board, village management board or health committee or other local authority exercises jurisdiction; or

(h) applying to land held at the commencement of the Act by any society carrying on, with the approval of the Governor-General, educational or missionary work amongst natives; or

(i) prohibiting the acquisition by natives from any

person whatever of land or interests in land in any township lawfully established prior to the commencement of this Act, provided it is a condition of the acquisition that no land or interest in land in such township has at any time been or shall in future be, transferred except to a native or coloured person; or

(*j*) permitting the alienation of land or its diversion from the purposes for which it was set apart if, under section *one hundred and forty-seven* of the South African Act, 1909, or any other law, such land could not be alienated or so diverted except under the authority of an Act of Parliament; or

(*k*) in any way modifying the provisions of any law whereby mortgages of or charges over land may be created to secure advances out of public moneys for specific purposes mentioned in such law and the interest of such advances, or whereunder the mortgagee or person having the charge may enter and take possession of the land so mortgaged or charged except that in any sale of such land in accordance with such law the provisions of this Act shall be observed.

(2) Nothing in this Act contained which imposes restriction upon the acquisition by any person of land or right thereto, interests therein, or servitudes thereover, shall be in force in the Province of the Cape of Good Hope, if and for so long as such person would, by such restrictions, be prevented from acquiring or holding a qualification whereunder he is or may become entitled to be registered as a voter at parliamentary elections in any electoral division in the said Province.

9. The Governor-General may make regulations for preventing the overcrowding of huts and other dwellings in the stadts, native villages and settlements and other places in which natives are congregated in areas not under the jurisdiction of any local authority, the sanitation of such places and for the maintenance of the health of the inhabitants thereof.

10. In this Act, unless inconsistent with the

context—

'scheduled native area' shall mean any area described in the Schedule to this Act;

'native' shall mean any person, male or female, who is a member of an aboriginal race or tribe of Africa; and shall further include any company or other body of persons, corporate or unincorporate, if the persons who have a controlling interest therein are natives;

'interest in land' shall include, in addition to other interest in land, the interest which a mortgage of, or person having charge over, land acquires under a mortgage bond or charge;

'Minister' shall mean the Minister of Native Affairs;

'farm labourer' shall mean a native who resides on a farm and is *bona fide*, but not necessarily continuously employed by the owner or lessee thereof in domestic service or in farming operations:

Provided that—

(a) if such native reside on one farm and is employed on another farm of the same owner or lessee he shall be deemed to have resided, and to have been employed, on one and the same farm;

(b) such native shall not be deemed to be *bona fide* employed unless he renders ninety days' service at least in one calendar year on the farm occupied by the owner or lessee or on another farm of the owner or lessee and no rent is paid or valuable consideration of any kind, other than service, is given by him to the owner or lessee in respect of residence on such farm or farms.

A person shall be deemed for the purposes of this Act to hire land if, in consideration of his being permitted to occupy that land or any portion thereof

(a) he pays or promises to pay to any person a rent in money; or

(b) he renders or promises to render to any person a share of the produce of that land, or any valuable consideration of any kind whatever other than his own labour or services or the labour or services of his family.

11. This Act may be cited for all purposes as the Natives' Land Act, 1913.

The foregoing result of a legislative jumble is 'the law', and this law, like Alexander the coppersmith, 'hath done us much harm'. Mr Sauer carried his Bill less by reason than by sheer force of numbers, and partly by promises which he afterwards broke. Among these broken promises was the definite assurance he gave Parliament that the Bill would be referred to the Select Committee on Native Affairs, so that the natives, who are not represented in Parliament, their European friends and the missionary bodies on behalf of the natives, could be able at the proper time to appear before this committee and state any objection which they might have to the Bill. But when that time came, the Minister flatly refused to refer it to the committee. This change of front is easily explained, because the weight of evidence which could have been given before any Parliamentary committee would have imperilled the passage of the Bill.

As might have been expected, the debate on the Bill created the greatest alarm amongst the native population, for they had followed its course with the keenest interest. Nothing short of a declaration of war against them could have created a similar excitement, although the hope was entertained in some quarters, that a body of men like the Ministerialists in Parliament (a majority of whom are never happier than when attesting the Christian character of their race) would in course of days attend the holy communion, remember the 11th commandment, and do unto others as they would that men should do unto them. Our people, in fact a number of them, said amongst themselves that even Dutchmen sing psalms—all the psalms, including the 24th; and, believing as they did that Dutchmen could have no other religion besides the one recommended in the New Testament and preached by the predikants of the Dutch Reformed Church, were prepared to commend their safety to the influence of that sweet and peaceable religion. However, some other natives, remembering what took place before the South African war, took a different view of these religious incidents. Those natives, especially of the old Republics, knew that the only dividing fence between the Transvaal natives and complete slavery was the London Convention; they, therefore, now that the London Convention in fact had ceased to exist, had evil forebodings regarding the average Republican's treatment of the natives, which was seldom influenced by religious scruples, and they did not hesitate to express their fears.

Personally we must say that if anyone had told us at the beginning of 1913, that a majority of members of the Union Parliament were capable of passing a law like the Natives' Land Act, whose object is to prevent the natives from ever rising above the position of servants to the whites, we would have regarded that person as a fit subject for the lunatic asylum. But the passing of that Act and its operation have rudely forced the fact upon us that the Union Parliament is capable of producing any measure that is subversive of native interests; and that the complete arrest of native progress is the object aimed at in their efforts to include the Protectorates in their Union. Thus we think that their sole reason for seeking to incorporate Basutoland, Swaziland and Bechuanaland is that, when they have definitely eliminated the imperial factor from South Africa, as they are unmistakably trying to do, they may have a million more slaves than if the Protectorates were excluded.

In this connexion, the realisation of the prophecy of an old Basuto became increasingly believable to us. It was to this effect, namely: 'That the Imperial Government, after conquering the Boers, handed back to them their old Republics, and a nice little present in the shape of the Cape Colony and Natal—the two English colonies. That the Boers are now ousting the Englishmen from the public service, and when they have finished with them, they will make a law declaring it a crime for a native to live in South Africa, unless he is a servant in the employ of a Boer, and that from this it will be just one step to complete slavery.' This is being realised, for today we have, extended throughout the Union of South Africa, a 'Free' State law which makes it illegal for natives to live on farms except as servants in the employ of Europeans. There is another 'Free' State law, under which no native may live in a municipal area or own property in urban localities. He can only live in town as a servant in the employ of a European. And if the followers of General Hertzog are permitted to dragoon the Union Government into enforcing 'Free' State ideals against the natives of the Union, as they have successfully done under the Natives' Land Act, it will only be a matter of time before we have a Natives' Urban Act enforced throughout South Africa. Then we will have the banner of slavery fully unfurled (of course, under another name) throughout the length and breadth of the land.

When the Natives' Land Bill was before Parliament, meetings were held in many villages and locations in protest against the Ministerial surrender to the Republicans, of which the Bill was the outcome. At the end of March 1913, the Native National Congress met in Johannesburg, and there a deputation was appointed to go to Capetown and point out to the Government some, at least, of the harm that would follow legislation of the character mapped out in Parliament on February 28 when the Land Act was first announced. They were to urge that such a measure would be exploitation of the cruellest kind, that it would not only interfere with the economic independence of the natives, but would reduce them for ever to a state of serfdom, and degrade them as nothing has done since slavery was abolished at the Cape. Missionaries also, and European friends of the natives, did not sit still. Resolution after resolution, telegraphic and other representations, were made to Mr Sauer, from meetings in various parts of the country, counselling prudence. Even such societies as the Transvaal Landowners, who had long been crying for a measure to separate whites from blacks, and vice versa, urged that the Bill should not be passed during the same session in which it was introduced, that the country should be given an opportunity to digest it, in order, if necessary, to suggest amendments. The missionary bodies, too, represent a following of natives numbering hundreds of thousands of souls, on whose behalf they pleaded for justice. These bodies urged that before passing a law prohibiting the sale and lease of land to natives, and expelling squatters from their homes, the Government should provide locations to which the evicted natives could go. But all these representations made no impression upon the Government, who, instead, preferred to act upon the recommendation of thirteen diminutive petitions (signed in all by 304 Dutchmen in favour of the Bill)[1] than to be guided by the overwhelming weight of public opinion that was against its passage. Thus it became clear that the native's position in his own country was not an enviable one, for once a law was made prohibiting the sale of landed property to natives, it would be almost impossible to get a South African Parliament to amend it.

The Government, which at the beginning assured Parliament of their humane intentions, proceeded to delete the mildest clauses of the measure and to insert some very harsh ones; and almost each time that the Bill came before the House, one or two fresh drastic clauses were added. But it is comforting to note that even Parliament was not entirely satisfied with this, its heroic piece of legislation. Thus Mr Meyler of Natal did, as only a lawyer could with a view to recasting the Bill, some very useful work in pointing out the possible harm with which the Bill was fraught. We wish that his clever speeches and observations (much of which have come true), might yet be sifted out of the big Parliamentary Reports, and published in a concise little pamphlet.

Sir David Hunter, another member of Natal, expressed himself as follows:

While every one seemed animated with a desire to do what was right and just to the natives, there was a feeling that certain of the details of the measure required amendment. He was more than pleased when the Minister closed the debate by a speech in which he seemed to be willing to meet the wishes of those in the House who thought that amendment was required. He could not have imagined that the Bill would develop into the shape into which it had developed, and had he known that so great an alteration would take place in the general effect of the measure from what was foreshadowed by the hon. Minister when he had made that interesting speech on the second reading he (the

[1] One of these thirteen petitions had only four signatures, which was but one better than that of the Tooley Street tailors.

speaker) could not have conscientiously voted for the second reading. He would have been better pleased had a resolution been taken not to bring in a Bill until the Commission had reported. That was the position he had taken up all through and he would much rather now that the matter should be dealt with in that way. If, however, the Bill was to be pressed through there should be guarantees in it which should allay all suspicion. Anything affecting the native people required to be done gradually and should be placed before them a long time before the change took place. He hoped there would yet be some steps taken to give them a greater sense of security. To give some idea of the feeling in the minds of the natives he read a letter from a gentleman in Natal, largely interested in the natives, which had expressed the opinion that the natives stood uncompromisingly against any change in their present status until the Commission had reported. He hoped the hon. Minister would even yet endeavour to do something to meet their views.

But alas! these and similar pleadings had about as much effect upon the Ministerial steamroller as the proverbial water on a duck's back. With a rush the Natives' Land Bill was dispatched from the Lower House to the Senate, adopted hurriedly by the Senate, returned to the Lower House, and went at the same pace to Government House, and there receiving the Governor-General's signature, it immediately became law. As regards the Governor-General's signature, His Excellency, if Ministers are to be believed, was ready to sign the Bill (or rather signified his intention of doing so) long before it was introduced into Parliament. This excited haste suggests grave misgivings as to the character of the Bill. Why all the hurry and scurry, and why the Governor-General's approval in advance? Other Bills are passed and approved by the Governor, yet they do not come into operation until some given day—the beginning of the next calendar year, or of the next financial year. But the Natives' Land Act became law and was operating as soon as it could be promulgated.

After desperately protesting, with individual members of

Parliament and with cabinet ministers, and getting nothing for their pains, the delegates from the Native Congress wrote to Lord Gladstone, from an office about two hundred yards distant from Government House, requesting His Excellency to withhold his assent to the Natives' Land Bill until the people mostly concerned (i.e. the natives) had had a chance of making known to His Majesty the King their objection to the measure. His Excellency replied that such a course 'was not within his constitutional functions'. Thereby the die was cast, and the mandate went forth that the land laws of the Orange 'Free' State which is commonly known as 'the only slave state', shall be the laws of the whole Union of South Africa. The worst feature in the case is the fact that, even with the Governments of the late Republics, the Presidents always had the power to exempt some natives from the operation of those laws, and that prerogative had been liberally used by successive Presidents. Now, however, without a President, and with the prerogative of the King (by the exercise of which the evils of such a law could have been averted) disowned by the King's own Ministers on the spot, God in the heavens alone knows what will become of the hapless, because voteless, natives, who are without a President, 'without a King', and with a Governor-General without constitutional functions, under task-masters whose national traditions are to enslave the dark races.

4 One night with the fugitives

'Pray that your flight be not in winter', said Jesus Christ; but it was only during the winter of 1913 that the full significance of this New Testament passage was revealed to us. We left Kimberley by the early morning train during the first week in July, on a tour of observation regarding the operation of the Natives' Land Act; and we arrived at Bloemhof, in the Transvaal, at about noon. On the river diggings there were no actual cases representing the effects of the Act, but traces of these effects were everywhere manifest. Some fugitives of the Natives' Land Act had crossed the river in full flight. The fact that they reached the diggings a fortnight before our visit would seem to show that while the debates were proceeding in Parliament some farmers already viewed with eager eyes the impending opportunity for at once making slaves of their tenants and appropriating their stock; for, acting on the powers conferred on them by an Act signed by Lord Gladstone, so lately as June 16, they had during that very week (probably a couple of days after, and in some cases, it would seem, a couple of days before the actual signing of the Bill) approached their tenants with stories about a new Act which makes it criminal for anyone to have black tenants and lawful to have black servants. Few of these natives, of course, would object to be servants, especially if the white man is worth working for, but this is where the shoe pinches: one of the conditions is that the black man's (that is the servant's) cattle shall henceforth work for the landlord free of charge. Then the natives would decide to leave the farm rather than make the landlord a present of all their life's savings, and some of them had passed through the diggings in search of a place in the Transvaal. But the higher up they went the more gloomy was their prospect as the news about the new law was now penetrating every part of the country.

One farmer met a wandering native family in the town of Bloemhof a week before our visit. He was willing to employ the native and many more homeless families as follows: A monthly wage of £2 10s for each such family, the husband working in the fields, the wife in the house, with an additional 10s a month for each son, and 5s for each daughter, but on condition that the native's cattle were also handed over to work for him. It must be clearly understood, we are told that the Dutchman added, that occasionally the native would have to leave his family at work on the farm, and go out with his wagon and his oxen to earn money whenever and wherever he was told to go, in order that the master may be enabled to pay the stipulated wage. The natives were at first inclined to laugh at the idea of working for a master with their families and goods and chattels, and then to have the additional pleasure of paying their own small wages, besides bringing money to pay the 'Baas' for employing them. But the Dutchman's serious demeanour told them that his suggestion was 'no joke'. He himself had for some time been in need of a native cattle owner, to assist him as transport rider between Bloemhof, Mooifontein, London, and other diggings, in return for the occupation and cultivation of some of his waste lands in the district, but that was now illegal. He could only 'employ' them; but, as he had no money to pay wages, their cattle would have to go out and earn it for him. Had they not heard of the law before? he inquired. Of course they had; in fact that is why they left the other place, but as they thought that it was but a 'Free' State law, they took the anomalous situation for one of the multifarious aspects of the freedom of the 'Free' State whence they came; they had scarcely thought that the Transvaal was similarly afflicted.

Needless to say the natives did not see their way to agree with such a one-sided bargain. They moved up-country, but only to find the next farmer offering the same terms, however, with a good many more disturbing details—and the next farmer and the next—so that after this native farmer had wandered from farm to farm, occasionally getting into trouble for travelling with unknown stock, 'across my ground without my permission', and at times escaping arrest for he knew not what, and further, being abused for the crimes of having a black skin and no master, he sold some of his stock along the way, besides losing many which died of cold and starvation; and after thus having lost much of his substance, he eventually worked his way back to Bloemhof with the remainder, sold them for anything they could fetch, and went to work for a digger.

The experience of another native sufferer was similar to the above, except that instead of working for a digger he sold his stock for a mere bagatelle, and left with his family by the Johannesburg night train for an unknown destination. More native families crossed the river and went inland during the previous week, and as nothing had since been heard of them, it would seem that they were still wandering somewhere, and incidentally becoming well versed in the law that was responsible for their compulsory unsettlement.

Well, we knew that this law was as harsh as its instigators were callous, and we knew that it would, if passed, render many poor people homeless, but it must be confessed that we were scarcely prepared for such a rapid and widespread crash as it caused in the lives of the natives in this neighbourhood. We left our luggage the next morning with the local mission school teacher, and crossed the river to find out some more about this wonderful law of extermination. It was about 10 a.m. when we landed on the south bank of the Vaal River—the picturesque Vaal River, upon whose banks a hundred miles farther west we spent the best and happiest days of our boyhood. It was interesting to walk on one portion of the banks of that beautiful river—a portion which we had never traversed except as an infant in mother's arms more than thirty years before. How the subsequent happy days at Barkly West, so long past, came crowding upon our memory!—days when there were no railways, no bridges, and no system of irrigation. In rainy seasons, which at that time were far more regular and certain, the river used to overflow its high banks and flood the surrounding valleys to such an extent, that no punt could carry the wagons across. Thereby the transport service used to be hung up, and

51

numbers of wagons would congregate for weeks on both sides of the river until the floods subsided. At such times the price of fresh milk used to mount up to 1s per pint. There being next to no competition, we boys had a monopoly over the milk trade. We recalled the number of haversacks full of bottles of milk we youngsters often carried to those wagons, how we returned with empty bottles and with just that number of shillings. Mother and our elder brother had leather bags full of gold and did not care for the 'boy's money'; and unlike the boys of the neighbouring village, having no sisters of our own, we gave away some of our money to fair cousins, and jingled the rest in our pockets. We had been told from boyhood that sweets were injurious to the teeth, and so spurning these details we had hardly any use for money, for all we wanted to eat, drink and wear was at hand in plenty. We could then get six or eight shillings every morning from the pastime of washing that number of bottles, filling them with fresh milk and carrying them down to the wagons; there was always such an abundance of the liquid that our shepherd's hunting dog could not possibly miss what we took, for while the flocks were feeding on the luscious buds of the haakdoorns and the orange-coloured blossoms of the rich mimosa and other wild vegetation that abounded on the banks of the Vaal River, the cows, similarly engaged, were gathering more and more milk.

The gods are cruel, and one of their cruellest acts of omission was that of giving us no hint that in very much less than a quarter of a century all those hundreds of heads of cattle, and sheep and horses belonging to the family would vanish like a morning mist, and that we ourselves would live to pay 30s per month for a daily supply of this same precious fluid, and in very limited quantities. They might have warned us that Englishmen would agree with Dutchmen to make it unlawful for black men to keep milch cows of their own on the banks of that river, and gradually have prepared us for the shock.

Crossing the river from the Transvaal side brings one into the Province of the Orange 'Free' State in which, in the adjoining division of Boshof, we were born thirty-six years back. We remember the name of the farm, but not having been in this neighbourhood since infancy, we could not tell its whereabouts, nor could we say whether the present owner was a Dutchman, his lawyer, or a Hebrew merchant; one thing we do know, however: it is that even if we had the money and the owner was willing to sell the spot upon which we first saw the light of day and breathed the pure air of heaven, the sale would be followed with a fine of one hundred pounds. The law of the country forbids the sale of land to a native. Russia is one of the most abused countries in the world, but it is extremely doubtful if the statute book of the empire contains a law debarring the peasant from purchasing the land whereon he was born, or from building a home wherein he might end his days.

At this time we felt something rising from our heels along our back, gripping us in a spasm, as we were cycling along; a needle-like pang, too, pierced our heart with a sharp thrill. What was it? We remembered feeling something nearly like it when our father died eighteen years ago; but at that time our physical organs were fresh and grief was easily thrown off in tears, but then we lived in a happy South Africa that was full of pleasant anticipations, and now—what changes for the worse have we undergone! For to crown all our calamities, South Africa has by law ceased to be the home of any of her native children whose skins are dyed with a pigment that does not conform with the regulation hue.

We are told to forgive our enemies and not to let the sun go down upon our wrath, so we breathe the prayer that peace may be to the white races, and that they, including our present persecutors of the Union Parliament, may never live to find themselves deprived of all occupation and property rights in their native country as is now the case with the native. History does not tell us of any other continent where the Bantu lived besides Africa, and if this systematic ill-treatment of the natives by the colonists is to be the guiding principle of Europe's scramble for Africa, slavery is our only alternative; for now it is only as serfs that the natives are legally entitled to live here. Is it to be thought that God is using the South African Parliament to hound us out of our ancestral homes in order to quicken our pace heavenward?

But go from where to heaven? In the beginning, we are told, God created heaven and earth, and peopled the earth, for people do not shoot up to heaven from nowhere. They must have had an earthly home. Enoch, Melchizedek, Elijah, and other saints, came to heaven from earth. God did not say to the Israelites in their bondage: 'Cheer up, boys; bear it all in good part for I have bright mansions on high awaiting you all.' But he said: 'I have surely seen the affliction of my people which are in Egypt, and have heard their cry by reason of their taskmasters; for I know their sorrows, and I am come down to bring them out of the lands of the Egyptians, and to bring them up out of that land unto a good land and a large, unto a land flowing with milk and honey.' And he used Moses to carry out the promise he made to their ancestor Abraham in Canaan, that 'unto thy seed will I give this land'. It is to be hoped that in the Boer churches, entrance to which is barred against coloured people during divine service, they also read the Pentateuch.

It is doubtful if we ever thought so much on a single bicycle ride as we did on this journey; however, the sight of a police-man ahead of us disturbed these meditations and gave place to thoughts of quite another kind, for—we had no pass. Dutchmen, Englishmen, Jews, Germans, and other foreigners may roam the 'Free' State without permis-sion—but not natives. To us it would mean a fine and imprisonment to be without a pass. The 'pass' law was first instituted to check the movement of livestock over sparsely populated areas. In a sense it was a wise provision, in that it served to identify the livestock which one happened to be driving along the high road, to prove the *bona fides* of the driver and his title to the stock. Although white men still steal large droves of horses in Basutoland and sell them in Natal or in East Griqualand, they, of course, are not required to carry any passes. These white horse-thieves, to escape the clutches of the police, employ natives to go and sell the stolen stock and write the passes for these natives, forging the names of magistrates and justices of the peace. Such native thieves in some instances ceasing to be hirelings in the criminal busi-ness, trade on their own, but it is not clear what purpose it is intended to serve by subjecting native pedestrians to the degrading requirement of carrying passes when they are not in charge of any stock.

In a few moments the policeman was before us and we alighted in presence of the representative of the law, with our feet on the accursed soil of the district in which we were born. The policeman stopped. By his looks and his familiar 'Dag jong' we noticed that the policeman was Dutch, and the embodiment of affability. He spoke and we were glad to notice that he had no intention of dragging an innocent man to prison. We were many miles from the nearest police station, and in such a case one is generally able to gather the real views of the man on patrol, as distinct from the written code of his office, but our friend was becoming very companionable. Naturally we asked him about the operation of the plague law. He was a Transvaaler, he said, and he knew that Kaffirs were inferior beings, but they had rights, and were always left in undisturbed possession of their property when Paul Kruger was alive. 'The poor devils must be sorry now,' he said, 'that they ever sang "God save the Queen" when the British troops came into the Transvaal, for I have seen, in the course of my duties, that a Kaffir's life nowadays was not worth a —, and I believe that no man regretted the changes of flags now more than the Kaffirs of Transvaal.' This information was superfluous, for personal contact with the natives of Transvaal had convinced us of the fact. They say it is only the criminal who has any reason to rejoice over the presence of the Union Jack, because in his case the cat-o'-nine-tails, except for very serious crimes, has been abolished.

'Some of the poor creatures,' continued the policeman, 'I knew to be fairly comfortable, if not rich, and they enjoyed the possession of their stock, living in many instances just like Dutchmen. Many of these are now being forced to leave their homes. Cycling along this road you will meet several of them in search of new homes, and if ever there was a fool's errand, it is that of a Kaffir trying to find a new home for his stock and family just now.'

'And what do you think, Baas Officer, must eventually be the lot of a people under such unfortunate circumstances?' we asked.

'I think,' said the policeman, 'that it must serve them right. They had no business to hanker after British rule, to cheat and plot with the enemies of their Republic for the overthrow of their Government. Why did they not assist the forces of their Republic during the war instead of supplying the English with scouts and intelligence? Oom Paul would not have died of a broken heart and he would still be there to protect them. Serve them right, I say.'

So saying he spurred his horse, which showed a clean pair of hoofs. He left us rather abruptly, for we were about to ask why we, too, of Natal and the Cape were suffering, for we, being originally British subjects, never 'cheated and plotted with the enemies of our colonies', but he was gone and left us still cogitating by the roadside.

Proceeding on our journey we next came upon a native trek and heard the same old story of prosperity on a Dutch farm: they had raised an average 800 bags of grain each season, which, with the increase of stock and sale of wool, gave a steady income of about £150 per year after the farmer had taken his share. There were gossipy rumours about somebody having met some one who said that some one else had overheard a conversation between the Baas and somebody else, to the effect that the Kaffirs were getting too rich on his property. This much involved tale incidentally conveys the idea that the Baas was himself getting too rich on his farm. For the native provides his own seed, his own cattle, his own labour for the ploughing, the weeding and the reaping, and after bagging his grain he calls in the landlord to receive his share, which is fifty per cent of the entire crop.

All had gone well till the previous week when the Baas came to the native tenants with the story that a new law had been passed under which 'all of my oxen and cows must belong to him, and my family to work for £2 a month, failing which he gave me four days to leave the farm'.

We passed several farmhouses along the road, where all appeared pretty tranquil as we went along, until the evening which we spent in the open country, somewhere near the boundaries of the Hoopstad and Boshof districts; here a regular circus had gathered. By a 'circus' we mean the meeting of groups of families, moving to every point of the compass, and all bivouacked at this point in the open country where we were passing. It was heartrending to listen to the tales of their cruel experiences derived from the rigour of the Natives' Land Act. Some of their cattle had perished on the journey, from poverty and lack of fodder, and the native owners ran a serious risk of imprisonment for travelling with dying stock. The experience of one of these evicted tenants is typical of the rest, and illustrates the cases of several we met in other parts of the country.

Kgobadi, for instance, had received a message describing the eviction of his father-in-law in the Transvaal Province, without notice, because he had refused to place his stock, his family, and his person at the disposal of his former landlord, who now refuses to let him remain on his farm except on these conditions. The father-in-law asked that Kgobadi should try and secure a place for him in the much dreaded 'Free' State as the Transvaal had suddenly become uninhabitable to natives who cannot become servants; but 'greedy folk hae lang airms,' and Kgobadi himself was proceeding with his family and his belongings in a wagon, to inform his people-in-law of his own eviction, without notice, in the 'Free' State, for a similar reason to that which sent his father-in-law adrift. The Baas had exacted from him the services of himself, his wife and his oxen, for wages of 30s a month, whereas Kgobadi had been making over £100 a year, besides retaining the services of his wife and of his cattle for himself. When he refused the extortionate terms the Baas retaliated with a Dutch note, dated the 30th day of June 1913, which ordered him to 'betake himself from the farm of the undersigned, by sunset of the same day, failing which his stock would be seized and impounded, and himself handed over to the authorities for trespassing on the farm'.

A drowning man catches at every straw, and so we were again and again appealed to for advice by these sorely afflicted people. To those who were not yet evicted we counselled patience and submission to the absurd terms, pending an appeal to a higher authority than the South African Parliament and finally to His Majesty the King who, we believed, would certainly disapprove of all that we saw on that day had it been brought to his notice. As for those who were already evicted, as a Bechuana we could not help thanking God that Bechuanaland (on the western boundary of this quasi-British Republic) was still entirely British. In the early days it was the base of David Livingstone's activities and peaceful mission against the Portuguese and Arab slave trade. We suggested that they might negotiate the numerous restrictions against the transfer of cattle from the western Transvaal and seek an asylum in Bechuanaland. We wondered what consolation we could give to those roving wanderers if the whole of Bechuanaland were under the jurisdiction of the relentless Union Parliament.

It was cold that afternoon as we cycled into the 'Free' State from Transvaal, and towards evening the southern winds rose. A cutting blizzard raged during the night, and native mothers evicted from their homes shivered with their babies by their sides. When we saw on that night the teeth of the little children clattering through the cold, we thought of our own little ones in their Kimberley home of an evening after gambolling in their winter frocks with their schoolmates, and we wondered what these little mites had done that a home should suddenly become to them a thing of the past.

Kgobadi's goats had been to kid when he trekked from his farm; but the kids, which in halcyon times represented the interest on his capital, were now one by one dying as fast as they were born and left by the roadside for the jackals and vultures to feast upon.

This visitation was not confined to Kgobadi's stock. Mrs Kgobadi carried a sick baby when the eviction took place, and she had to transfer her darling from the cottage to the jolting ox-wagon in which they left the farm. Two days out the little one began to sink as the result of privation and exposure on the road, and the night before we met them its little soul was released from its earthly bonds. The death of the child added a fresh perplexity to the stricken parents. They had no right or title to the farm lands through which they trekked: they must keep to the public roads—the only places in the country open to the outcasts if they are possessed of a travelling permit. The deceased child had to be buried, but where, when and how?

This young wandering family decided to dig a grave under cover of the darkness of that night, when no one was looking, and in that crude manner the dead child was interred—and interred amid fear and trembling, as well as the throbs of a torturing anguish, in a stolen grave, lest the proprietor of the spot, or any of his servants, should surprise them in the act. Even criminals dropping straight from the gallows have an undisputed claim to six feet of ground on which to rest their criminal remains, but under the cruel operation of the Natives' Land Act little children, whose only crime is that God did not make them white, are sometimes denied that right in their ancestral home.

Numerous details narrated by these victims of an Act of Parliament kept us awake all that night, and by next morning we were glad enough to hear no more of the sickening procedure of extermination voluntarily instituted by the South African Parliament. We had spent a hideous night under a bitterly cold sky, conditions to which hundreds of our unfortunate countrymen and countrywomen in various parts of the country are condemned by the provisions of this Parliamentary land plague. At five o'clock in the morning the cold seemed to redouble its energies; and never before did we so fully appreciate the Master's saying: 'But pray ye that your flight be not in the winter.'

5 Another night with the sufferers

We parted sadly from these unfortunate nomads of an ungrateful and inhospitable country, after advising them to trek from the Union into the arid deserts of Bechuanaland. In our advice we laid special stress upon the costliness of such an expedition as theirs and upon the many and varying regulations to be complied with, on such a trek, through the western Transvaal. But, cost whatever it may, they, like ourselves, understood that as the law stood they would be better off and safer beyond the boundaries of the Union.

From here we worked our way into the Hoopstad district. There we saw some natives who were, as it were, on pins and needles, their landlords having given them a few days in which to consider the advisability of either accepting the new conditions or leaving their houses. Our advice to these tenants was to accept, for the time being, any terms offered by their landlords, pending an appeal to His Majesty the King; we also passed through a few farms where the white farmers were visibly sympathetic towards the harried natives. Some of the white farmers were accepting natives as tenants on their farms in defiance of the law. We naturally thanked these for their humanity and went our way, promising never to disclose their magnanimity to the Government officials. 'What has suddenly happened?' one of these landlords asked. 'We were living so nicely with your people, and why should the law unsettle them in this manner?'

We may here mention that a fortnight later we were in General Botha's constituency in the Transvaal. A few days before we arrived there a meeting of white farmers was held at one of the Dutch farmhouses at which it was resolved to take the fullest advantage of the new law, which had placed the entire native population in the hands of the farmers. It was further resolved that a Kaffir who refused to become a servant should at once be consigned to the road.

A similar resolution was passed at another meeting of land-lords at another place. Part of the proceedings of this meet-ing was reported in some, though not all, of the Dutch news-papers. Without breaking our promise not to disclose any names of landlords who felt it a duty to resist injustice, even though it bears the garb of law, we will mention Mr X, a Boer farmer, of the farm —, near Thingamejig, between the town of — and the river —. He protested at the meet-ing, stating that the Transvaalers were not compelled to turn the natives out, and that they were only debarred from taking any new native tenants; that it was wicked to expel a Kaffir from the farm for no reason whatever, and so make him homeless, since he could not, if evicted, go either to another farm or back to his old place. For expressing his views so frankly Mr X was threatened by his compatriots with physical violence! His opponents also said that if he continued to har-bour Kaffirs on his farm as tenants, they would hold him responsible for any stock that they might lose. The incidents of the meeting were related to the natives by Mr X himself. He told the natives, further, that he would go to the expense of fencing his farm with the natives inside, so that they may be out of the reach of his infuriated neighbours.

We spent the next night in some native huts on a farm in the district of Hoopstad. On that occasion we met a man who had had a month's notice to leave his farm, and was going from farm to farm in search of a new place. He had heard alarming stories about evictions wherever he went. During that evening we were treated to some more pitiful stories concerning the atrocities of the wretched Land Act. Many native wanderers had actually passed that farm during the preceding few days, trudging aimlessly from place to place in search of some farmer who might give them a shelter. At first they thought the stories about a new law were inven-tions or exaggerations, but their own desperate straits and the prevailing native dislocation soon taught them otherwise.

The similarity in the experiences of the sufferers would make monotonous reading if given individually, but there are instances here and there which give variety to the painful record, and these should yield the utmost satisfaction to the promoters of the Act, in proving to them the full measure of their achievement. One example of these experiences was that of a white farmer who had induced a thrifty native in another district to come and farm on his estate. The contract was duly executed about the end of May 1913. It was agreed that the native should move over to the new place after gathering his crops and sharing them with his old landlord, which he did in the third week in June. On his arrival, however, the new landlord's attitude towards him aroused his suspicions; his suspicions were confirmed when, after some hesitation, the landlord told him that their contract was illegal. Having already left his old place the legal embargo was also against his return there, and so his only course was to leave that place and wander about with his stock and family. They went in the direction of Kroonstad, and they have not been heard of since.

The next example is that of the oldest man in the 'Free' State. He had been evicted (so we were told during that evening on the farm) along with his aged wife, his grey-headed children, the children's children and grandchildren. We may here add that we read a confirmation of this case in the English weekly newspaper of Harrismith. The paper's reference to this case will also illustrate the easy manner in which these outrageous evictions are reported in white newspapers. There is no reference to the sinister undercurrent and hardships attending these evictions. The paper in question, the *Harrismith Chronicle*, simply says:

An Ancient Couple

A venerable native whose age is no less than 119 years, accompanied by his wife, aged 98, and a son who is aproaching 80, left Harrismith on Tuesday by train for Volksrust. The old man acquired some property in the Transvaal, and is leaving this district to start a new home with as much interest in the venture as if he were a stripling of twenty. The old lady had to be carried to the train, but the old man walked fairly firmly. The aged couple were the centre of much kindly attraction, and were made as comfortable as possible for their journey by the railway officials. It is difficult to realise in these days of rapid change that in the departure from the 'Free' State of this venerable party we are losing from our midst a man who was born in 1794, and has lived in no less than three centuries of time. Good luck to them both; and may they still live long and prosper!

Now, as a matter of fact, this 'ancient couple' had not left the 'Free' State of their own free will. Their stock had been expelled from their grazing areas, and they were told that they could only continue to graze if the centenarian tenant agreed to supply a certain number of labourers to work on the landowner's farm and with his sons ceased to do any ploughing as tenants. This system of sharing the crops has been followed ever since the Boers planted themselves in the 'Free' State, and the family had had no other means of support. Happily the aid of providence in the case of this 'ancient couple' was speedy, as the old people quickly found an asylum on the farm of Mr P. ka I. Seme, a native solicitor in the Transvaal.

At the same place on the same evening we were told of a conversation between a well-known Dutchman and a native. 'The object of this law,' said the Burgher, 'is to goad the natives into rebellion, so that the Government may legally confiscate what little ground was left to them, and hand over the dispossessed Kaffirs and their families to work for the farmers, just for their food.' The policy of goading the natives into rebellion is not wholly foreign to colonial policy; but the horrible cruelty to which livestock is exposed under the new Act is altogether a new departure. King Solomon says, 'The righteous man regardeth the life of his beast, but the tender mercies of the wicked are cruel'; but there is a Government of professed bible readers who, in defiance of all scriptural precepts, pass a law which penalizes a section of the community along with their oxen, sheep, goats, horses and donkeys on account of the colour of their owners. The penalty clause (Section 5) imposes a fine of £100 on a landowner who accommodates a native on his farm; and if after the fine is paid the native leaves his stock on the farm to go and look for a fresh place, there will be an additional fine of £5 for every day that the native's cattle remain on that farm. They must take the road immediately and be kept moving day and night until they die of starvation, or until the owner (who is debarred, by Section I, from purchasing a pasturage for his cattle) disposes of them to a white man.

Such cruelty to dumb animals is as unwarranted as it is unprecedented. It reads cruel enough on paper, but we wish that the reader had accompanied us on one journey, say, during the cold snap in the first week in August, when we travelled from Potchefstroom to Vereeniging, and seen the flocks of those evicted natives that we met. We frequently met those roving pariahs, with their hungry cattle, and wondered if the animals were not more deserving of pity than their owners. It may be the cattle's misfortune that they have a black owner, but it is certainly not their fault, for sheep have no choice in the selection of a colour for their owners, and no cows or goats are ever asked to decide if the black boy who milks them shall be their owner, or but a herd in the employ of a white man; so why should they be starved on account of the colour of their owners? We knew of a law to prevent cruelty to animals, but had never thought that we should live to meet in one day so many dumb creatures making silent appeals to heaven for protection against the law. 'What man has nerve to do, man has not nerve to see,' and oh! if those gifted Parliamentarians could have been mustered here to witness the wretched results of one of their fine day's work for a fine day's pay! But 'they bind heavy burdens and grevious to be borne', then draw their Parliamentary emoluments and retire to the quiet of their comfortable homes, to enjoy more rest than is due to toilers who have served both God and humanity.

During this same night in Hoopstad district we were also told of the visit of a Dutch farmer in the middle of June 1913, to his native tenants. One of the natives—named Kgabale— was rather old. His two sons are delving in the gold mines of Johannesburg, and return home each spring-time to help the old man and their two young sisters to do the ploughing. The daughters tend the fields and Kgabale looks after the stock. By this means they have been enabled to lead a respectable life and to pay the landowner fifty per cent of the produce every year, besides the taxes levied by the Government on natives. Three weeks before our visit, the farmer came to cancel Kgabale's verbal contract with him and to turn the family into unpaid servants, in return for the privilege of squatting on his farm. As Kgabale himself was too old to work, the farmer demanded of him that his two sons should return immediately from Johannesburg to render manual service on his farm, failing which, the old man should forthwith betake himself from the place. He gave Kgabale seven days to deliver his two sons.

Naturally this decision came upon Kgabale and his daughters like a bolt from the blue. The poor old man wandered from place to place, trying to find some one—and it took him two days to do so—who could write, so as to dictate a letter to his sons in Johannesburg, informing them of what had happened. The week expired before he could get a reply from Johannesburg. The landlord, in a very abusive mood, again demanded the instant arrival of his two sons from Johannesburg, to commence work at the farm-house the very next morning. Kgabale spent the whole night praying that at least one of his sons might come. By day-break next morning no answer had arrived, and the Dutch-man came and set fire to the old man's houses, and ordered him then and there to quit the farm. It was a sad sight to see the feeble old man, his aged wife and his daughters driven in this way from a place which they had regarded as their home. In the ordinary course, such a calamity could have been made more tolerable by moving to the next farm and there await the arrival and advice of his sons; but now, under the Natives' Land Act, no sympathetic landowner would be permitted to shelter them for a single day. So Kgabale was said to have gone in the direction of Klerksdorp.

One of the sons arrived a week after the catastrophe. He found his old home in ruins, and that his aged parents and their children had become victims of the turpitude of an Act of Parliament. The son went in search of his relatives across the Vaal, but it was not known if they succeeded in finding the refuge which the law had made unlawful.

Among the squatters on the same farm as Kgabale was a widow named Maria. Her husband in his lifetime had lived as a tenant on the farm, ploughing in shares until his death. After his death Maria kept on the contract and made a fair living. Her son and daughter, aged fourteen and sixteen respectively, took turns at herding her cattle and assisting the mother in other ways. During the ploughing season, they hired assistance to till the fields, but they themselves tended and reaped the harvest and delivered 50 per cent of the produce to the landowner. Such were the conditions on which she was allowed to live on the farm. Maria, being a widow, her son being but a youth, it was hoped that the landlord would propose reasonable terms for her; but instead, his proposal was that she should dispose of her stock and indenture her children to him. This sinister proposal makes it evident that farmers not only expect natives to render them free labour, but they actually wish the natives to breed slaves for them. Maria found it difficult to comply with her landlord's demand, and as she had no husband, from whom labour could be exacted, the Dutchman ordered her to 'clear out, and,' he added with an oath, 'you must get another man before you reach your next place of abode, as the law will not permit you to stay there till you have a man to work for the Baas.' Having given this counsel the landlord is said to have set fire to Maria's thatched cottage, and as the chilly south-easter blew the smoke of her burning home towards the north-west, Maria, with her bedclothes on her head, and on the heads of her son and daughter, and carrying her three-year-old boy tied to her back, walked off from the farm, driving her cows before her. In parting from the endeared associations of their late home, for one blank and unknown, the children were weeping bitterly. Nor has any news of the fate of this family been received since they were forced out on this perilous adventure.

6 Our indebtedness to white women

Some farmers (unfortunately too few) who had at first intended to change the status of their native tenants, had been obliged to abandon the idea owing to the determined opposition of their wives. One such case was particularly interesting. Thus, at Dashfontein, the wife of a Dutch farmer, a Mr V, on whose property some native families were squatting, got up one morning, and found the kitchen-maid very disagreeable. The morning coffee had been made right enough, but the maid's 'Morre, Nooi' (Good morning, ma'am) was rather sullen and almost bordering on insolence. She did her scullery work as usual, but did not seem to care, that morning, about wasting time inquiring how baby slept, and if Nonnie had got rid of her neuralgia, and so on. She spoke only when spoken to and answered mainly in monosyllables. Mrs V was perplexed.

'What is the matter, Anna?' she asked.

'Nothing, Nooi,' replied Anna curtly.

Mrs V tried some of her witty jokes, but they seemed to be wasted on Anna. After jesting with the servant had failed, scolding was next tried, but nothing seemed to bring back the girl's usual cheerfulness. 'Oh, Anna,' said the mistress at length, 'you make me think of the olden days, when such disagreeable whims on the part of frowning maids used to be cured by —'

Anna was evidently not listening, and, if she had heard the mistress, she did not care two straws (or one straw for that matter) what cures Mrs V's great-grandmother had prescribed for sullen servant girls. In fact, Anna had become a wild Kaffir, for though she went about her work in silence, her face bore an expression which seemed to speak louder than her mouth could have done. She was clearly engaged in serious thought. The mistress tried to dismiss from her mind the inexplicable attitude of her servant, but the frowning look on Anna's face made the attempts unsuccessful. The fact that when Anna went home, the previous night, she was happiness personified, did not decrease Mrs V's perplexity.

'There must be something wrong,' Mrs V concluded, after vainly trying ruse after ruse to get a smile out of her servant girl. 'Something is amiss. I wonder if one of those well-dressed Kaffirs from Potchefstroom has been prowling about the farm and instilling in Anna's simple mind all kinds of silly notions, about town flirts and black dandies, silk dresses in Potchefstroom and similar *vuilgoed*. And if a town Kaffir is going to marry Anna, where on earth am I going to get a reliable servant to whom I could securely entrust my home when I have occasion to go to town or to the seaside on a shorter or longer vacation? Who could cook and attend to my husband's and children's peculiar wants, if Anna is going to leave us? It seems certain that Anna's heart is not on the farm,' she said to herself. 'It was there right enough when she went home last night, but it is clear that some one has stolen it during the night. Anna is helplessly lovesick. I must find out who it is. The swain must be found and induced to come and join, or supervise, our squatters. We cannot let him take her away, for what will the homestead be without Anna? I was looking forward to her marrying on the farm and giving her a superior cottage so that other Kaffir girls may see how profitable it is to be good. Anna leaving the farm, *O, nee wat!* (Oh, no). We must find out who it is; but wait, there is old Gert (her father) coming, with old Jan (her uncle). I must find out from them who had been intruding into the company of their daughters last night. I should warn them to be on the alert lest Anna elopes to Potchefstroom with somebody, probably to take the train and go farther—to Johannesburg or Kimberley, as did Klein Mietje, whom I had hoped to train as our housemaid—'

'Good morning, Auta Gert, how is Mietje and the *kleintjes*?'

Auta Gert's demeanour was a greater puzzle to Mrs V than his daughter's when he replied, 'So, so.'

Mrs V (between horns of the same dilemma): 'And you,

Auta Jan?'

'Ja, Missus,' replied Jan.

Mrs V's perplexity was intense, for it became evident that the two natives were there as a deputation, charged with some grave mission. Before she uttered another word the two natives asked for an interview.

'Not to waste much time, Missus,' began old Gert, 'a thunderbolt has burst on the native settlement on the farm, and Dashfontein is no longer a home to us—'

'No longer a home!' exclaimed Mrs V 'I hope you idiotic Kaffirs are not going to be so foolhardy as to leave me, leave the Baas, and leave the farm upon which your fathers and mothers lie buried. Do not you know that during this very week numbers of natives have been calling on the Baas, asking him for places of abode, complaining that they have been turned adrift, with their little ones and their hungry animals, for refusing to become servants to farmers on whose property they had been ploughing on shares? White men have suddenly become brutes and have expelled natives with whom they have lived from childhood—natives whose labour made the white man wealthy are turned away by people who should treat them with gratitude. And are you going to leave your old home just when the Devil appears to have possessed himself of the hearts of most farmers? In your own interest, apart from my own and the Baas's, Auta Gert, you should have left us long ago when you could find a place elsewhere. Are you so deaf and blind as not to hear and see the change which has come over the country of late? White men formerly punished a Kaffir who had done some wrong, now they worry him for sheer cussedness. You must be mad, Auta Gert, to try and leave us. What is going to become of your family and your beautiful cattle. No wonder that Anna is so upset. I have been thinking that some *rondlooper* from the towns had been trying to take her away.'

As Mrs V spoke she was agreeably surprised to find the sobering effect which her rebuke seemed to have upon her husband's native tenants. She knew her influence over them, especially over the old native families, but in all her dealings and close association with them she could not remember an impromptu speech of hers that produced such immediate results. The faces of the two natives brightened up, and they kept looking at one another as she spoke. At length she turned round towards the stoep and there was Anna, for the first time that morning, interested in and delighted by what she said. Usually it would have been a serious breach of the rules of the house for Anna to listen when the Missus was speaking about something that did not immediately concern her scullery duties; but Mrs V's satisfaction was unbounded on seeing the bright look on her servant's face, which she had hitherto vainly sought.

'Now, you see,' said Anna to her father, 'I told you it would never happen if the Missus can help it.'

At this, the men could scarcely suppress a laugh. The Missus looked round again, and said:

'Anna, have you Kaffirs plotted to fool me this morning? Because I take such a deep interest in your welfare, you have so far forgotten yourselves that you connived with your parents to come over to my house and fool me on my own farm? What is the meaning of all this?'

Auta Gert unfolded his story. The Baas was at the native settlement the previous day. He called a meeting of the native peasants and told them of the new law, under which no Kaffir can buy a farm or hire a farm. He added that, according to this law, their former relations of landlord and tenants have been made a criminal offence, for which they could be fined a hundred pounds, and he gave them ten days to decide whether they would become his servants or leave the farm.

'Go away, Auta Gert; you were dreaming, my husband would never talk such nonsense. You have been with him from childhood, long before I ever knew him, and yet you do not know that my husband is incapable of uttering anything half so wicked?'

'He said it was the law, the new law.'

'Of course you need some stringent measures against the useless, sneaking and prowling loafers, but there is no fear that such laws could apply to natives like you and Mietje and your children.'

'But, Nooi, the Baas told us to leave the farm as the law did not permit him to—'

'Get you gone, Auta Gert, he was joking. You must know that the law did not buy this farm. The old Baas purchased it from Baas Philander. I personally helped to add up the number of morgen and to calculate the money, and there was not a penny piece from any Government. Go home, Auta Gert, and leave everything to me, and do not let me hear you saying Dashfontein is no longer your home.'

'Well, Nooi,' assented the natives with some relief, 'if you say it is all right, then it must be so, and we will go back and reap our mealies in peace, and if a policeman comes round demanding a hundred pounds we will tell him to arrest us and take us to the Nooi of the farm. Good-bye, Nooi.'

'Good-bye, Auta Gert; good-bye, Auta Jan—Poor Anna, my dear little maid, why did you not tell Nooi this morning that you were worried over this matter. Really, Anna, I was thinking that you were lovesick. How did poor old Mietje take it? Sadly, did she. Well, I will speak to the Baas about it. He had no business to attempt to bring bad luck over us by disturbing our peaceful natives with such godless tidings. Tell your mother that Nooi says it will be all right.'

A few days later, Hendrik Prins, the farm manager in the employ of Mr V, was due at the native settlement to see the steam sheller at work and also to receive the landowner's share of the produce. Instead of Prins, Mr V attended in person. Each native regarded this unusual occurrence as the signal for their impending eviction and thought that day would see their last transaction with their old master and landlord.

Mr V counted the separate bags filled with mealies and Kaffir corn placed in groups around the sheller. He counted no fewer than 12,300 bags, and knew that his share would total 6,150, representing about £3,000 gross. Could he ever succeed in getting so much, with so little trouble, if poor whites tilled his lands instead of these natives? he thought. After all, his dear Johanna was right. This law is blind and must be resisted. It gives more consideration to the so-called poor whites (a respectable term for lazy whites), than to the owners of the ground. He, there and then, resolved to resist it and take the consequences.

The grain was all threshed; a number of native girls were

busy sewing up the bags, and the engine-driver ordered his men to yoke his oxen and pull the machine away. Mr V ordered Auta Gert to call all the 'volk' together as he had something to tell them. Auta Gert, knowing the determination of his mistress, did so in confidence that they were about to receive some glad tidings. But the other folk came forward with a grievous sense of wrong. The fact that some natives on the adjoining property had been turned away three days before and sent homeless about the country, their places being taken by others, who, tired of roaming about and losing nearly everything, had come in as serfs did not allay their fears. Auta Hans was already conjuring up visions of a Johannesburg speculator literally 'taking' his Cape short-horns for a mere bagatelle, as they did to William Ranco, another evicted squatter from Hoopstad.

Mr V, the farmer, mounted a handy wagon hard by and commenced to address the crowd of blacks, who gathered around the wagon at the call of Gert.

'Attention! Listen,' he said. 'You will remember that I was here last month and explained to you the new law. Well, I understand that that explanation created the greatest amount of unrest amongst the natives in the huts on my farm. Personally, I am very sorry that it ever came to that, but let me tell you that your Nooi, my wife, says it is not right that the terms under which we have lived in the past should be disturbed. I agree with her that it is unjust, and that the good Lord who has always blessed us, will turn his face from us if people are unsettled and sent away from the farm in a discontented mood.' (Loud and continued applause, during which Mr V took out his pouch of Magaliesburg tobacco and lit his pipe.) 'The Nooi,' he continued after a few puffs, 'says we must not obey this law: she even says, if it comes to physical ejectment, or if they take me to prison, she is prepared to go to Pretoria in person and interview General Botha.' (More cheers, during which the natives dispersed to cart away their mealies amidst general satisfaction.)

The writer visited Dashfontein in July 1913, when the above narrative was given him word for word by old Gert.

As old Gert narrated the story, Aunt Mietje, his wife, who

had had timely notice of the impending visit of the *morulag-anyi* editor from her husband (who slaughtered a sheep in honour of the occasion), superintended with interesting expectations over frizzling items in the frying-pan on her fireplace. Her bright eyes, beaming from under her head-kerchief, suggested how she must have been the undisputed belle of her day. The rough wooden table was covered with the best linen in the native settlement, and on it were laid some clean plates, and the old yet shining cutlery reserved for special occasions, besides other signs of an approaching evening meal. Having learnt the art from an experienced housewife on whose farm her people were squatting, and improved upon her teaching, she was famous in the neigh-bourhood for the excellence of her cooking. Her only worry in that department was her seeming lack of success in train-ing her daughters up to her elevation. She is usually sent for when important visitors come to Dashfontein, and would then don her best costume of coloured German print, and carry down with her the spotless apron which Mrs V gave her the preceding New Year; and in spite of her advancing years, she would cause Anna, and every other upstart at the homestead, instinctively to play second fiddle to her. And when we suggested that our wife could measure swords (or, shall we say, forks) with her as a cook, she giggled and remembered some white man's proverb about the proof of the pudding being in the eating.

After the harrowing experience of the previous week, during which we were forced to see our fellow-beings hounded out of their homes, and the homes broken up; their lifelong earnings frittered away by a law of the land, their only crime being the atrocious one of having the same colour of skin as our own, and finding ourselves suddenly landed on an oasis, the farm of a kind Dutchman and his noble wife, on whose property, and by whose leave, little black piccanin-nies still played about in spite of the law, it can be readily understood with what comfort we sat down and did justice to the good things provided by Aunt Mietje. In the course of her preparation every step of her suggested that she enter-tained no sort of misprised opinion about her superiority over her compeers; and nothing pleased her better than when she dazzled her husband and family connexions with deeds which proved her superiority over her contemporaries, in everything that tends to make the virtuous and industrious housewife. She gave a dramatic ending to her husband's narrative when she said—

'Who would have thought that Hannetje, naughty little Hannetje, who was so troublesome when my sister used to nurse her—who would have thought that she would ever prove to be the salvation of our people? Who ever anticipated that all the strong Boers, on whom we had relied, would desert us when the fate of our whole tribe hung in the balance? Natives have been moving from north to south, and from south to north, all searching at the same time for homes and grazing for their cattle. During the last few weeks the roads were hidden in clouds of dust, sent up by hundreds of hoofs of hundreds of cattle, their owners with them, vainly seeking places of refuge; but in the case of Dashfontein, we reclined on a veritable Mount Ararat, by grace of naughty little Hannetje, whom God in his mysterious foresight had raised up to be Mrs van V, proprietress of Dashfontein. If my prayers are of any value, God will appoint in heaven a special place for her when she gets there, though, for the sake of our people, I hope that time is very far distant. However, I hope to be somewhere near: in truth, I should like to accompany her, when Elijah's chariot comes for her soul, so as to render her what little aid I can on board, when she soars through unknown tracts of space to the spirit world on high, so that if there be any uncomfortable questions about her maiden vagaries, I may be there to attest that she has since atoned a hundredfold for each, and thus accelerate her promotion. No no, Hannetje is not a Boer *vrouw*, she is an angel.'

7 Persecution of coloured women in the Orange 'Free' State

When the 'Free' State ex-Republicans made use of the South African constitution—a constitution which Lord Gladstone says is one after the Boer sentiment—to ruin the coloured population, they should at least have confined their persecution to the male portion of the blacks (as is done in a milder manner in the other three provinces), and have left the women and children alone. According to his class legislation, no native woman in the Province of the Orange 'Free' State can reside within a municipality (whether with or without her parents, or her husband) unless she can produce a permit showing that she is a servant in the employ of a white person, this permit being signed by the Town Clerk. All repressive measures under the old Republic (which, in matters of this kind, always showed a regard for the suzerainty of Great Britain) were mildly applied. Now, under the Union, the Republicans are told by the imperial authorities that since they are self-governing they have the utmost freedom of action, including freedom to do wrong, without any fear of imperial interference. Of this licence the white inhabitants of the Union are making the fullest use. Like a mastiff long held in the leash they are urging the application of all the former stringent measures enacted against the blacks, and the authorities, in obedience to their electoral supporters, are enforcing these measures with the utmost rigour against the blacks because they have no votes.

Hence, whereas the pass regulations were formerly never enforced by the Boers against clergymen's wives or against the families of respectable native inhabitants, now a minister's wife has not only to produce a pass on demand, but, like every woman of colour, she has to pay a shilling for a fresh pass at the end of the month, so that a family consisting of, say, a mother and five daughters pay the municipality 6s every month, whether as a penalty for the colour of their skins or a penalty for their sex it is not clear which.

There is some unexplained anomaly in this woman's pass business. If the writer were to go and live in the 'Free' State, he could apply for and obtain letters of exemption from the ordinary pass laws; but if his wife, who has had a better schooling and enjoyed an older civilisation than he, were to go and reside in the 'Free' State with her daughters, all of them would be forced to carry passes on their persons, and be called upon to ransack their skirt pockets at any time in the public streets at the behest of male policemen in quest of their passes. Several white men are at present undergoing long terms of imprisonment inflicted by the Orange 'Free' State circuit courts for criminally outraging coloured women whom the pass laws had placed in the hollow of the hands of these ruffians. Still many more mothers are smothering evidence of similar outrages upon innocent daughters—cases that could never have happened under ordinary circumstances.

The natives of the 'Free' State have made all possible constitutional appeals against these outrages. In reply to their petitions the provincial government blames the municipalities. The latter blame the law and the Union Parliament, and there the matter ends. We have read the 'Free' State law which empowers the municipalities to frame regulations for the control of natives, etc., but it must be confessed that our limited intelligence could discern nothing in it which could be construed as imposing any dire penalties on municipalities which emancipate their coloured women from the burden of the insidious pass law and tax. Hon. Mr H. Burton, as already stated, was Minister of Native Affairs before the Union Government surrendered to the 'Free' State reactionaries. A deputation consisting of Mrs A. S. Gabashane, Mrs Kotsi and Mrs Louw, women from Bloemfontein—the first-named being a clergyman's wife—waited on him in Cape Town on the subject of these grievances, and he assured them that in response to representations made by the Native Congress, he had already written to Dr

Ramsbottom, the Provincial Administrator, asking him to persuade the 'Free' State municipalities to relieve the native women from this burden. And if to relieve native women in the 'Free' State from a burden which obtains nowhere else in the Union were unlawful, as the municipalities aver, Mr Burton—a K.C.—would have been the last person to ask them to break the law.

Subsequently the women petitioned Lady Gladstone for her intercession. But we wonder if the petition was ever handed to Lady Gladstone by the responsible authority who, in this instance, would have been the Department of Native Affairs. Notwithstanding all these efforts, native women in the 'Free' State are still forced to buy passes every month or go to prison, and they are still exposed to the indecent provision of the law authorising male constables to insult them by day and by night, without distinction.

After exhausting all these constitutional means on behalf of their women, and witnessing the spread of the trouble to the women and children of the country districts under the Natives' Land Act, the male natives of the municipalities of the Province of the Orange 'Free' State saw their women-folk throwing off their shawls and taking the 'law' into their own hands. A crowd of 600 women, in July 1913, marched to the municipal offices at Bloemfontein and asked to see the Mayor. He was not in, so they called for the Town Clerk. The Deputy-Mayor came out, and they deposited before him a bag containing their passes of the previous month and politely signified their intention not to buy any more passes. Then there occurred what *John Bull* would call, '—l with the lid off'.

At Jagersfontein there was a similar demonstration, led by a jet-black Mozambique lady. She and a number of others were arrested and sentenced to various terms of imprisonment. The sentences ranged from about three weeks to three months, and the fines from 10s to £3. They all refused to pay the fines, and said their little ones could be entrusted to the care of providence till their mothers and sisters have broken the shackles of oppression by means of passive resistance. As the prison authorities were scarcely prepared for such a sudden influx of prisoners there was no sufficient accommodation for fifty-two women, who were conveyed on donkey carts to the adjoining village of Fauresmith.

When this happened, Winburg, the old capital of the 'Free' State, also had a similar trouble. Eight hundred women marched from the native location to the Town Hall, singing hymns, and addressed the authorities. They were tired of making friendly appeals which bore no fruit from year's end to year's end, so they had resolved, they said, to carry no more passes, much less to pay a shilling each per month, *per capita*, for passes. A procession of so many women would attract attention even in Piccadilly, but in a 'Free' State dorp it was a stupendous event, and it made a striking impression. The result was that many of the women were arrested and sent to prison, but they all resolutely refused to pay their fines, and there was a rumour that the central government had been appealed to for funds and for material to fit out a new jail to cope with the difficulty.

This movement served to exasperate the authorities, who rigorously enforced the law and sent them to jail. The first batch of prisoners from Bloemfontein were conveyed south to Edenburg; and as further batches came down from Bloemfontein they had to be retransferred north to Kroonstad. In the course of our tour in connexion with the Natives' Land Act in August, 1913, we spent a week-end with the Rev. A. P. Pitso, of the last-named town. Thirty-four of the women passive resisters were still incarcerated there, doing hard labour. Mrs Pitso and Mrs Michael Petrus went with us on the Sunday morning to visit the prisoners at the jail.

A severe shock burst upon us, inside the prison walls, when the matron withdrew the barriers and the emaciated figures of ladies and young girls of our acquaintance filed out and greeted us. It was an exceptionally cold week, and our hearts bled to see young women of Bloemfontein, who had spent all their lives in the capital and never knew what it was to walk without socks, walking the chilly cemented floors and the cold and sharp pebbles without boots. Their own boots and shoes had been taken off, they told us, and they were, throughout the winter, forced to perform hard labour barefooted.

Was ever inhumanity more cold-blooded?

Do these 'Free' Staters consider their brutality less brutal because it happens to be sanctioned by law?

Is heaven so entirely unmindful of our case that it looks on with indifference when indignity upon indignity is heaped, not only upon our innocent men, but even upon our inoffensive women?

Tears rolled down our cheeks as we saw the cracks on their bare feet, the swellings and chronic chilblains, which made them look like sheep suffering from foot-and-mouth disease. It was torture to us to learn the kind of punishment to which they were subjected and the nature of the work they were called upon to perform; these facts were stated to us in the presence of the prison officials, and they were communicated by us to the Native Affairs Department merely as a matter of course. But what must be the effect of this brutal punishment upon girls who knew only city life? To our surprise, however, they vowed never to buy passes, even if they had to come back.

A month later, when we visited Bloemfontein, a majority of those who were at the Kroonstad jail had already returned to their homes, and the family doctors were doing a roaring trade. Their practice, too, was most likely to continue to boom as the sufferers were still determined to buy no more women's passes.

This determination caused a white man to suggest that 'instead of being sent to prison with hard labour, these madcaps should be flogged'—and this because the women refuse to be outraged by law.

Our visit to Kroonstad took place just after the circuit court had convicted the white superintendent of the Kroonstad Native Location for an outrage upon a coloured woman. He arrested her in the location ostensibly because she could not produce her residential pass, and in the field between the location and the town through which he had to escort her to prison he perpetrated the atrocity. In sentencing him to four years' hard labour, the Chief Justice said for a similar crime upon a white woman a black man would be liable to the death penalty.

When General Botha assumed the portfolio of Native Affairs at the time of this trouble, the writer, as General

Secretary of the Congress, telegraphed to him the greetings of the South African Native Congress, and pointed out to him that over two hundred coloured women were at that time languishing in jail for resenting a crime committed upon them, a crime which would have been considered serious in any other place outside the 'Free' State. The chivalrous General replied in a Dutch telegram containing this very courteous reply: 'It shall be my endeavour, as hitherto, to safeguard the just interests of the inhabitants of this land irrespective of colour.'

General Botha's assurances are so sweet, especially when they are made to persons who are not in a position to influence his electoral support. The natives, who know the 'sweets' of these assurances cannot be blamed if they analyse the Premier's assurances, in the light of their past experience, especially the phrase 'as hitherto'. To them it conveys but one idea, namely, 'If the future policy of the South African Government found it convenient to send coloured women to prison in order to please the ruling whites, they will, *as hitherto*, not hesitate to do so.'

While on the subject of native women, it is deeply to be regretted that during this year, while the empire is waging a terrible war for the cause of liberty, His Excellency the Governor-General in South Africa should have seen his way to issue a Basutoland Proclamation—No. 3 of 1915. This law decrees that under certain penalties, no native woman will be permitted to leave Basutoland 'without the permission of her husband or guardian'. The Proclamation on the face of it may look comparatively harmless, but its operation will have wide and painful ramifications amounting to no less than an entrenchment of the evils embraced in polygamy; and in carrying out this decree civilisation will have to join hands with barbarism to perpetuate the bondage, and accentuate the degradation of Basuto women.

It is a fact that no respectable Mosuto woman wants to leave her husband or guardian; but the economic conditions of today press very heavily on polygamous wives. Their lord and master finding himself no longer able to provide for half-a-dozen houses at a time, bestows on them the burden and anxieties of wifehood without its joys, namely, a husband's

undivided care and the comforts due to wives in mono-
gamous marriages.

Some of these polygamous wives have from time to time
sought relief in emigrating to European centres where they
could earn their own living and send food and raiment to
their little ones. A woman cannot always be blamed for
having entered into a polygamous marriage. More often than
not, she did so in obedience to the wishes of her aged parents.
The old people, in many instances, have judged present day
economics from the standard of their own happy days when
there was plenty of land and rainfalls were more regular;
when the several wives and children of a rich cattle-owner
could always have enough grain, eat meat, drink milk and
live happily. But times are altered and even a monogamist
finds the requirements of one wife quite a stupendous handful. The country is so congested that the little arable land
left them yields hardly any produce. I have seen it suggested
in official documents that sheep-breeding should be limited
in Basutoland as there is not enough grazing for the flocks.
And under this economic stress these surplus wives are sometimes driven to accept the overtures of unscrupulous men
who gradually induce them to wallow in sin; hence too, they
give birth to an inferior type of Basuto.

That such a law should be adopted during the reign of
Chief Griffith, their first Christian Chief and the first
monogamist who ever ruled the Basuto, is disappointing.
And while we resent the policy of the British authorities in
the Union, who promote the interests of the whites by repressing the blacks, we shall likewise object to an attempt on the
part of the same authorities in the native territories to protect
the comfort of black men by degrading black women. God
knows that the lot of the black woman in South Africa is
bad as it is. One has but to read the report of the commission recently appointed by the Union Government to inquire
into cases of assault on women to find that their condition
is getting worse. Presumably the evidence was too bad for
publication, but the report would seem to show that in South
Africa, a country where prostitution was formerly unknown,
coloured women are gradually perverted and demoralised
into a cesspool for the impurities of the family lives of all

the nationalities in the sub-continent.

In her primitive state, the native girl was protected against seduction and moral ruin by drastic penalties against the seducer, which safeguards have since the introduction of civilised rule been done away with. With tribes just groping their way from barbarism towards civilisation natural hygienic and moral laws have been trampled upon, and for this state of affairs the white man's rule is not wholly free from blame. It should be a crime to defile a potential mother and a woman should continue to be regarded as the cradle of the race and her person remain sacred and inviolate under the law, as was the case in former times.

The only charge that could be brought up against primitive native socialism was that by tolerating polygamy it had incidentally legalized concubinage; but taking all circumstances into consideration, it is doubtful if the systematic prostitution of today is a happy substitution for the polygamy of the past.

There were no mothers of unwanted babies; no orphanages, because there were no stray children; the absence of extreme wealth and dire poverty prevented destitution, and the natives had little or no insanity; they had no cancer or syphilis, and no venereal diseases because they had no prostitutes.

Have we not a right to expect a better state of affairs under civilised European rule?

It is apparently in revolt of similar horrible conditions that when the war broke out, British and Continental women were fighting for the vote with a view to liberating their sex and race from kindred impurities, for the soul rises up in 'divine discontent' against a state of affairs which no nation should tolerate—evils to which the coloured women of South Africa are now a prey.

To this kind of degeneracy may also be traced the undoing of the finer elements of the native social system, the undermining of their health and of the erstwhile splendid physique of the African race and the increasing loss of the stamina of our proverbially magnificent men and women. The effect of these evils and of the abuses inherent to the liquor traffic is manifest in several of the tribes who are today but shadows of their former selves.

The safeguarding of our maidens and women-folk from the evils of drink, greed and outrages resulting from indefensible pass laws, and the elimination of bad habits among men by a rightful policy, will restore that efficiency, loyalty, and contentment which aforetime were the boast of pioneer administrators in British South Africa, and which if fostered will render them a magnificent asset to the empire for all time.

But as often as the coloured woman has been attacked she has humbly presented 'the other cheek'. Evidence of her characteristic humility is to be found in the action of the coloured women of the 'Free' State, whose persecution by the South African Government, at the instance of certain 'Free' State municipalities, prompted the writing of this chapter. After the war broke out (the Bloemfontein *Friend* tells us) the native women of that city forgot their own difficulties, joined sewing classes, and helped to send clothing to the afflicted Belgians in Europe. Surely such useful members of the community deserve the sympathy of every right-minded person who has a voice in the conduct of British colonial administration; so let us hope that this humble appeal on their behalf will not be in vain.

8 At Thaba Ncho: a secretarial fiasco

The beginning of September 1913 found us in the Ladybrand district. Besides numerous other sufferers of the land plague, the writer was here informed of one case that was particularly distressing, of a native couple evicted from a farm in the adjoining district. After making a fruitless search for a new place of abode, they took out a travelling pass to go to Basutoland with their stock. But they never, so the story went, reached their destination. We were told that they were ambushed by some Dutchmen, who shot them down and appropriated their stock. To a stranger the news would have been incredible, but, being a 'Free' Stater born, it sounded to us uncommonly like the occurrences that our parents said they used to witness in the early days of that precious dependency. We were further told that one of the Dutch murderers had been arrested and was awaiting his trial at the next criminal sessions. As both the native man and woman were shot, it seemed difficult to conceive how the prosecution could find the necessary evidence to sustain a charge of murder.

The trial duly came off at Bloemfontein a month or two later, and the evidence in court seemed more direct and less circumstantial than we had expected. For, not only were the stolen cattle found in the possession of the prisoner, but the bullet picked up near the bodies of the dead refugees (according to the evidence given in court) fitted the prisoner's pistol. General Hertzog personally attended the court at Bloemfontein and conducted the defence; and presumably more by his eloquence than anything else, he convinced a white jury of the guiltlessness of the accused, who was acquitted and acclaimed outside the court by his friends as a hero. In justice to the police it must be added that they re-arrested this man and charged him with the theft, or with being in possession of the deceased natives' cattle. On this charge the prisoner was convicted before the circuit court a few months later, and in sentencing him to three years, with hard labour, the presiding judge is said to have made some references to the previous trial and the manner in which the prisoner had escaped the capital sentence.

From Ladybrand we travelled south towards Wepener, not far from the Basuto frontier. Evictions around here were numerous, but beyond the inevitable hardships of families suddenly driven from home, they had not suffered any great amount of damage. Being near to the Basuto border, a native in these parts, when ejected, can quickly take his stock across the boundary, and leaving them in friendly pastures, under sympathetic laws, go away to look for a new place. But it became abundantly clear that the influx of outsiders into Basutoland could not continue at the rate it was then proceeding without seriously complicating the land question in Basutoland, where chieftains are constantly quarrelling over small patches of arable land.

A pitiable spectacle, however, was the sight of those who had been evicted from the centre of the Orange 'Free' State. It was heartrending to hear them relate the circumstances of their expulsions, and how they had spent the winter months roaming from farm to farm with their famishing stock, applying in vain for a resting place. Some farmers were apparently sympathetic, but debarred from entertaining such applications by the sword of Damocles— the £100 fine in Section 5 of the Natives' Land Act—they had perforce to refuse the applicants. The farms hereabout are owned by Boers and English settlers, but many are owned by Germans, Jews, Russians, and other Continentals. Some of the proprietors do not reside on the farms at all; they are either Hebrew merchants or lawyers, living in the towns and villages away from the farms. Many have no wish to part with the natives, who seem invariably to have treated their landlords well, but they are forced to do so by the law.

It seems a curious commentary on the irony of things that South Africa, which so tyrannically chases her own natives from the country, receives at this very time with open arms Polish, Finnish, Russian and German Jews, who themselves

are said to have fled from the tyranny of their own governments in Europe. With a vengeance, it looks like 'robbing
Peter to pay Paul'.

Standing by the side of a kopje, very early on that
September morning, it was a relief to see the majestic tops
of the mountains of Basutoland, silhouetted against the rising
sun, beyond the Caledon River, which separates the 'Free'
State from Basutoland.

A number of fugitives were at that time driving little lots
of stock across the broad and level flats which extended in
the direction of the Basutoland Protectorate. How comforting to know that once they crossed the river, these exiles could
rest their tired limbs and water their animals without breaking any law. Really until we saw those emaciated animals,
it had never so forcibly occurred to us that it is as bad to
be a black man's animal as it is to be a black man in South
Africa.

To think that this 'Free' State land from which these people
are now expelled was at one time, and should still be, part
and parcel of Basutoland; and to remember that the fathers
of these natives, who are now fleeing from the 'Free' State
laws, were allies of the Boers, whom they assisted to drive
the Basutos from this habitable and arable part of their land;
that with their own rations, their own horses, their own rifles,
and often their own ammunition they helped the Boers to
force the Basutos back into their present mountain recesses,
and compelled them to build fresh homes in all but uninhabitable mountain fastnesses, in many instances inaccessible to
vehicles of any kind, in order (as was said at the time) to
give themselves 'more elbow-room'; to see them today fleeing
from the laws of their perfidious Dutch allies, expelled from
the country for which they bled and for which their fathers
died; and to find that, at the risk of intensifying their own
domestic problems in their now diminutive and overcrowded
mountain state, the Basutos are nobly offering an asylum
to those who had helped to deprive them of their country;
and to remember that this mean breach of faith, on the part
of ex-Republicans towards their native allies, is facilitated
by the protection of the Union Jack, sheds in regard to the
Basutos, a glorious ray of light upon black human nature.

Look at these exiles swarming towards the Basuto border, some of them with their belongings on their heads, driving their emaciated flocks attenuated by starvation and the cold. The faces of some of the children, too, are livid from the cold. It looks as if these people were so many fugitives escaping from a war, with the enemy pressing hard at their heels.

It was a distressing sight. We had never seen the likes of it since the outbreak of the Boer War, near the Transvaal border, immediately before the siege of Mafeking. Even that flight of 1899 had a buoyancy of its own, for the Boer War, unlike the present stealthy war of extermination (the law which caused this flight), was preceded by an ultimatum. But the sight of a people who had loyally paid taxation put to flight in these halcyon times, by a Parliament the huge salaries of whose members these very exiles, although unrepresented in its body, have meekly helped to pay, turned one's weeping eyes to heaven, for, as Jean Paul says, 'There above is everything he can wish for here below.' But if the native of other days has been sold by the perfidy of his Dutch allies of the day, the British soldiers and British taxpayer of the present day have been deceived by 'we don't know who'. They fought and died and paid to unfurl the banner of freedom in this part of the globe, and the spectacle before us is the result. This must be what A. H. Keene referred to when he said, 'The British public were also dumb, and with that infinite capacity for being gulled which is so remarkable in a people proud of their common sense, acquiesced in everything.'

Visiting the farms, we found some native tenants under notice to leave. We informed them that Mr Edward Dower, the Secretary for Native Affairs, would be in Thaba Ncho the following week, and advised them to proceed to the town and lay their difficulties before this high representative of the Union Government, with a request for the use of his good offices to procure for them the Governor-General's permission to live on farms, a course provided in Section 1 of the Natives' Land Act. We made no promises, as previous requests for such permission had been invariably ignored. But we hoped that the Government Secretary's meeting with the sufferers and speaking with them face to face would soften

87

the implacable red-tape and official circumlocution, and perhaps even open the way towards a modification of the administration of this legislative atrocity; but we were mistaken.

The meeting duly took place on Friday, September 12, 1913. A thousand natives gathered at the racecourse on the wide level country between the railway station and Thaba Ncho town. A few historical facts relative to Thaba Ncho might not be out of place.

Thabo Ncho (Mount Black) takes its name from the hill below which the town is situated. Formerly this part of Africa was peopled by Bushmen and subsequently by Basutos. The Barolong, a section of the Bechuana, came here from Motlhanapitse, a place in the western 'Free' State to which place they had been driven by Mzilikazi's hordes from over the Vaal in the early 'twenties. The Barolongs settled in Thaba Ncho during the early 'thirties under an agreement with Chief Noshweshwe. The Seleka branch of the Barolong nation, under Chief Moroka, after settling here, befriended the immigrant Boers who were on their way to the north country from the south and from Natal during the 'thirties. A party of immigrant Boers had an encounter with Mzilikazi's forces of Matabele. Up in Bechuanaland the powerful Matabele had scattered the other Barolong tribes and forced them to move south and join their brethren under Moroka. Thus during the 'thirties circumstances had formed a bond of sympathy between the Boers and Barolongs in their mutual regard of the terrible Matabele as a common foe.

But the story of the relations between the Boers and the Barolong needs no comment: it is consistent with the general policy of the Boers, which, as far as natives are concerned, draws no distinction between friend and foe. It was thus that Hendrik Potgieter's voortrekkers forsook the more equitable laws of Cape Colony, particularly that relating to the emancipation of the slaves, and journeyed north to establish a social condition in the interior under which they might enslave the natives without British interference. The fact that Great Britain gave monetary compensation for the liberated slaves did not apparently assuage their strong feelings on the subject of slavery; hence they were anxious to get beyond the hateful reach of British sway. They were sweeping through the country with their wagons, their families, their cattle, and their other belongings, when in the course of their march, Potgieter met the Matabele far away in the northern Free State near a place called Vechtkop. The trekkers made use of their firearms, but this did not prevent them from being severely punished by the Matabeles, who marched off with their horses and livestock and left the Boers in a hopeless condition, with their families still exposed to further attacks. Potgieter sent back word to Chief Moroka asking for assistance, and it was immediately granted.

Chief Moroka made a general collection of draught oxen from amongst his tribe, and these with a party of Barolong warriors were sent to the relief of the defeated Boers, and to bring them back to a place of safety behind Thaba Ncho Hill, a regular refugee camp, which the Boers named 'Moroka's Hoek'. But the wayfarers were now threatened with starvation; and as they were guests of honour amongst his people, the Chief Moroka made a second collection of cattle, and the Barolong responded with unheard-of liberality. Enough milch cows, and sheep, and goats were thus obtained for a liberal distribution among the Boer families, who, compared with the large numbers of their hospitable hosts, were relatively few. Hides and skins were also collected from the tribesmen, and their tanners were set to work to assist in making *veldschoens, velbroeks*, and *karosses* for the tattered and footsore Boers and their children. The oxen which they received at Vechtkop they were allowed to keep, and these came in very handy for ploughing and transport purposes. No doubt the Rev. Mr Archbell, the Wesleyan Methodist missionary and apostle to the Barolong, played an active part on the Barolong relief committee, and, at that time, there were no more grateful people on earth than Hendrik Potgieter and his party of stricken voortrekkers.

After a rest of many moons and communicating with friends at Cape Colony and Natal, the Dutch leader held a council of war with the Barolong chiefs. He asked them to reinforce his punitive expedition against the Matabele. Of course they were to use their own materials and munitions and, as a reward, they were to retain whatever stock they might capture from the Matabele; but the Barolongs did not quite like the terms. Tauana especially told Potgieter that he himself was a refugee in the land of his mother Moroka. His country was Bechuanaland, and he could only accompany the expedition on condition that the Matabele stronghold at Coenyane (now western Transvaal) be smashed up, Mzilikazi driven from the neighbourhood and the Barolong returned to their homes in the land of the Bechuana, the Boers themselves retaining the country to the east and the south (now the 'Free' State and the Transvaal). That this could be done Tauana had no doubt, for since they came to Thaba Ncho, the Barolong had acquired the use of firearms—long-range weapons—which were still unknown to the Matabele, who only used hand-spears. This was agreed to, and a vow was made accordingly. To make assurance doubly sure, Tauana sent his son Motshegare to enlist the co-operation of a Griqua by the name of Pieter Dout, who also had a bone to pick with the Matabele.

Pieter Dout consented, and joined the expedition with a number of mounted men, and for the time being the Boer-Barolong-Griqua combination proved a happy one. The expedition was successful beyond the most sanguine expectations of its promoters. The Matabele were routed, and King Mzilikazi was driven north, where he founded the kingdom of Matabeleland—now Southern Rhodesia—having left the allies to share his old haunts in the south.

This successful expedition was the immediate outcome of the friendly alliance between the Boers in the 'Free' State and Moroka's Barolong at Thaba Ncho. But Boers make bad neighbours in Africa, and, on that account, the Government of the 'Free' State thereafter proved a continual menace to the Basuto, their neighbours to the east. Pretexts were readily found and hostile inroads constantly engineered against the Basuto for purposes of aggression, and the friend-liness of the Barolong was frequently exploited by the Boers in their raids, undertaken to drive the Basuto further back into the mountains. This, however, must be said to the honour of the mid-nineteenth century 'Free' Staters, in con-trast to the 'Free' Staters of later date: that the earlier 'Free' Staters rewarded the loyalty of their Barolong allies by recognising and respecting Thaba Ncho as a friendly native state; but it must also be stated that the bargain was all in the favour of one side; thereby all the land captured from the Basuto was annexed to the 'Free' State, while the dusky warriors of Moroka, who bore the brunt of the battles, got nothing for their pains. So much was this the case, that Thaba Ncho, which formerly lay between the 'Free' State and Basutoland, was subsequently entirely surrounded by 'Free' State territory.

Eventually Chief Moroka died, and a dispute ensued between his sons concerning the chieftainship. Some Boers took sides in this dispute and accentuated the differences. In 1884, Chief Tspinare, Moroka's successor, was murdered after a night attack by followers of his brother Samuel, assisted by a party of 'Free' State Boers. It is definitely stated that the unfortunate chief valiantly defended himself. He kept his assailants at bay for the best part of the day by shooting at them through the windows of his house, which they had surrounded; and it was only by setting fire to the house that they managed to get the chief out, and shoot him. As a matter of fact the house was set on fire by the advice of one of the Boers, and it is said that it was a bullet from the rifle of one of these Boers that killed Chief Tsipinare.

President Brand, the faithful ally of the dead chieftain, called out the burghers who reached Thaba Ncho after the strife was over. He annexed Thaba Ncho to the 'Free' State, and banished the rival chief from 'Free' State territory, with all his followers. The Dutch members of the party which assassinated the chief were put upon a kind of trial, and discharged by a white jury at Bloemfontein.

Of course, Boers could not be expected to participate in any adventure which did not immediately lead to land grabbing. But, fortunately for some Barolongs, the dead chief had in his lifetime surveyed some farms and granted free-hold title to some of the tribesmen. In fact, his death took place while he was engaged in that democratic undertaking. The Boer Government, which annexed the territory, confiscated all the land not yet surveyed, and passed a law to the effect that those Barolongs who held individual title to land could only sell their farms to white people. It must, however, be added that successive Boer Presidents have always granted written exemptions from this drastic measure. So that any native who wanted to buy a farm could always do so by applying for the President's permission, while, of course, no permission was necessary to sell to a white man; several natives, to the author's knowledge, have thus bought farms from natives, and also from white men, by permission of the State President, and the severity of the prohibition was never felt. But after the British occupation in 1900, the natives keenly felt this measure, as the Governor, when appealed to by a native for permission to buy a farm, always replied that he had no power to break the law. Thus, under the Union Jack, sales have gone on from black to white, but none from white to black, or even from black to black. In the crowd which met Mr Dower that morning were two Barolong young men who had lately inherited a farm each under the will of their deceased uncle, and the law will not permit the Registrar of Deeds to give them title to their inheritance; their numerous representations to the Union authorities have only met with promises, while lawyers have taken advantage of the hitch to mulct them in more money than the land is worth. The best legal advice they have received is that they should sell their inheritance to white men.

Now the Natives' Land Act, as applied to the whole Union of South Africa, is modelled on these highly unsatisfactory conditions relating to land in the 'Free' State. The six months' imprisonment, the £100 fine, and other penalties for infringement of the Land Act, are borrowed from Chapter XXXIV of the 'Free' State laws, to which reference is made in Section 7 of the Natives' Land Act. Section 8 of the Natives' Land Act is a re-enactment of some of the reprehensible 'Free' State land laws which had been repealed by the Crown Colony Government after the British occupation in 1900. When the Natives' Land Bill was before Parliament the opposition moved that the remaining native farms be scheduled as a native area, where natives might purchase farms, of course from other natives. The passage of such an amendment was more than could be expected as the real object of the Natives' Land Bill was to block every possible means whereby a native may acquire land from a native, or from any one else; but when the motion was rejected the natives of Thaba Ncho were exceedingly alarmed. They telegraphed their fears to Mr Sauer, who promised to visit them when Parliament rose, but his purpose was frustrated by his death, immediately after the passage of the Act.

To return to Mr Dower's meeting, the Native Affairs Secretary received a warm welcome from the natives, who hoped that his coming would show them a way out of their dilemma. As already stated, a thousand natives came from the surrounding farms, some on horseback, others on bicycles, and other conveyances such as carts, wagons, etc.; they included evicted wanderers and native tenants under notice to leave their farms, with letters of eviction and other evidence in their pockets; they included some refugees, who had likewise been evicted from other districts —refugees who, as one of them put it, were 'constantly on the move, and hurried hither to plead for shelter for our homeless families, now living in wagons'.

The morning was showery. Thaba Ncho Hill in the background, always visible for scores of miles in every direction, towered high above the surrounding landscape. Its stony slopes covered with a light mist from peak to base, it stood like a silent witness to the outraged treaty between the Barolong and the Boers.

Mr Dower, who was accompanied by his secretary (Mr Apthorpe) and the Thaba Ncho magistrate (Major Robertson) and the location-superintendent, addressed the natives for half an hour. The speeches were correctly interpreted by Mr Jeremiah Makgothi, a native farmer, and formerly a local school teacher, who collaborated with Canon Crisp in the translation of the scriptures into Serolong for the world-renowned S.P.C.K. The Rev. P. K. Motiyane, the local Wesleyan minister, also assisted in the task of interpretation.

Mr Dower made some pathetic references to the life and work of the late Hon. J. W. Sauer, the great Cape politician who had just passed away; then he proceeded to refer at length to sundry inconsequential topics of minor local significance; and, having repeated his great pleasure at seeing them, without making a single reference to the momentous measure that was ravaging the natives of the country, the Government Secretary resumed his seat amidst looks of astonishment and consternation from the assembled natives.

The Rev. J. D. Goronyane, a gentleman who, as secretary to the late chiefs, played a leading part in the Boer-Barolong relations of the nineteenth century, was the next speaker. He thanked the Secretary for coming. No people, he said, regretted Mr Sauer's death more than the Barolong; they had looked forward to meeting him in connexion with the new cloud now looming over the country in the shape of the Land Act, and they were sorry that his coming had been frustrated by a higher power. Turning to Mr Dower, he said: 'All the people you see before you are frightened by the new law. They have come here for nothing else but to hear how they are expected to live under it.'

Other speakers followed, but when the actual sufferers began to narrate their experiences there were so many who wished to come forward that the leaders decided that, their cases being more or less similar, they should wait and hear how the representative of the Government would deal with the cases of those who had already spoken.

MR DOWER'S REPLY

He regretted that, as one speaker had said, some people read the Act through the spectacles coloured by their desires. Others seemed to be glad at the uncertainty and endeavoured to keep on turning the wheel of discontent. It was true that some people were imposing on the natives, but, on the whole, there was a reasonable desire to comply with the Act, although it was not always properly understood. Few individuals had been evicted, though many had received notice. Some of the notices given under a misapprehension, and with a desire not to contravene the Act, had, since the magistrates' explanations, actually been withdrawn. 'So your best course is to explain the facts to your magistrates, if possible, in the presence of the master.' (A voice: 'Who'll bring him there?') After explaining that the principle of the Act was a first step towards territorial segregation, Mr. Dower said it gave protection to some parts of the country which formerly were not so protected. He mentioned as an instance that more than one-half of the farms formerly owned by natives in that district were no longer in their possession. In other Provinces *the Act was restrictive*, while *in the Free State it was prohibitive*. The old practice of 'sowing on the halves' might continue so long as the lawfully executed contracts lasted; but at the expiration of those contracts the practice should cease, as Parliament had decided on its abolition. It amounted to a partnership beween a white man and a black man. With a civilised native the system might have been good, but a raw native always got the worst of the partnership. He would advise them to make the best temporary arrangements within the four corners of the law. It might be by adopting one of three alternatives: (1) Become servants (in which case it would be legal for a master to give them pieces of land to plough and graze a number of stock); or (2) move into the reserve— (voices: 'Where is the reserve?'); or (3) dispose of the stock for cash. (Sensation.) The arrangement would only be temporary until Parliament took further steps in terms of the Commission's report. It would be better than trekking from pillar to post, till all the cattle had died out, and eventually returning penniless. Farmers always had the right to evict their native tenants. (A voice: 'But we could go elsewhere.') Because some old laws which had been repealed had now been re-enacted, let them not think that there was a desire to oppress. 'They may have been unjust, as you say, but understand that this law is not the last thing said by Parliament. A final settlement must depend on the recommendations of the Commission, and such action will be taken as will be to the lasting interests of white and black. The Lands Commission has already held its first sitting, and you will be serving your best interests by bringing all your information to the magistrate, so that it be laid before the Commission. Show by your wise action that you are inspired by the justice of your case. The course of agitation will not help you. Remove suspicions and mistrust from your minds, and bring cases of real hardships to the magistrate, who will see that this Act is administered as smoothly as possible. But *the Act does not provide for any special cases in the Free State* being submitted to the Governor-General under the first section of the Act.'

The concluding statement settled the minds of those who had not expected from the Government any protection against the law, and the disappointment under which the meeting broke up was indescribable. This law is full of rude shocks, and this day this spokesman of the Government told the natives that in the other three provinces the Governor-General will only exercise his right in exceptional cases, while in the 'Free' State the law did not permit him to exercise it even in such cases, so that the Government alone knows why that provision was inserted.

9 The fateful thirteen

The natives of South Africa, generally speaking, are intensely superstitious. The fact that they are more impressionable than tractable causes them, it seems, to take naturally to religion, and seems a flat contradiction of Junius's assertion that 'there are proselytes from atheism, but none from superstition'. With some South African tribes it is unlucky to include goats amongst the animals paid by a young man's parents as the dowry for his bride; it was equally bad to pay dowry in odd numbers of cattle. The payment must be made in even numbers of oxen, sheep, or other animals or articles, such as two, four, six, eight, ten, and so on. The man who could not afford more than one sheep to seal the marriage contract would have to exchange his goat for a sheep to make up a presentable pair. If he were too poor to do that, a needle or any other article was admissable to make up the dowry to an even number, and so avoid giving one or three, or more odd numbers of articles. Conscious as they were of the existence of some supreme being, but worshipping no god, true or false, the white man's religion which makes such a worship obligatory through a mediator found easy access among so susceptible a people; and with equal ease they likewise adopted the civilisation of the white man. But the natives received not only the white man's civilisation and his religion, but have even gullibly imbibed his superstitions. Thus is their dread of the figure 13 accounted for. The native witch-doctors in the early days took advantage of their credulity, whilst civilised people trade on their susceptibilities, and the semi-civilised natives also trade upon the fears of their more impressionable brethren.

To give a concrete case or two, we might say that when the main reservoir of the Kimberley water-works was built, one of the labourers one week-end lost the whole of his weekly pay. He inquired, and searched everywhere he could think of, but nobody had seen his missing purse. But on Monday morning he conceived a plan for the recovery of his lost purse. In pursuance of this plan, on the Monday he asked for and obtained a day off; then he declared to the gang of labourers that he was going to the nearest location to consult a bone-thrower. Instead of going to the location, however, he went to the open country, gathered some plants, returned to the dormitories while the others were at work, boiled the herbs in a pot of water and put it aside to cool. When the workmen returned for their midday meal he announced an imaginary consultation he had had with the bone-thrower, and that that functionary had divined the whereabouts of the purse; it was to the effect that the purse had been stolen and was in the possession of a fellow-worker. 'The doctor,' he said 'gave me some herbs. I have cooked them, and by his direction each of you is invited to immerse his hands in the decoction which is now cool. If you are not the thief, nothing would happen to you, but to the one who has stolen my money,' he added with emphasis, 'the doctor said that the medicine will snap the thief's fingers clean off and leave him only with the palm.'

One by one the men dipped their hands in the 'medicine,' and as they took turns at the pot, one young fellow at length became visibly disturbed, and believing that the concoction was true, he confessed to the theft and undertook to refund the money, rather than lose his fingers.

Another case was this. A Transkeian missionary once heard of the serious indisposition of a native. It was not a natural sickness, it was believed, but was the effect of sorcery, and news in that sense was noised abroad. Such cases primitive natives believe to be beyond the skill of a medical man. White doctors, they would say, know next to nothing at all about such things. They do not believe in witchcraft and how could they be expected to be able to smell it out of a patient. Only a witch-doctor—if he is more skilful—can smell out and subdue the charm directed by another witch-doctor into the body of the bewitched.

Having heard this piece of native philosophy on witchcraft, the missionary startled the natives by telling them in their own tongue that he could cure the disease. And he did cure it. He captured a baby lizard from the rocks which abound in the craggy undulations of most parts of the Transkei. He hid it in the inside pocket of his coat and proceeded to the sick-bed with some real medicines in his hand. 'When a man who is not sick imagines himself sick,' says Dr Kellog, 'he must be sick indeed,' and truly in accordance with this saying, the native was dangerously ill. A bone-thrower, who had in the presence and hearing of the sick man divined his malady, pronounced that he was not only bewitched by a snake, but also that the reptile was within him and was eating him to death. In these circumstances the missionary administered an emetic to the reluctant patient, in the presence of some incredulous spectators, who had never known a white man to extract a reptile from the person of a bewitched native. Further, by some agility of the hand, the missionary produced from his pocket unobserved, just as the emetic was acting, the baby lizard he had taken from the rocks. So smartly was this done that everybody, including the patient, believed the reptile to have been extracted from his body by the power of the medicine administered by the missionary. The sick man at once stood up and walked, and the missionary was known, by all who witnessed the marvel, as the greatest witch-doctor of the neighbourhood.

In like manner, when some civilised Christians made remarks on New Year's Day about the figure 13, there was much gossiping among the more superstitious natives as to the form of trouble which the year 1913 had in store for the natives, although none knew that a revolutionary law of Draconian severity would be launched in their midst during this eventful year.

The powerful African potentate, Menelik of Abyssinia (whose death had been falsely circulated no fewer than seven times during the past dozen years), really died in 1913.

Letsie II, paramount chief of the semi-independent Basuto nation, departed this life during this same year.

Dinizulu (son of the great Cetewayo, whose impis slew the Prince Imperial in 1879), who was born to inherit the throne of his fathers, and who lived to be one of the most disappointed men of his day, spent many years in prison and in exile, and was known in his lifetime as the Black Napoleon; was released from prison by the Union Government, and given back his pension of £500 per annum. He shared the hopes of his people that in accordance with the Government's erstwhile good intentions now tottering before a growing republicanism, Zululand would be restored to the Zulus, and he established as their ruler under the crown. He, too, died in the year 1913.

An unusually large number of good and noble men of greater or lesser renown were gathered to their fathers during this year.

It is perhaps not generally known that few British statesmen did so much for the South African natives, in so short a term of service at the Colonial Office, as the Hon. A. Lyttleton. And he, too, left us rather suddenly during this troublous year of 1913. In this year, too, South Africa was visited by a drought which for severity was pronounced to be unprecedented in the knowledge of all the old inhabitants. Remarks—some pithy, some ugly—were made upon the drought by Dutchmen. They all remembered how the God of their fathers used to send them nice soaking rains regularly each spring-time, and that it usually continued to nourish the plants and other of the country's vegetation throughout the summer, and they concluded that there must be some reason why he does not do it now. The majority of Dutchmen whom the writer thus overheard attributed the visitation to the sins of the foreigners, who are fast buying up the country, and cursing it by settling godless people upon it. One or two saw in it the vengeance of the supreme being for the unnecessary persecution of his black creatures, but they were afraid to say this aloud. 'See,' said one, 'is the drought not worse in the "Free" State where Kaffirs seem to be very hard hit by this new law?' This was true. Dutchmen's cattle were dying of poverty in the 'Free' State, and the land was so parched in some parts that it seemed difficult to believe that grass could ever grow in these places again, supposing the long-looked-for rain came at last.

On our birthday, October 9, 1913, they hanged four murderers who had been condemned to death at the preceding criminal sessions. The selection of the morning of our birthday for the execution of four prisoners at our home was curious as executions in Kimberley take place only about once or twice in ten years. The event, of course, was purely accidental; but middle-aged natives seemed to have an aptitude for remembering catastrophes which, in the lives of their fathers and their fathers' fathers, followed such coincidences. Whilst the executions were taking place, on the morning of our birthday, an ugly ocean tragedy was taking place away out on the Atlantic. The *Vulturno* was ablaze with a number of passengers on board. Innocent white men and women were being roasted alive, because the sea was too rough to permit their transfer from the burning ship to the rescuing liners; and so they perished, literally, 'between the devil and the deep sea'—within full view of relief.

Dutchmen as a rule are like natives in that they live as long as they can, and die only when they must; but in the Transvaal a Dutch farmer all but exterminated his family on this day with a revolver, which he had previously secured for the purpose. On this day also the mind of an English miner at Randfontein having suddenly become unhinged, he shot his wife, his baby, and his aunt, then coolly pocketing the pistol, he cycled down to the school, called out his two children, shot them down in cold blood, and retired to a quiet place where he put an end to his own life. During that fateful week in which disaster followed disaster in rapid succession, there occurred the following, namely, the colliery disaster at Cardiff, which left a thousand dependents without breadwinners, to say nothing of the damage to property, which is estimated at over £100,000. There were also railway accidents and aviation disasters, causing damage to life and property. There were commercial troubles due to the Johannesburg strike in July, and this effect of the strike indicates the influence exercised by the 'golden city' over South African commerce. In that sad upheaval in the labour world many innocent people lost their lives and property, and unfortunately, as is always the case, besides adding largely to the taxpayer's burdens, seriously affected people who had nothing to do with the strike. Yet when some of our friends expressed thankfulness that the year did not have thirteen months, we were obstinate enough to refuse to waste valuable time in considering the subject.

Individuals, like communities, suffered heavily from one cause or another in the year 1913. Thus the writer's little family also had its baptism of sorrow. On New Year's Day of that year 1913, his little boy, a robust child of three months, was prattling in the house. He first saw the light in the last quarter of 1912, on the very day we opened and christened our printing office, so we named him after the great inventor of printing type: he was christened Johann Gutenburg. Somehow or other he could never keep well after the New Year, for though he tried to look pleasant, it was visibly under serious difficulties. It had been our fortune, during a married life of fifteen years, to keep our children in remarkably good health; but the health of this little fellow showed unmistakable evidence that this immunity was reaching its end. Vehement attacks of whooping cough now overtook the little ones. The others got rid of it during the winter months, but with Gutenburg the disease developed into inflammation of this organ, and of that; and taking the whole year from January to December, it would not be too much to say that the little boy scarcely enjoyed three full months of good health. And by the end of the year it was clear that he was going the way of half-a-dozen cousins who were gathered into eternity all during one month— December, 1913. Before the New Year was a week old, the doctor, who had then become a regular member of the family, gave us the final warning.

For a month past, loving aunts had tenderly relieved the child's inexperienced parents of the daily ministrations and of the more exacting night watches. After the doctor's warning there came 'the calm before the storm'. It only lasted for one day; the deceptive strength which had temporarily buoyed the little patient up was now passing away and the inevitable reaction was setting in. Oh, if he were only a year older so that he could have communicated to us by speech his feelings and his wants! His little body, which stood the long sickness with such fortitude, got frail. His bright eyes, high forehead and round cheeks remained, however, to defy the waste of the disease. The parson came and uttered words of encouragement. 'Symptoms of death,' he said, pointing to the sick-bed (and he was no novice in such matters) 'were very far from there,' but the surroundings of the sick-bed seemed to us to ring out the command with a force as strong as six peals of thunder, saying 'Suffer little children to come unto me,' and such divine orders, comprehensible only to those to whom they are issued, took precedence of any words of encouragement that may be uttered by a mortal minister of religion. That these good men of God know the ways of their master is patent in that they always couple the encouragement to the sick, or to the friends of the sick, with the advice to surrender to the divine injunction. The grandmother of the child was composed, 'no mortal can stay it,' but his aunts were restless. 'Go, call the doctor at once,' they demanded. He came, gave a solemn look and stood silent. After feeling the pulse he said: 'The child has collapsed. I have done all I could and can do no more.' Next came the anxious looks of the other attendants, the footfalls of inquiring neighbours, messages to nearer and further relatives about the pronounced 'collapse'.

This was at noon, and each one expected that he could hold out for two hours at the most; but he breathed throughout the afternoon with a gallantry that was wonderful in its way. His large round eyes turned upward as though they had become blind to their immediate surroundings. It seemed that those eyes could no longer see the objects in the room and its anxious inmates; truly they could no longer see the sun or the moon and stars that night. Kimberley was no longer a home to the little chap whose short lease of life was clearly drawing to an end. A new outlook seemed to have dawned over his now brightening face. His eyes were riveted on the new Jerusalem, the city of God, and he seemed to be in full communion with the dear little cousins who preceded him thither during the previous month. Evidently they were beckoning him to leave this wicked South Africa and everything in it, and come to eternal glory. In this condition we left him early in the afternoon to answer the call of our daily and nightly drudgery—it would be gross extravagance to call it 'duty'—an occupation which has no reverence for mournful occasions. At 9.15 p.m., just about the time of his birth sixteen months before, the little soul was relieved of its earthly bonds.

There he lay robed in a simple white gown, his motionless form being an eloquent testimony of the indelible gap left in our domestic circle as a visitation of 1913. But the celestial expression of his face, his deep-brown colour, and his closed eyelids, seemed to say to us: 'Be at ease, I have conquered.'

Still, it must be confessed that to us this wrench was a most painful experience, and that the doctrine of 'Thy will be done' was found to be a great deal more than a mere profession of faith. The sympathies of relatives, friends and other mourners, their deeds and words of condolence, followed by a solemn religious service, took the sting out of the affliction, although it must again be confessed that so deep was our sorrow for the dead child's mother that for some time we could not bear to look her in the face.

Painful and unusual solemnities and formulae were gone through during the next day, and these again were lightened by the kind and sympathetic assistance of genuine friends, like Messrs Joseph Twayi, H. S. Poho, and others, some of them delegates to a temperance conference then sitting in Kimberley.

In the absence of the pastors of St. Paul's Mission, who were both attending the annual synod at Pniel, two Wesleyan ministers—Rev. Jonathan Motshumi of Kimberley, and Rev. Shadrach Ramailane of Fauresmith—took charge of the funeral service, and a row of carriages followed the hearse to the West End cemetery.

As the procession turned round Cooper's corner into Green Street, Kimberley, something caused us to look out of the carriage window; we then caught sight of one of the carriages that formed the procession in which some little girl friends and relatives of the deceased were driving, their plain white dresses relieved only by a scrap of black ribbon here and there. Their silent sympathy, expressed with girlish shyness, was evident, though their snow-white dresses were in striking contrast to the colour of their carriage and of the horses, and the sombre black of the rest of the funeral party. As we saw the solemn procession and heard the clank of the horses' hoofs, we were suddenly reminded of that journey in July 1913, when we met that poor wandering young family of fugitives from the Natives' Land Act. A sharp pang went through us, and caused our heart to bleed as we recalled the scene of their night funeral, forced on them by the necessity of having to steal a grave on the moonless night, when detection would be less easy. Every man in this country, we thought, be he a Russian, Jew, Peruvian, or of any other nationality, has a claim to at least six feet of South African soil as a resting place after death, but those native outcasts, who in the country of their birth, as a penalty for the colour of their skin, are made by the Union Parliament to lead lives like that awarded to Cain for his crime of fratricide, they might, as in the case of that wandering family, be even denied a sepulchre for their little ones.

The solemnity of the funeral procession, of which we formed the mainmast, almost entirely disappeared from our mind, to be succeeded by the spirit of revolt against this impious persecution as these things came before us. What have our people done to these colonists, we asked, that is so utterly unforgivable, that this law should be passed as an unavoidable reprisal? Have we not delved in their mines, and are not a quarter of a million of us still labouring for them in the depths of the earth in such circumstances for the most niggardly pittance? Are not thousands of us still offering up our lives and our limbs in order that South Africa should satisfy the white man's greed, delivering £50,000,000 worth of minerals every year? Have we not quarried the stones, mixed, moulded and carried the mortar which built the cities of South Africa? Have we not likewise prepared the material for building the railways? Have we not obsequiously and regularly paid taxation every year, and have we not supplied the Treasury with money to provide free education for Dutch children in the 'Free' State and Transvaal, while we had to find additional money to pay the school fees of our own children? Are not many of us toiling in the grain fields and fruit farms, with their wives and their children, for the white man's benefit? Did not our people take care of the white women—all the white women, including Boer fraus—whose husbands, brothers and fathers were

away at the front—in many cases actively engaged in shatter-
ing our own liberty? But see their appreciation and gratitude!
Oh, for something to

Strike flat the thick rotundity o' the world!
Crack Nature's moulds, all germens spill at once!
That make ungrateful man!

When one is distressed in mind there is no greater
comforter than an appropriate scriptural quotation. Our
bleeding heart was nowhere in the present procession, which
apparently could take care of itself, for we had returned in
thought to the July funeral of the veld and its horrid
characteristics; and a pleasant reaction set in when we
recalled a verse of Matthew which says: 'The foxes have
holes, and the birds of the air have nests, but the Son of Man
hath not where to lay his head.' How very Christ-like was
that funeral of the veld. It resembled the messiah's in that
it had no carriages, no horses, no ordained ministers, nor
a trained choir singing the remains into their final resting
place. The veld funeral party, like the funeral party of the
Son of Man, was in mortal fear of the representatives of the
law; it, like that party, had not the light of the sun, nor the
light of a candle, which charitable friends in our day would
usually provide for the poorest of the poor under ordinary
circumstances. Still, it was not cold at Golgotha, or should
not be today as it was on the first Good Friday; but even
the Madonna and the disciples must have had some house
in which to gather to discuss the situation.

One of the most astounding things in connexion with the
unjust treatment of the natives by the whites of South Africa
is the profound silence of the Dutch Reformed Church, which
practically is now the state church of South Africa. This
Christian body does not only exclude coloured worshippers
from participating in its services, but would arraign them
before the law, or otherwise violently assault them should
they visit its places of worship at other times.

When it is remembered that the predikants of the Dutch
Reformed Church in the old Republics dare not pronounce
the benediction on a coloured congregation, we think it will
not be considered unfair to say that the calculatingly
outrageous treatment of the coloured races of South Africa

by the Boer section of that community is mainly due from the sanction it receives from the Dutch Reformed Church. If the predikants of the Dutch Reformed Church would but tell their congregations that it was gross libel on the Christian faith, which they profess, to treat human beings as they treat those with loathsome disease—except when it is desired to exploit the benefits, such as their taxes and their labour which these outraged human beings confer upon the Dutch: we say that if the predikants would but instruct their congregations so, then this stain, which so greatly disfigures the Christian character of the Boers would be removed.

The Dutch almost worship their religious teachers; and they will continue these cruelties upon the natives as long as they believe that they have the approval of the Church. Let the predikants then tell their people that tyranny is tyrannical even though the victims are of a different race, and the South African Dutch will speedily abandon that course.

Just two instances by way of illustration. Ten years ago we attended an election meeting at Burghersdorp, a typical Dutch constituency at the Cape. The present Minister of Railways and Harbours was wooing the constituency, and he appeared to be the favourite candidate among three others. Dutchmen from the surrounding farms flocked to attend the meeting. The speeches were all in the Taal. No hall in the town was large enough to hold the number that came, so the four candidates addressed the gathering in the Market Square. This was how Mr Burton asked the Dutch electors for their votes: 'Whenever you speak of making South Africa comfortable to Afrikanders, do not forget that the blacks are the original Afrikanders. We found them in this country, and no policy can possibly succeed which aims at the promotion of the interests of one section of the Afrikander race to the neglect of another section.'

There were a few native listeners in the throng, and we blacks at once thought that the speaker had held out the red rag to the bull, and that every word of this candid statement would cost him at least fifty Dutch votes. But we were agreeably surprised, for the open air rang with the loud cheers and 'Hoor, hoors'[1] from hundreds of leather-lunged Boers.

[1] 'Hear, hear.' in Dutch.

One old farmer turned round to Tommy—the blackest native in the crowd—held him by the shoulders, and shouted as brusquely as his tongue could bend to the vernacular, 'Utloa, utloa, utloa!'[2]

Mr Burton was returned at the head of the poll.

A more recent instance: in 1913, the South African Asiatic laws operated so harshly against British Indians that Westminster and Bombay demanded instant reform. In deference to this outside intervention the Union Government appointed the Solomon Commission to inquire into the matter. While the investigations were in progress, emphatic protests were constantly uttered against this 'outside interference'. Some of the South Africans went as far as to assert that 'if imperialism meant a "coolie" domination in South Africa, then it was about time that South Africa severed her imperial bonds'. The clamourers who designated the inquiry as a concession to outsiders seemed almost to dictate to the Commission not to recommend anything that 'savours of a surrender to the coolies'.

But when General Smuts, in terms of the Commission's report and as a concession to Anglo-Indian feeling, tabled a bill in 1914, to amend the hardships before they had been a year in operation, the clamour at once died down; and we have not heard that anyone in South Africa was a penny the poorer as a result of this 'outside interference', and its consequent 'surrender to the coolies'.

Dutchmen only follow their leaders. Hence, let the leaders direct them into cruel ways as they are seemingly doing at the present time, then if Mr Burton's assertions be right (and we think no one will deny that he is right when he says the one-sided policy can never succeed), these leaders, instead of producing a South Africa which is rich and contented, will only succeed in producing a South Africa which is poor and discontented. Those, too, who wish well for South Africa and are at the same time sympathizers of the present Government, let them also strive to induce the Ministry to cease its policy of dilly-dallying and of equivocation at the expense of the coloured taxpayers. So that the Dutch throughout South Africa, as did the Dutch of Cape Colony, under the

[2] 'Hear, hear,' in Sesuto.

able leadership of Jan Hendrik Hofmeyr, may pursue a fresh course—the course of political righteousness. When the Labour Party discover that white votes alone will not give it the reins of Government, its leaders will most probably advocate a native franchise in the northern colonies similar to the native franchise of the Cape. And we can assure them that the first man who would successfully tackle such a problem will not only secure for his party the votes thus created, but that sheer gratitude will in future place at his disposal the coloured vote of the Cape as well.

It is also our belief, in regard to the Dutch, that if a trusted leader from among them were to propose a native franchise for the northern provinces, the proposal would ultimately be accepted.

The predikants of the Dutch Reformed Church, who largely influence the leadership of the South African Dutch, ought to know that the English colonist can be just as devilish as the Boers on questions of colour; and that some of them, with their superior means and education have almost out-Boered the Boer in this matter; but that even they have been held in check by the restraint imposed upon them by the English churches in the country. Thus, knowing the Dutchman's obedience to the commands of his pastor, we are afraid that if ever there come a day of reckoning for the multifarious accumulation of wrongs done to the natives, the Dutch Reformed Church, owing to its silent consent to all these wrongs, will have a lot to answer for.

10   The Natives' Land Act in Cape Colony

During the month of October, 1913, the fell work of the iniquitous provisions of the Natives' Land Act was done so remorselessly that the British blood of certain editors of Natal dailies rose superior to their colonial prejudices and they lashed out against such wicked and wholesale injustice on the part of the legislation against the peaceful native population. It has already been pointed out that when the Secretary for Native Affairs started to tour the districts, to teach magistrates how to enforce the new plague act, some people thought that the tour was part of a scheme to alleviate the distress that followed the enforcement of the Natives' Land Act, but the natives and those of their sympathisers who followed Mr Dower's itinerary very soon discovered that the authorities were waging a war of extermination against the blacks; and that they were bent upon reducing the independent black peasantry to a state of thraldom. Commenting on Mr Dower's visit to the 'Free' State, the *Natal Advertiser* of October 4, 1913, said:

The explanation of the Natives' Land Act, given to the Barolongs of Thaba Nchu by Mr Dower, is so illuminative of the wretched unsatisfactoriness of the Act that the occasion certainly merits notice. It would be difficult to conceive a more thoroughgoing and drastic condemnation of the Act than this attempt at faint praise of it, delivered by the Secretary of the Native Affairs Department. All he can say to these unfortunate natives is, that it would be better to engage as labourers or sell up than to trek from pillar to post, till all their cattle had died. As to saying that farmers always had power to evict, the interrupting native hit the nail on the head by his ejaculation: 'But we could go elsewhere.'

On October 5, the daily papers published the following telegram from Johannesburg:

As a result of the passing of the Natives' Land Act, groups of natives are to be seen in the different provinces seeking for new land. They have crossed over the Free State into Natal, from Natal into the Transvaal, and from the Transvaal into British Bechuanaland . . .

Yesterday a native arrived in Johannesburg from the Umvoti district, Natal, and reported that a chief, together with his tribe, had been evicted from a farm in the Greytown district, Natal, and that feeling in the matter had become acute.

In the Western Transvaal hundreds of natives are crossing over into the Bechuanaland Protectorate, and in the Eastern Transvaal they are concentrating on three farms in the Wakkerstroom district that have been bought by a native land company.

At present the attention of those working for the repeal of the law is being concentrated on the collection of funds for the purpose of sending a deputation to England. They hope to arouse public opinion there by lectures and other means.

It must not be supposed, however, that all English colonial journalists regretted the operation of this atrocious law. The *Cape Times*, for instance, vied with the Hertzog press in congratulating the minister on having successfully passed it, and in belittling the hardships of the victims of the Act. One English farmer wrote to the *Farmer's Weekly* that the evictions were effective, but at the same time he regretted that 'as long as the native kept to the public road he still had a resting place for the hollow of his foot'. The native had been successfully legislated off the land, and apparently this farmer wanted him to be legislated off the roads as well. Another English journalist wrote to the *Sunday Post* that the hardships are exaggerated, as he had himself seen only twelve families evicted in one day and on one farm. The question which this statement suggests is: How many families must be ejected from one farm in one day to constitute a hardship; and whether this journalist would view with the same coolness a law which forcibly turned twelve white families off a farm, against the wishes of themselves and the landowner?

Again, it cannot be said that South African politicians as a whole were indifferent to the suffering of the luckless victims of the Land Act, but they eased their consciences with the palliative thought that the sufferers were not so many. However this blissful though erroneous self-satisfaction was nailed to the counter by the Rev. A. Burnet of Transvaal, when he said: 'I have yet to learn that a harsh law becomes less harsh, and an act of injustice less unjust, because only a few people are affected by it.'

The section of the law debarring natives from hiring land is particularly harsh. It has been explained that its major portion is intended to reduce the natives to serfs; but it should also be noted that the portion of the Act that is against natives acquiring any interest whatsoever in land aims directly at dispossessing the natives of their livestock. Section 5 provides for a fine of £100, or six months imprisonment, to a farmer convicted of accommodating a native on his farm. And if after the fine is paid, the native leaves the stock on the farm, for a number of days, while he goes to search for another place, there will be a fine of £5 *per diem* for each day the cattle remain on the farm. The cattle should be consigned to the road immediately the order is given for ejection, and they should remain without food till their owner sells them, or finds employment under a farmer as a wage-earner. Thus it would seem that the aim of Section 5 is not only to prohibit native occupation of land, but, in addition to it, makes it impossible for him to be a cattle-owner.

When this harsh provision of the law was brought to the notice of Cape politicians, they shrugged their shoulders and remarked that they were happy that things in the Cape were not so bad. But this is no excuse at all, for in accordance with the wording of the Act, as substantiated by its results upon the Cape natives, the condition of these natives is worse in many instances than it is among the natives of Natal, or the Transvaal. In these two provinces a European who has no intention of evicting his natives may retain their services under certain restrictions (see Sub-section 6 [c]); but in the

Cape and the Orange 'Free' State, the native, according to Section 1, may retain no interest whatever in the land, including the 'ploughing on shares'.

Well-to-do natives, from Grahamstown to the Transkeian boundaries, mainly derived their wealth from this form of occupation. It enabled them to lead respectable lives and to educate their children. The new prohibitions tended to drive these natives back into overcrowded locations, with the logical result that sundry acute domestic problems, such as disordered sanitation caused by the smallness of the location, loss of numerous heads of cattle owing to the too limited pasturage in the locations, are likely to arise. These herds of cattle have been the natives' only capital, or the natives' 'bank', as they truthfully call them, so that, deprived of this occupation, the down-grade of a people, under an unsympathetic quasi-Republic Government like the present Union Administration, must be very rapid.

The fact that the traditional liberal policy of Cape Colony has broken down through this law can no longer be disputed: indeed, the only comfort that had been held out to the natives was that Mr Sauer would make the Natives' Land Act a dead letter. This statesman having since died, we were anxious to see how the Cape natives were faring under the Act, so we left Kimberley on November 1, 1913, on a tour of observation in the eastern districts of the Cape Province. Our programme included visits to two alleged defenders of the Act, in the persons of Rev. James Henderson of Lovedale, and Mr Tengo Jabavu of King Williamstown, editor of the Xosa ministerial newspaper. Our object in visiting these gentlemen was to acquaint ourselves with their point of view, and if possible to arrive at an agreement with them.

We reached Alice in the forenoon and walked through the town to the famous native institution. We made our first acquaintance with Lovedale, and we hardly remember having seen so many native boys housed in any one place before. But it pained us to think what must be the future lot of this great gathering of young fellows, who are now debarred by law from the rights of ownership of the soil of South Africa, their own homeland.

During our three hours' stay at Lovedale we had an interview with Mr Henderson, the Principal, about things in general, and the Native College Scheme in particular, and lastly, but not least, about the Natives' Land Act. Unfortunately we could learn nothing from the eminent educator, for we found that his conclusions were based on second-hand information. He had never met any member of the Government, or their representatives, in fact it was news to the Principal that in going to Lovedale, that morning, we had met men on their way from the magistrate's office in Alice, not far away, who had been definitely warned by the magistrate against re-ploughing their old lands on the farms. Of course Mr Henderson was moved with sympathy for a people so ruthlessly treated by a Government they had loyally served. And it would seem that the Principal of Lovedale had since made independent inquiries, for we have read in the Lovedale paper other evidence of the operation of this drastic law that had not come under our own observation. Thus in supporting the case of the native deputation in the Imperial Parliament on July 28, 1914, Sir Albert Spicer effectively read passages from the *Christian Express,* the organ of Lovedale.

One of the instructors at Lovedale very kindly lent us a horse, and Mr Moikangoa accompanied us to an all-night meeting at Sheshegu, a famous political 'rendezvous' which has acquired this distinction because it is the centre of numerous little locations, within easy reach of four surrounding magistracies. At the all-night meeting at Sheshegu there were chiefs, headmen, and other natives from the Peddie, Fort Beaufort and Alice districts. There were a number of schoolteachers also from these districts, and two or three native storekeepers. The disclosures made by the several speakers concerning the operation of the Land Act among the natives made one's heart bleed. The chieftain Kapok Mgijima, who entertained many of the visitors to the meeting, had his own peculiar experience under the Act. Not only he had been debarred from re-ploughing his own lands, but he had also been ordered to move his oxen from a farm owned by a European, where for fourteen years he had grazed his oxen. Another native, who had been ploughing in the direction of King Williamstown, was warned by the authorities not to resume his ploughing in 1913. He could only do so as a servant in the employ of a white landowner. He was further warned that if he connived with the white man to cheat the law, by representing themselves as master and servant, they would, when found out to be still carrying on their old relation of landlord and tenant, be dealt with very severely.

The landlord was furious. 'Why,' he asked, 'did you tell them of your intention? You should have done your business quietly; now that you have apprised them they will watch us, you fool.'

'But,' said the native, 'owing to the existence of the east coast fever in Transkei, no animals can be taken from one plantation to another without a magisterial permit disclosing the object of the removal. I had to tell what I wanted to come here for. I was asked at the magistrate's office if I did not know the law. I said that I was aware of such a new law, which had created a lot of disturbance in the Northern provinces, but I had never heard that it was applicable to the Cape. To this the magistrate's clerk replied that it was not a provincial law, it was a law of the Union, of which the Cape formed part. There were certain exemptions, the clerk added, but they did not exempt the Cape natives from the prohibition of ploughing on white men's farms and grazing their cattle on those farms.'

Other speakers narrated their experiences under the Act, and these experiences showed that the Plague Act was raging with particular fury in the old Cape districts of Fort Beaufort, Grahamstown, King Willliamstown, and East London. At this meeting it was resolved to support a movement to send an appeal to His Majesty the King, against the law.

Our visit to these places took place just after the glorious showers of the early summer. On the wider tracts of land owned by Europeans the grass looked invitingly green. The maiden soil, looking beautiful and soft after the soaking rains, cried silently for cultivation. The people who had hitherto depended on such cultivation for their subsistence were now prohibited by reason of their colour from earning their usual livelihood, as directed by Almighty God, 'In the sweat of thy brow shalt thou eat bread'.

115

This prohibition seems particularly contemptible when it is remembered that the majority of the natives of these locations are Fingoes, and that their fathers in the early days joined the British in fighting most of the Kaffir Wars, side by side with British troops. They shared in all the massacres and devasting raids committed upon the British settlers by unfriendly native tribes. As a mark of recognition of their loyalty to the Government, and of their cooperation with the British forces in the field of battle, this country was given, in the name of Her late Majesty Victoria, to their chiefs by a British governor. But in spite of this treaty, the people have been gradually dispossessed of the land during the past three-quarters of a century. Hence the occupation, now crystallised into ownership, passed bit by bit into white hands. Hitherto the right to live on, and to cultivate, lands which thus formerly belonged to them was never challenged, but all that is now changed. Naturally the ingratitude meted out to these people by the authorities in return for services consistently rendered by three successive generations of them will be a blow, not only to the economic independence of a loyal and patriotic people, but to the belief in British sense of justice.

11 The passing of Cape ideals

From the great meeting place—Sheshegu— we went through the Alice district. In this district we met several men who would get no crops—their annual income—the next year, as the law had placed an embargo on their ordinary avocation. King Williamstown was also visited, and there at a meeting held in the Baptist Church, which was kindly lent for the purpose by the Rev. Mr Pierce, it was unanimously resolved to appeal to His Majesty the King against the Natives' Land Act. Mr W. Sebe presided over this meeting of representative natives, and Mr Bassie translated the Act.

At Queenstown a similar resolution was passed by practically the whole meeting. Beyond answering questions at each of these meetings, the writer said little else besides reading the Act, which told its own tale. Many natives who have never seen a copy of the Act before, but who had heard its praises sung by interested parties and had believed the false teachers, attended the meetings to oppose any undue interference with 'the law'. But these men were appalled when the law was read to them, sentence by sentence, and translated by their own teachers in their own tongue. Then a discussion would follow, invariably ending with the query: 'Can a Parliament capable of passing such a law still be trusted by the community concerned?'

The Queenstown meeting, which was held in the native Baptist school kindly lent by Messrs Damane and Koti, was more interesting than the others because it is the only one of the many native meetings we attended where there was any dissent. There were four dissentients at Queenstown, and we take this opportunity of congratulating all genuine enemies of native welfare on the fact that they had four staunch protagonists of colour, who showed more manliness than Mr Tengo Jabavu because they attended the meeting. Still, if the courage of these opponents was admirable, we confess we did not like the gross callousness, and what seemed to us an indecent disregard of native suffering that was manifest in their conduct: when the story of the hardships of unfortunate victims of the Land Act was narrated they laughed, and repeated the newspaper excuse that the evictions were not directly due to the Act.

We agree with them that evictions have always taken place, since the first human couple was sent out of the garden of Eden, yet they must admit that until the Union Parliament passed the Natives' Land Act there never was a law saying to the native population of South Africa, 'You must not settle anywhere under a penalty of £100, unless you are a servant.' These unsympathetic natives made no effort to defend the Act itself, but attempted to bluff the meeting with the supposed danger of reprisals by spiteful Boers, who, they said, 'will be more vindictive if natives dared to appeal to the King, over the heads of the Boer Government.' But the meeting would not be bluffed. One speaker especially re- marked that the Act embodied the very worst form of vindictiveness, and the sooner the whole world understood the Union Parliament's attitude towards the blacks the bet- ter it would be. The meeting agreed that no slavery could be worse than to be outlawed in your own homes, and the motion was carried against the said four dissentients.

We interviewed a number of the natives passing through Queenstown, and the result showed that many and varied were the vicissitudes of the natives in the eastern districts of the Cape Province.

From Queenstown we touched some of the north- eastern districts of the Cape Province. In one of these districts a fairly prosperous native was farming as a tenant on a farm. By sheer industry he had earned and enjoyed the respect of all who knew him. His landlord, a white man, was particularly proud of him. This native went into town one morning and as he passed the magistrate's court on his way to the stores, a messenger hailed him inside. Having entered the office, the assistant magistrate served him with a notice to leave his hired farm, on which he had been a tenant since his youth, and which was as much a home to him as to the proprietor. The landlord, on hearing of this, naturally resented this usurpation on the part of the authorities, who, he said, had unduly interfered with his private affairs. Next day the Baas drove into the town to interview the magistrate, and to remonstrate with him on what he though to be the un-authorised interference of the assistant magistrate.

He and the magistrate read and re-read the Natives' Land Act, and both came to the conclusion that it was a law that was as complicated as it was unnecessary; but the magistrate, being a representative of the law, decided that, rightly or wrongly, it must be obeyed.

This visit of the Baas to the magistrate had made our native friend hopeful that it would result in averting the calamity that threatened him and his family, but, to his utter dismay, the landlord on returning soon undeceived him and gave his own opinion of 'the most peculiar and wicked law' that he had ever heard of. Although Dutchmen had known and had heard of some strange laws, yet this Dutchman was so full of indignation at the strangeness of this law that his des-cription of it was made up of largely untranslatable Dutch adjectives. These adjectives, however, could not relieve the suffering of his native tenant from the wound inflicted by the law in his sudden expulsion from his home. It seems clear that no South African native, on leaving a Dutch farm, had ever received a more respectable send-off than our friend did on leaving his farm in compliance with the Natives' Land Act. The white landlord accompanied him right up to the boundary of the farm which for seventeen years had been his home, and which he was so cruelly forced to leave. For the first time in his life, as the Dutchman said, he shook hands with a Kaffir. And, as he did so, he called down the direst curses upon the persons responsible for the impasse—curses, by the way, which seem to be liberally answered.

It would, perhaps, be interesting to add what has happened since. Our native friend took his family to the town, because the Act is not enforceable in municipal areas. Leaving his family there, he started roaming about the districts, looking for a place where he could graze his cattle. In the course of the wandering his stock thinned down, owing to death from starvation and other causes. At home his old master found he could not get on without him, so learning of the whereabouts of the native and also of his sad plight, the master sent out to him and advised him to return home, graze his stock there, and 'hang the legal consequences'. May they never be found out.

It has now amounted to this that white men who wish to deal humanely with their native friends must resort to clandestine methods, to enable a native and his stock to drink the fresh water and breathe the pure air in the wide tracts of South Africa, for by law natives have now less rights than the snakes and scorpions abounding in that country. Can a law be justified which forces the people to live only by means of chicanery; and which, in order to progress, compels one to cheat the law officers of the Crown? This case is but one of many that came under our own observation, and there may be many more of which we know nothing.

The *Cape Times*, the leading Bothaite daily newspaper of the Cape, has defended every action of the Union, including the dismissal of the English civil servants. It justifies the last act by alleging that the dismissed officials did not know Dutch. Consequently it could not be expected that this journal could have any qualms about a law enacted specifically to repress black men. It supported every harsh clause of the Natives' Land Bill, including Clause I. However, when the native deputation to England gave proofs of the ravages of the 'plague law' in Cape Colony, the *Cape Times,* instead of defending its pet law, said: 'The complaint to which they give precedence is particularly instructive,' and so, quoting from the deputation's appeal which says: 'In the Cape Colony, where we are repeatedly told that the Act is not in force, the Magistrates of East London, King Williamstown and Alice prohibited native tenants from reploughing their old hired lands last October, and also ordered them to remove their stock from grazing farms,' this ministerial daily adds: 'It is unnecessary to consider the justice or otherwise of this complaint for it is perfectly clear that if a magistrate oversteps the bounds of the law, it is a matter to be dealt with by the Union Government.'

It will be observed that this is an insinuation that the magistrates who administer the Land Act at the Cape are exceeding their authority and should be 'dealt with by the Union Government'. Now, what are the facts? It is well known that all magistrates, including those at the Cape, are paid to administer every legislative instrument, whether sensible or absurd, passed by the partly literate Parliament of the Union of South Africa. Hence, these magistrates, in ordering natives off their farms, and turning native cattle off the grazing areas, are only carrying out Section 1 of the Natives' Land Act. One Cape magistrate who ruled that to plough on a farm was a breach of the law, *was* 'dealt with by the Union Government', for a peremptory order came from Pretoria declaring such a decision to be illegal.

Therefore, so far from the Cape magistrate 'overstepping the bounds of the law' in expelling natives from the farms and native cattle from their pastures, these magistrates could legally have done worse, inasmuch as they could, under Section 5, have sent these natives to prison for contravening Section 1. In justification, then, of its own and of its party's share in this legislative achievement, the *Cape Times* should have sought a more worthy excuse than thus attempting to make scapegoats of a band of fair-minded men who presumably, prior to the Union, never thought it would be part of their duty to administer from the Cape bench an Act which inflicted such gross cruelty.

Who, in the days of the Murrays, Mr F.Y. St. Leger, and subsequently of Mr F.E. Garrett, could have thought that the *Cape Times* would in this manner have destroyed its great traditions, built up during the nineteenth century, by sanctioning a law under which Cape magistrates would be forced to render homeless the natives of the Cape in their own Cape of Good Hope? The one colony whose administration, under its wise statesmen of the Victorian era, created for it that tremendous prestige that was felt throughout the dark continent, and that rested largely upon the fact that among its citizens, before its incorporation with the Northern States, it knew no distinction of colour, for all were free to qualify for the exercise of electoral rights. The old Cape Colony of our boyhood days, whose administration, despite

121

occasional lapses, managed during a hundred years to steer clear of the familiar massacres and bloodshed of punitive expeditions against primitive tribes, massacres and bloodshed so common in other parts of the same continent; the old Cape Colony whose peaceful methods of civilisation acted as an incentive to the Bechuana tribes to draw the sword and resist every attempt at annexation by Europeans other than the British: a resistance so determined that it thwarted the efforts to link German South-West Africa with the Transvaal Republic, and so kept open the trade route to Rhodesia for the British. All this done without any effort on the part of the British themselves, and done by the natives out of regard for Cape Colony ideals. But alas! these natives are now debarred from tilling the soil of the Cape, except as Republican serfs. What would Sir George Grey, or Bishop Gray, or Saul Solomon, say of this? What would these empire builders say if they came back and found that the hills and valleys of their old Cape Colony have ceased to be a home to many of their million brawny blacks, whose muscles helped the conqueror to secure his present hold of the country? What would these champions of justice say if they saw how, with her entrance to the Union, Cape Colony had bartered her shining ideals for the sombre history of the Northern States, a history defiled with innocent blood, and a territory soaked with native tears and scandalised by burying natives alive; and that with one stroke of the pen the so-called federation has demolished the Rhodes' formula of 'equal rights for all civilised men, irrespective of colour'? How are the mighty fallen!

But while we sing the funeral dirge of Cape ideals, the Republicans sing songs of gladness. Thus, when Mr Sauer, a noted disciple of the late Mr Saul Solomon, died the *Bloemfontein Friend,* the leading ministerial daily of the 'Free' State, said:

He stood uncompromisingly for Rhodes' ideal of complete equality, and it was an open secret that Mr Sauer, who piloted the Natives' Land Act through Parliament last session would, had circumstances been different, have been its strongest opponent. It was the irony of fate that made him Minister of Native Affairs when a law had to be passed which appeared to be in entire conflict with his cherished lifelong convictions. The Act he passed embodied the hated northern principles which he had consistently opposed during the whole of his political career, and, as in the case of the Act of Union, it was only Mr Sauer's influence that allayed the feelings of the intransigent section of the native population.

Mr Sauer was a convinced disciple of the teachings of Saul Solomon, who founded and preached the gospel of the Cape native policy. In our view that was a mistaken policy. Its principal modern exponent has now been taken away, and if God, and not man, shapes the destinies of nations, we may be pardoned the belief that Mr Sauer's death at this juncture means something more than the mere passing from the finite into the infinite of one human being.

If this is a brutal utterance, it is at any rate more frank, and therefore more manly, than the vacillating policy of the *Cape Times,* the ministerial organ of the Cape Colony. It is said that 'politics make strange bed-fellows', but not even the shrewdest of our political seers could have predicted that in 1913 the *Cape Times* would be found in the same camp as its Republican contemporaries which sing glees over the demolished structure of Cape traditions, and over the passing away of Victorian statesmen and the principles they stood for—Victorian principles, which the *Cape Times* of other days helped to build up in another political camp! How are the mighty fallen!

> Sweet smiling village, loveliest of the lawn,
> Thy sports are fled and all thy charms withdrawn;
> Amidst thy bowers the tyrant's hand is seen
> And desolation saddens all thy green:
> And trembling, shrinking from the spoiler's hand,
> Far, far away, thy children leave the land.
> Ill fares the land, to hastening ills a prey,
> Where wealth accumulates and men decay.

The Cape native can thoroughly endorse these sentiments

of Oliver Goldsmith, which, however, compared with his own present lot, are mild in the extreme; for it could not have been amid scenes of this description, and with an outlook half as bad as ours, that the same author further sings:

> A time there was e'er England's grief began,
> When every rood of ground maintain'd its man;
> But times are altered: Trade's unfeeling train
> Usurp the land and dispossess the swain.

> Those gentle hours that plenty bade to bloom,
> Those calm desires that ask'd but little room,
> Those graceful sports that grac'd the peaceful
>   scene,
> Liv'd in each look and brighten'd all the green,
> These far departing seek a kinder shore,
> And rural mirth and manners are no more.

> In all my wand'rings round this world of care,
> In all my griefs—and God has giv'n my share—
> I still had hopes my latest hours to crown,
> Amidst these humble bowers to lay me down.

12 Mr Tengo Jabavu, the pioneer native pressman

There is issued in King Williamstown (Cape) *Imvo*, the second-oldest newspaper published in any one of the South African native languages. This paper formerly had a kind of monopoly in the field of native journalism, and it deserved a wide reputation. In later years the *Izwi*, another native journal, appeared on the scene; and then the King Williamstown pioneer could hardly hold its ground against the new rival. The *Izwi*, though somewhat too pronounced against the traditional policy of the Dutch, appealed to a large section mainly by reason of its Imperial sentiment. The result was that Mr Tengo Jabavu's paper began to sink into difficulties and had to cast about for a financial rescuer. Prominent supporters of the present ministry came to the rescue; three out of the ten members of the first Union cabinet became shareholders in the sinking *Imvo*, so that the editor, in a sense, cannot very well be blamed because his paper is native only in language. However, we do not think that he does full justice to his ministerial employers.

God forbid that we should ever find that our mind had become the property of someone other than ourselves. But should such a misfortune ever overtake us, we should at least strive to serve our new proprietor diligently, and whenever our people are unanimously opposed to a policy, we should consider it a part of our duty to tell him so; but that is not Mr Jabavu's way of serving a master. Throughout the course of a general election we have known him to feed his master (the South African Party), upon flapdoodle, fabricating the mess out of imaginary native votes of confidence for his masters' delectation, and leaving them to discover the real ingredients of the dish, at the bottom of the poll, when the result has been declared.

He did the same thing in the case of the Natives' Land Bill. Thus when he found that the trouble was organising the natives on an unprecedented scale, and that the native press and the Native Congress were unanimous in denouncing the Grobler-Sauer Bill, a Reuter's telegram appeared in the newspapers purporting to give the proceedings of a meeting of the natives of King Williamstown, who, it was alleged, approved of the Bill. When the author reached King Williamstown, during the visit, he found the King Williamstown natives disgusted with what they said was Reuter's speculation upon their feelings. But Reuter's agent on the spot, whose office we also visited, knew nothing about the meeting. The only meeting ever held in the place, we were told, was one of nineteen persons presided over by Mr Tengo Jabavu, and when Mr Jabavu asked the other eighteen natives present in the meeting besides him to signify their approval of the legislation, Mr W.D. Soga (a well-known native politician) asked the chairman to place a motion before the meeting, as he was ready to move an amendment. The temper of the meeting having already shown itself unfavourable to the chairman's suggestion, the latter, instead of challenging a positive defeat, suggested an adjournment. This was agreed to for the simple reason that nineteen persons were too few to express the wishes of the 100,000 natives of King Williamstown. But, the next morning, the message 'from Reuter's agent at King Williamstown' appeared in all the daily papers, except that of King Williamstown, conveying the natives' approval of the Bill, and Mr Sauer, in Parliament, made capital out of the 'mess'-age. But Mr Tengo Jabavu lived to rue his action in this matter before very long. His authority, or rather his leadership of the natives, was put to the test in March 1914, when he contested the Tembuland seat against Dr W.B. Rubusana. Dr Rubnusana had always been supposed to occupy the second place, and Mr Jabavu the first place, in the estimation of the natives of the Cape Province: yet, to the surprise of everybody, Mr Jabavu, although assisted by the Dutch vote, polled only 294 votes, while Dr Rubusana, who relied entirely on the coloured vote, polled 852.

We mentioned, in a previous chapter, the names of

Principal Henderson and Mr Tengo Jabavu, as those whom we especially desired to interview during our trip. Having stated the fulfilment of this desire in regard to Mr Henderson, we now proceed to state it in regard to Mr Jabavu.

There was to be a meeting of the natives of King Williamstown, in the Baptist Chapel, on November 3, 1913, to discuss the Natives' Land Act. To this meeting we had been invited by telegram; and in going to King Williamstown we made up our mind to invite Mr Jabavu to this meeting of natives of this town, and in fact, to treat him with the same respect as we had shown the Principal of Lovedale with such happy results; but, to our horror, we found that Mr Jabavu was not only preaching the Backvelders' dangerous politics, that were ruinous to native interests, but that, besides their dangerous politics, he had imbibed their baser quality of ingratitude. For this man had not only enjoyed our free hospitality on three occasions, when he visited up-country, and the hospitality of our relatives at various times in other parts, but when he was about to leave for Europe, on a holiday jaunt, and wanted someone to take charge of his work, we left our own affairs and went to King Williamstown, at our own expense, to fill that post, and we filled it without a fee; but, see his retaliation.

We reached King Williamstown on Saturday evening and called at Mr Jabavu's house on Sunday afternoon. Mrs Jabavu said her husband had gone to Stutterheim, and would be back by a late train. On Monday morning we called at Mr Jabavu's office, and his son whom we saw said his father would be there in the afternoon. We called in the afternoon and were told that he was inside and would see us later. We waited from 2.30 till nearly 4 pm, chatting with his son, while Mr Jabavu was closeted in the next room, evidently unwilling to see us. As his son had to leave we also went away, but returned to his office at 6 pm, just an hour before the opening of the public meeting to which we wished to invite him. Mr Jabavu sent a verbal message, with the young lady who had taken in our card to him, to the effect that he was not prepared to see us. That in brief was our reception by the man who edits 'a native paper'.

We went to the meeting at the Baptist Chapel, which was

a huge success. Mr W. Sebe presided. The editor of the King Williamstown daily paper, an Englishman, attended the meeting in person and took notes for his paper, while no reporter represented the *soi-disant* native paper of King Williamstown.

When the proceedings of the meeting appeared in the King Williamstown English paper, Mr Jabavu attempted to discount the report by writing in his own paper that 'the *Cape Mercury* evidently does not know that there are natives and natives, as well as King Williamstown and King Williamstown, there being town and country,' etc. This being a veiled insinuation that the rural native view was opposed to the urban native view at King Wiliamstown, we could not leave the matter unchallenged, so we posted the following challenge to Mr Tengo Jabavu, which he evidently found it impossible to accept:

Dear Sir,

Imvo comments disparagingly on Monday's meeting, and adds that the natives who composed the meeting were a handful drawn by curiosity. Now, I challenge *Imvo*, or Mr Tengo Jabavu, to call a series of three public meetings, anywhere in the district of King Williamstown. Let us both address these meetings immediately after the Natives' Land Act has been read and interpreted to each. We could address the meetings from the same platform, or separately, but on the same day and at the same place. For every vote carried at each of these meetings in favour of his views on the Act I undertake to hand over £15 to the Grey Hospital (King Williamstown) and £15 to the Victoria Hospital (Lovedale), on condition that for every vote I carry at any of the meetings, he hand over £15 to the Victoria Hospital (Mafeking), and £15 to the Carnarvon Hospital (Kimberley).

That is £30 for charity, if he will accept.

I will not place difficulties in his way by inviting him to meetings up here, but leave him to call meetings among his own people (if he has any) in his own district, and I will attend at my own expense.

Mr Tengo Jabavu

Yours, etc

(Sgd) Sol. T. Plaatje,

Editor of *Tsala ea Batho* and Secretary S.A. Native
National Congress,
14, Shannon Street, Kimberley.

IMVO'S REPLY

Dear Sir,

I am instructed by the Editor of *Imvo* to acknowledge
the receipt of your letter, and to inform you that as he
has not been reading and following your writings, etc.,
he cannot understand what you mean by it. In short,
to let you know that he takes no interest in the matter.

I am Sir,

Yours truly,

(Sgd) A.M. Jabavu

Imvo Office, King Williamstown
November 24, 1913.

Poor fellow! He had not met a single member of the Government since the plague law was so rudely sprung upon an
unsuspecting country, and since it sent unprotected widows
and innocent children adrift, to wander about with their
belongings on their heads. Mr Jabavu had not met any
member of Parliament and discussed the measure with him
or with a responsible Government official; so he found it
awkward to accept a challenge to substantiate his arguments,
in the presence of one who had not only discussed the
measure with members of Parliament, with Cabinet
Ministers and their representatives, but who had also witnessed the ravages of the Act amongst the natives in the
country.

The general complaint of the natives of King Williamstown, his fellow-townsmen, is that he refuses to attend their
meetings and relies on the white daily papers for information
about the natives at large.

But Mr Jabavu is nothing if he is not selfish. We are
informed, and have every reason to believe, that, months

129

after the Act was passed, he wanted to raise a loan of £200 on landed security, but was debarred by the Natives' Land Act. The next issue of his paper praised the Act for the sixtieth time and noted the following exception: 'There is only one flaw in this otherwise useful Act, which is occasioning a manifest hardship through harsh administration, and that is the provision relating to lending money.'

Now, from our point of view, this seems to be the only defensible provision, as it would tend to discourage usury, a common evil in money transactions between Europeans and natives; but because it interfered with Mr Jabavu's personal aims, that is the only flaw. The cold-blooded evictions and the Draconian principle against living anywhere, except as serfs, are inconsequential because they have not yet touched Mr Jabavu's person.

13   The Native Congress and the Union Government

A native meeting was called to meet at Johannesburg on July 25, 1913, under the auspices of the South African Native Congress.

The Congress was attended by natives from as far south as East London and King Williamstown, and from as far north as the Zoutpansbergen in Northern Transvaal, and also from Natal, Zululand, and from Bechuanaland; in fact from nearer and distant centres in all parts of the country they had gathered to discuss the situation arising from the serious conditions created by the Natives' Land Act. Thus the proceedings of the meeting were conducted under a grave sense of responsibility. There was little of the customary loquaciousness which characterises native gatherings; and there was much less free translation of the speeches for the benefit of the European visitors. Translations, as a rule, take up a great deal of valuable time, and it was their curtailment on this occasion, apparently, which caused the *Transvaal Leader*—a morning paper of the Rand—to complain that natives had become unusually secretive and had ceased to be as communicative as at previous meetings. The *Rand Daily Mail*, on the other hand, referred to the closing session in a very few lines. It said: 'Last evening, a number of native women attended the Native Congress, attired as befitting the solemnity and importance of the occasion. The orderly behaviour of the 200 or more delegates was attributable to the presence on the platform of Mr Dube, an able chairman, supported by two native solicitors who passed their B.A. in London.'

Mr R.W. Msimang is a solicitor who was articled to a firm of solicitors in England; but the reference to the second 'native solicitor' and 'London B.A.' is about the most undeserved compliment ever paid to the author, who, until 1914 (a year after the Congress reported by the *Mail*), had never been on board a ship, nor inside a London college.

At the annual Congress, March 1913, a deputation had been appointed to proceed to Cape Town and to present to the Government the native objections against the proposed embargo on the purchase and lease of land. The deputation consisted of Mr J.L. Dube, Dr W.B. Rubusana, Mr Advocate Mangena, Rev. L. Dlepu, Messrs W.Z. Fenyang, S. Msane, L.T. Mvabaza, D. Letanka, and S.T. Plaatje; the writer, however, was not able to proceed to Cape Town at the time. The July Congress was specially called to receive the report of the delegates to Cape Town, and further to consider what other steps it might be necessary to take.

Dr Rubusana gave a report on the deputation to Cape Town. They had four interviews with the Minister of Native Affairs, and several interviews with members of Parliament, urging the setting aside of some Government farms, to which evicted native tenants might go, as the effect of the Bill, then under discussion, would inevitably be to make numbers of them homeless. The Minister, he said, never denied the possible hardship that would follow the enforcement of such a law, but he seemed to be driven by a mysterious force in the face of which the native interest did not count. What that force was, he said, could only be surmised. General Hertzog, who had always advocated some such measure (though he had never been able to carry it out), had just been excluded from the Botha cabinet; to placate his supporters, who were very angry over his dismissal, the Government carried out this alleged policy of his, so that while General Hertzog in office was not able to bring about the enslavement of the blacks, General Hertzog out of office succeeded in getting the Government to sacrifice their principles of right and justice and to force the Act through Parliament, in order to retain the support of the 'Free' State malcontents.

When every effort with the ministry failed, the delegates asked for a postponement of the Bill pending the report of the Commission. This also was refused by the Government. Finally he wrote a letter to Lord Gladstone, asking him to withold his assent to the Bill until he had heard the native view. To this His Excellency replied that such a course was 'not within his constitutional functions'. All took place in May 1913.

In July, Mr Dube, the president of the Congress, wrote to Lord Gladstone asking for an interview to lay before him the nature of the damage that the Act was causing among the native population. Again His Excellency replied that it was 'not within his constitutional functions'.

The Natives' Land Act, which was then law, was read to the assembled natives, most of whom narrated their experiences and the result of their observations to the effect of the Act during the six weeks that it had been in force. Congress considered these, and as a result of their deliberations it was resolved to appeal to His Majesty's Government; and also to take steps to apprise the British public of the mode of government carried on in British South Africa under the Union Jack, and to invoke their assistance to abrogate the obnoxious law that had brought the Congress together.

The Congress considered at length how His Majesty the King and the British public could best help the natives in these matters; and it was concluded that if South Africa were really British, then any suffering taking place in that country must be of concern to His Majesty the King and the British public. The next point for inquiry by the Congress was the journey of a deputation to be chosen to proceed on this mission, a journey consisting of six thousand miles by sea and a thousand miles by rail. When the Europeans of South Africa went to England to ask the Imperial Government for a constitution, their delegates were easily sent, because the native taxpayers, although with hardly any hope of benefiting by the gift—which amounted to a curtailment of their rights—were compelled to contribute to the travelling and other expenses of these envoys; but in the native's own case no such funds are at his disposal, even though he goes to the Imperial Government to point out that his taxes had been used by a Parliament in which he is unrepresented as a rod for his back. In order to meet this necessary demand for ways and means, Mr Msane was deputed to tour the country and ask for funds from the natives. A Johannesburg committee was appointed to superintend this effort and take charge of the funds which he might raise. The members of the said committee were: Messrs W.F. Jemsana (chairman), Elka M. Cele (treasurer), D.S. Letanka, R.W. Msimang, H.D. Mkize, B.G. Phooko, D.D. Tywakadi, D. Moeletsi, M.D. Ndabezita, H. Selby Msimang (hon. sec.), S. Msane (organiser). Finally a deputation was appointed to proceed to Pretoria to lay before the Union Government three resolutions that the Congress passed. The first, condoling with the Government on the death of Hon. J.W. Sauer, late Minister of Justice and Native Affairs, who died just as the Congress was about to meet; the second resolution, that the natives dissociated themselves entirely from the industrial struggles on the Witwatersrand and elsewhere, and preferred to seek redress for their grievances through constitutional rather than by violent means.

The third resolution, that humble representations to the authorities against the eviction of natives from farms, having proved unavailing, the natives had now decided to raise funds for the purpose and convey their appeal to His Majesty the King and to the British public. That Mr Msane had been appointed organiser of the appeal fund and that a safe conduct was requested for him to tour the native villages. The following deputation was appointed to present these resolutions to the Union Government at Pretoria: Chief Karl Kekana and Mr S.M. Makgatho of the Transvaal, Mr E. Mamba of the Transkei (Cape), Mr Saul Msane and Rev. R. Twala (Natal), Mr S.T. Plaatje (Kimberley) and Mr J.M. Nyokong of the Orange 'Free' State.

Mr S.F. Malan, the Minister for Native Affairs *pro tem,* received the deputation in the Government Buildings, which were the Transvaal Houses of Parliament before Union. With the Minister of Native Affairs, were Messrs E. Barrett, Assistant Secretary for Native Affairs, Mr Pritchard, the Johannesburg Commissioner, and Mr Cross, a Rand magistrate. The Minister readily received the resolutions and confessed to a feeling of relief at the moderation of their tone. Further, he listened to the story of hardships already suffered by the natives, as a result of the enforcement of the Land

Act, specific instances of which were given, some being of natives not far from Pretoria, who, after being evicted from their old homes and having found new homes, were told by the Commissioner that they could not settle therein.

The delegates submitted to the Minister that their complaint was not a sentimental grievance, but real physical suffering. The Minister having listened to these statements, pointed out that this Act was the law of the land, which must be obeyed. He was not so sure, he said, that the natives could achieve anything by means of a deputation to England as the law had already been signed by His Majesty's representative on the spot without hesitation. He could not see why the natives should be interfered with when holding meetings and organising a deputation to go to the King, as long as they kept within the four corners of the law. But it seemed to him that they should have waited until a commission had been appointed under Sections 2 and 3 of the Act. An appeal to the Sovereign, he added, was the inherent right of every British subject; but he expressed the desire that the appeal to England should be dropped until the commission had first made its report. The delegates explained that as the law had in six weeks done so much harm, it was alarming to think what it might do in six months, while there was nothing definite to hope for from the report of a commission not yet appointed, and whose report might conceivably take six years.

The deputation made it clear that the appeal to the King would be dropped if the Government undertook to amend the law pending the report of the commission.

THE NATIVE'S LAND ACT IN NATAL

In the following months both the Minister in charge of Native Affairs and the Chief Native Commissioner of Natal asked Rev. John L. Dube, president of the S.A. Native National Congress, to furnish them with information and particulars of natives in misery as a result of the Natives' Land Act. Mr Dube had been collecting some concrete cases of hardship, including Chief Sandanazwe of Evansdale, Waschbank, who stated that he and fifty members of his tribe 'are given notice to remove, and that he has made representations to the authorities in Maritzburg asking for land without success.'

Mr Dube sent the following letter to the Secretary for Native Affairs, with a list of evicted farm tenants, on September 12, 1913.

Sir,

The Chief Native Commissioner for Natal approached me shortly after the publication in the press of my open letter[1] with a request similar to that made by you, viz., that I should furnish him with particulars and information. From time to time I did so furnish those names to the Chief Commissioner, and I send you herewith a list of those names and also additional names which have come to my knowledge since my correspondence with the Chief Native Commissioner.

In regard to the concluding paragraph of your letter to the effect that the only result of the Chief Native Commissioner's request was the submission of the case of a native in the Weenen County who received notice from his landlord over a year ago, you must be misinformed. As you will see from the list, scores of names were furnished to the Native Commissioner, and furthermore, some of the individuals themselves who were suffering hardship were sent by me to the Chief Commissioner and were interviewed by him. The trouble has been that the Chief Commissioner, instead of dealing with these individual cases himself, has, I am informed, in many instances, sent the individuals on to the magistrates, and my letters also have been forwarded to the magistrates, with the request that magistrates would go into the matter. However anxious the magistrates may be to help in this matter they are but human and in cases, I am informed, they are overweighed with other work and have been unable to give the attention to these matters that they required.

[1] Mr Dube was here referring to an open letter which he sent to the *Natal Press*, explaining the hard lot of the native victims of the Act, and appealing to the colonists to intercede with the South African Government on behalf of the sufferers.

Moreover the magistrate acts purely as an official, and the native who is wandering about the country helpless does not get the immediate sympathy and attention which his case deserves and demands. In many cases the individuals I sent on are under the impression, rightly or wrongly, that nothing is being done for their relief.

If I might make a suggestion, it would be that some independent gentleman should be appointed to investigate these cases—some gentleman who would have sufficient time to devote to the investigation of the various instances of hardship that would come before him, and who would be empowered to do what was necessary to relieve the deserving.

I may say further that since the introduction of the Squatters' Bill during the 1912 session of Parliament eviction by farmers has been much increased, possibly in view of the impression that prevailed generally among the farming community that the Squatters' Bill or some similar measure was to be re-introduced by the Government, the result being that those natives who had been evicted by farmers now the Natives' Land Bill has become law, are prevented from entering into agreements with landowners as rent-paying tenants, and only under servile conditions, with the result that in many cases they become wandering and helpless vagrants.

Another form of hardship which prevails very generally as the result of the Natives' Land Act is this: the younger natives do not receive the wage from farmers as can be easily earned, say, on the Rand mines, with the result that the younger men leave their homes and their fathers and proceed to the mines; the father is unable to supply the labour demanded by the landlord owing to the absence of his sons, and as a result he is evicted—many cases of this sort can be cited.

I may here cite two cases within my personal knowledge: (1) Bhulose was living on Mr R. Miller's farm, 'Dalmeny', near Phoenix. He was evicted with his wife and family in June last. He is seeking a place now to reside on, but cannot obtain one. (2) A native woman Vatplank, a widow with her family, was evicted from the property of a farmer, Mr Adendorff, near Newcastle; this woman with all her household goods and her family had to camp out on the veld. She was barred by the Act from going to neighbouring farmers for a residence.

I have done my utmost to give you concrete examples and names of persons suffering hardship. If I can supplement the information contained in this letter and in the accompanying list I shall only be too happy to do so.

Might I suggest further that you should ask the Chief Native Commissioner to forward to you all my correspondence with him on this matter? This will show you and the Government that the statements contained in my open letter are not mere fabrications, but are based upon solid facts.

John L. Dube

Mr Dube's list includes evictions from the districts of Greytown, New Hanover, Ekukanyeni, Homeless (a very appropriate name in the circumstances), Howick, Estcourt, and Mid-Illovu.

Here is a specimen of notice:

I hereby give you Mandwasi notice to leave my farm Blinkwater by the end of July, 1913.

(Sgd.)
July 20, 1913. Freestone Ridge.

'The wheels of administration moved slowly' (to borrow an official phrase) between the Native Affairs Department and the other departments of State. Thus, while the authorities were temporising with this and similar representations, the Natives' Land Act was scattering the natives about the country, creating alarm and panic in different places. The high officials of State, instead of relieving the distress thus caused, were interviewing natives and urging them not to send a deputation to Europe. The natives received this advice hopefully. They believed it was an indication that the

Government was about to amend the law, in which case, of course, the deputation would be unnecessary; but, besides this advice, the officials in each instance promised no relief.

The Natal Native Commissioner held a similar meeting with a number of Zulus. The meeting asked for some relief for the evicted tenants who were roaming about the country, but the official significantly evaded the point. The disappointment of the meeting, created by his evasive replies, having overcome the proverbial native timidity when in the presence of authority, resulted in one petty chief saying to the Commissioner: 'Local authorities levy a tax every year on each of our dogs. We don't know what they do with the money. You have never complained against that waste, so why should you complain if our money is spent in sending a deputation to the King?' The answer, if there was one, is not reported.

General Botha, until then, never met native taxpayers to discuss their grievances with them. But in the latter part of 1913 he actually met some natives in the Eastern Transvaal, who desired to inform him of the ravages of the Act. But instead of holding out any hope that an asylum would be found for the wanderers, he proceeded to advise them against sending a deputation to England. The natives having given specific instances of the plight of certain evicted tenants in the neighbourhood, asked for an abode for them. The Government's indifference to native sufferings being thus revealed, the natives of Vryheid became more eager to help to organise the proposed deputation.

General Botha's effort against the deputation, without offering any homes to the evicted natives, was probably the best stimulus towards the deputation fund. The Premier visited a northern tribe some time after and was said to have warned the chief and his people against the pretensions of the Native Congress. When Mr Dube called there a few days later, they handed him £200 towards the deputation fund, which they had collected since General Botha's visit. Mr Saul Msane similarly raised £360 for the fund in the Eastern Transvaal where the Premier first warned the natives against the deputation without offering them any relief.

Those natives who were not immediately affected by the

Act were rather lukewarm regarding the proposed deputation. But when the officials warned them against wasting their money on a deputation and told them in the next breath that it was a breach of the law to find an abode for the evicted wanderers, these natives, perceiving the hollowness of the Government's advice, determined that as a last resort a deputation should be sent to England.

14   The Kimberley Congress

When everything was ready another special Congress was called to meet at Johannesburg in February, to carry out the deputation's scheme and appoint the delegates to proceed to England. In view of the dissatisfaction of the Government after the July Congress, the author considered it his duty to inform the Government that a meeting was about to take place. This information called forth a peremptory intimation from the Government that because of the recent strike of white men (from which the natives had publicly dissociated themselves) the native Congress could not be held. But at the time that this telegraphic prohibition reached us, General Smuts, Minister of Defence, was announcing in Parliament that the embargo on public meetings, in areas where, owing to the recent strike (of January 1914), martial law was proclaimed, had been removed. Logically, then, General Botha's decision made the previous day in regard to the Congress meeting fell to the ground; and so we telegraphed to Senator Schreiner and Dr Watkins, members of Parliament, to ascertain if this was so. Both these gentlemen answered that in spite of the removal of the prohibition of public meetings of whites, the Prime Minister directs that the one in regard to the 'Native Congress' must stand. Thereupon the writer, after consulting a few native residents in Kimberley, intimated to the executive of the Congress that:

> Kimberley, my home, is not yet a Republic in its sentiments. There we have not reached the stage where someone's permission must be asked before a meeting can be held. So we invite the Congress to hospitable and British Kimberley, where public meetings close

with singing the British National Anthem and not with singing the 'Volkslied' or the 'Red Flag' as is the case' in meetings at some other South African centres.

After the notices were out the Government sent an intimation to the effect that the Congress was not actually prohibited. That it was only deemed undesirable to allow it to be held at Johannesburg, where a strike had taken place; and that even there the Government no longer objected, provided it be held indoors. But this belated reconsideration was unnecessary as the Kimberley preparations were far advanced and some of the delegates were already on their way to Kimberley.

The Congress was opened in St. John's Hall at 10 a.m. on Friday morning, February 27, 1914, by the Rt. Rev. W. Gore-Browne, Bishop of Kimberley and Kuruman. His lordship was accompanied by Archdeacon de Rougemont and Rev. I.I. Hlangwana of St. Paul's Mission, who gave out the native hymns. In the absence of the president, who reached Kimberley in the afternoon of that day, the Bishop was received by Mr Makgatho, vice-president of the Congress. After the religious exercise had ended, the Bishop counselled the Congress not to ask for a repeal of the whole Act, but only for relief from the oppressive clauses, and then to wait for the Commission's report in regard to the remainder of the Act. 'There may be something good in it,' added the Bishop, 'as the glittering diamonds of Kimberley are found in blue clay.'

Mr Makgatho, in thanking the Bishop for opening the Congress, thanked him for the allegory, but added, however, that he had never heard of a father who said to his child, 'You are hungry my son, and I am going to prepare some dinner for you, but meanwhile you had better wait outside in the rain.' After the Bishop gave the Congress his benediction, Prince Malunge-Ka-Mban-deni of Swaziland was introduced to him, as were the Chiefs Molotlegi and Mamogale of Transvaal, Moiloa of the Bahurutshe, and Messrs Elka M. Cele of Natal, Meshack Pelem from the Cape, J. M. Nyokong, S. Litheko of the O.F.S., and other native leaders.

In the evening a large public reception was held in the City Hall in honour of the delegates. Kimberley joined wholeheartedly in the function. De Beers Company, which had hitherto shown the greatest hospitality only to European assemblies and not to native conferences and organisations, acted otherwise in the case of this Congress and its requirements. Presumably Mr Pickering, the secretary of de Beers, had had information that even the mining labourers in the enclosed mining compounds were heart and soul with their countrymen outside; and so the Company's hospitality was extended to the native delegates.

Bioscope films were projected by Mr I. Joshua, the chairman of the A.P.O., Messrs Lakey and September, other A.P.O. committee men, acting as masters of ceremonies. The coloured people attended in their hundreds, and cheered the musicians of their native brethren who entertained the people who thronged the City Hall till many were refused admission. The Coloured People's Organisation sent a speaker, Mr H. van Rooyen, to welcome the delegates on behalf of the African Political Organisation. The president of their Ladies' Guild, Mrs van der Riet, a schoolteacher and musician of long standing, attended and played the accompaniment for the Greenport Choir on the pianoforte; Miss M. Ntsiko, who had borne the brunt of the evening's accompaniment, was thus relieved.

Mr Joseph Kokozela, on behalf of the Kimberley and Beaconsfield branches of the Congress, welcomed the Congress to Kimberley, and presented Mr Dube, the president, with an address, which was beautifully illuminated by the Sisters of St. Joseph Convent, of Mafeking. Mr H. van Rooyen associated his people with the natives in their present struggle for existence, and Dr J. E. Mackenzie, who spoke on behalf of the Europeans, made a fine speech. He said that nobility was not confined to any particular race or colour; that men with black skins have been known to be just as noble as men with white skins. Amongst other questions he asked, 'What could be more noble than the Bedford boy leader who subsequently became the St. Augustine of Central Africa, or what could be more noble than the action of the two servants of Dr Livingstone, who carried his body, for hundreds of miles, through difficult forests, to the coast, and thus ensured his burial in Westminster Abbey?'

Dr Mackenzie's speech was afterwards referred to by several native delegates to the Congress. They said that before they came to Kimberley they felt certain that English ideas were utterly obliterated in the Union of South Africa, and that English sentiments were things of the past; but that Dr Mackenzie's speech had given them fresh hope, as it was like cold water to a traveller in the desert. It was, they said further, like a dream to hear a white man talk like that in a mixed audience.

The Congress received sympathetic telegrams from such old residents of Kimberley as Sir David Harris and Dr Watkins. Both these gentlemen telegraphed their felicitations from Parliament.

Mr H. A. Oliver, member for Kimberley, a great Wesleyan and Sunday School leader, who was at Cape Town for the Parliamentary session, instructed his manager at Kimberley to book seats on his account for the senior classes of the Newton Wesleyan Sunday School to attend the Congress entertainment.

The Resident Magistrate of Kimberley telephoned to us on this same day that he had received the following telegram from the Secretary for Native Affairs: *'Leaving tonight for Kimberley to attend the Native Congress. Inform Plaatje.'*

It had never previously happened that a representative of the Government attended a coloured political assembly, and it was felt that wiser councils had prevailed with the Government, and that as a result it had decided to meet the natives, at least half-way. If gambling was one of the indulgences of the natives, some at least of the delegates would have wagered that Mr Dower was conveying a concession to the Native Congress, by which it would be unnecessary for the latter to send a deputation to England. So thoroughly was the idea of a concession associated in the mind of the Congress with the approaching visit of Mr Dower that it postponed the election of delegates for the mission to England. This anticipation was a reasonable one as the Union's recent legislation was in the melting-pot.

The law against British Indians, passed at the same time as the Natives' Land Act, was just then recommended for modification, under pressure brought to bear upon the Imperial Government by the Government of India and other agencies. Again, the Labour members were creating difficulties both at Cape Town and Westminster over General Smuts's Deportation Bill, which compelled the Government to amend its conditional banishment clause—a hardship that was not as vital or as absolute as the banishment clauses against black tenants in the Natives' Land Act. Consequently, the native delegates to Congress, representing as they did an overwhelming majority of the inhabitants of South Africa—a section that had received nothing but violent legislation from the South African Parliament since the inauguration of Union—had every reason to expect that, for the first time, a Government emissary was carrying an olive branch to the natives; but, alas! unlike the industrial strikers, the natives had no votes to create a constitutional difficulty; unlike the British Indians, they have no Indian Government at their back; therefore, their vital interests, being negligible, could comfortably be relegated to the regions of oblivion, and this hope, like all its predecessors, was falsified.

Mr Dower attended the Congress on Saturday, February 28, and again on Monday, March 2, and made speeches.

He was profuse in expressions of the gratitude of the Government to the natives, their leaders and their chiefs, for the loyal co-operation they have always rendered the authorities, and he came to ask them, he said, to perpetuate that loyal co-operation and to refrain from appealing to Great Britain on the Natives' Land Act. To appeal would be to put back the clock of the Native Affairs Department for many years. Of course, it did not matter about the putting back of the natives' own clock, since its only use is that of an index for the registration of Government taxes, municipal pass fees at one shilling or more per month per native, and similar phases of the black man's burden. Thus, in answer to questions put by the members of the Congress, Mr Dower was not able to say that one iota of the provisions of that Draconian law would be modified before the Commission made its report, nor could he give a pledge in the name of the Government that if the Commission reported favourably to the natives, Parliament would carry into effect the Commission's report, even though the pledge sought took no account of the possibility of the Commission's report being hostile to the interests of the natives. This then was the character of the visit which the Government Secretary paid to the Native Congress. It was entirely barren of results, and as such it left the Congress as it found it, in bewilderment and gloom.

Fresh fears took hold of the Congress. When the commissioners' names were gazetted, they were not received with any great amount of enthusiasm by the native population, for the best that could be thought of the Natives' Land Commissioners was that they were not associated with any political party. With such a view, it can be understood what were the feelings of the Congress when it thereafter learnt that four of the five commissioners were present, as delegates, at the conference of the ministerial party held at Cape Town two months before (the conference at which Generals Hertzog and De Wet definitely severed their connection with General Botha), nor was there anything to show that the fifth commissioner was not there also. Therefore, the situation amounted to this, that this Land Commission, which should be composed of impartial members, or, if made up of party politicans, it should at any rate represent the three political parties as well as the natives, was in reality but a branch of the ministerial party which foisted this very Land Act upon the country.

It was finally resolved to appoint a deputation of five to accompany the president, Mr Dube, to England if further efforts failed. The Congress nominated nine names; and the election of five delegates from these was entrusted to a committee of fourteen members of the Congress, who balloted for five and reported the result to the full Congress as follows:

S. T. Plaatje	13	Dr W. B. Rubusana	2
S. M. Makgatho	9	A. K. Soga	2
Saul Msane	6	M. Pellem	2
W. Z. Fenyang	3	Chief Mamogale	1
T. M. Mapikela	3		

The first-named five were therefore declared elected. Mr Fenyang subsequently stood down in favour of Dr Rubusana; Mr Makgatho was not able to reach Cape Town in time for the steamer's departure, so the deputation that eventually accompanied the president to England were:

1. Dr Rubusana.
2. S. T. Plaatje.
3. Saul Msane.
4. T. M. Mapikela.

Their instructions were first to approach the Prime Minister and ask him to undertake on behalf of his parliamentary majority to repeal the Natives' Land Act, failing that, to endeavour at least to get the clause rescinded which prevents evicted native tenants from finding settlements anywhere except as servants, and that if the Prime Minister should refuse to grant this request, they were forthwith to appeal to the Imperial Parliament and the British public.

It may be added that the Congress, before it rose, received telegraphic advices from Mr Gibson of the Cape Church Council, and also from the Hon. W. P. Schreiner, not to appeal to England. These communications encouraged the delegates to believe that intermediate relief was being arranged for, to ameliorate the condition of the wandering evicted natives, in which case there would, of course, be no occasion to appeal to England. But it subsequently transpired that the natives were advised against making an appeal to England without the offer of any relief.

Before Congress rose votes of thanks were passed in favour of the Bishop of Kimberley and Kuruman, the de Beers Company, the *Diamond Fields Advertiser* for its liberal reports of the proceedings, Mr Dower for entertaining the delegates to a dinner on Monday, and also to the residents of Kimberley.

The special thanks of the Congress were voiced by Mr Makgatho to the various committees, whose strenuous efforts for the comfort of the delegates left nothing to be desired.

An honorarium of £10 was voted in favour of the honorary secretary, Mr S. T. Plaatje.

After the deputation reached Cape Town on May 13, 1914, we wrote to Lord Gladstone informing him that we were bearers of a petition from the native population to His Majesty the King, which we would ask His Excellency to graciously convey. Of course we expected a short note from His Excellency to the effect that 'it was not within his constitutional functions' to meet us, but to our surprise this time His Excellency wrote appointing a meeting with us at noon on May 15 at Government House. But, in the interview, the reason why that particular appointment came within the pale of His Excellency's constitutional functions became apparent: for the Governor-General only made it the opportunity to urge the deputation not to go to England.

The deputation replied that, even in native politics there was always an appeal from the action of an induna to the native chief and from the latter to the ruler; that it was straining the loyalty of the black millions of South Africa to tell them that there was no appeal to His Majesty the King against the oppressive laws of a Parliament in which they had no representatives.

It must be added that although the Governor-General did not say so, yet the barbarous cruelties of this relentless law appeared to have produced a sympathy that was visible in his facial expression. Astonishment and pity were amongst the sensations which seemed to be depicted on Lord Gladstone's face.Still, he held out no hope that his good offices would be used to secure an amelioration of the conditions complained of. All His Excellency advised us to do was to abandon the appeal to England.

'But, your excellency, what about these cruelties that are now in progress?' we asked.

'Oh, well,' said Lord Gladstone, 'the natives are not the only sufferers, even in England people have suffered hardships from time to time, till they were compelled to emigrate to America and other places.'

'That is true, your lordship, but it is to avert such a contingency, if possible, that the natives appointed a deputation to lay their case before His Majesty the King, as they have no means to emigrate to America, or any other country.'

'Oh, no,' he answered, 'don't misunderstand me; I only use that as an instance, not that natives must emigrate.'

The Governor-General then repeated the advice not to appeal to the Crown, but he held out no hope of an amendment in the Act, and so the deputation sailed for England.

Previous to this interview, no less a personage than General Botha himself—Premier and Minister of Native Affairs—condescended to meet the deputation. Prior to this meeting, the deputation entertained strong hopes that the Premier would come to it with an offer of, say, at least allowing the hiring of land by natives, pending the report of the Commission, even though the prohibition to buy land remained in force. But instead of such a minimum, the only hope that General Botha held out was that he had not evicted the natives on his own farm, and that he had further told some farmers not to evict their natives. These personal acts of the Premier on his own farm, and with regard to some other farmers, had not helped the entire native population of the Union since the Act was promulgated. Nor would they assist those native wanderers who are now without a home on earth, as General Botha himself could not allow any of them to settle on his farm without breaking the law. Again, it did not seem quite clear how General Botha's efforts in this direction could make any impression on private landowners when his own officials were carrying out wholesale evictions of native tenants, on the Government farms at Standerton and elsewhere, and sending them adrift about the country. The only remedy, and that a partial one, would be to legalise the settlement of tenants who have been evicted. But to this General Botha said, 'If I went to Parliament now with a Bill to amend this law they will think I'm mad.'

That statement confirmed the decision of the deputation to proceed to England, and accordingly they at once made arrangements for sailing.

One painful fact which these interviews revealed was the ignorance of the Government in matters relating to the natives. The 5,000,000 blacks of the Union are taxed to maintain what is called the most expensive civil service in the world. The officials of the Native Affairs Department, in return for their huge salaries, paid out of the proceeds of taxes levied from relatively the most poorly paid manual labourers in the world, namely, the native taxpayers, are called 'the guardians of the natives'; but General Botha, the Minister of Native Affairs, 'Father of the natives' and supreme head of the Civil Service, seemed (or pretended) to know absolutely nothing of the manner in which his official underlings play battledore and shuttlecock with the interests of the native population. To mention but one instance: at one stage of the interview we attempted to enlist his sympathy on behalf of the 'Free' State natives in particular, who, in spite of prohibitive laws in the Boer statute books, had not to our knowledge been debarred by the Boer Government from buying or leasing land. General Botha not only denied that his was the first Boer administration which definitely enforced these prohibitions but he also asserted, with all the dignity of his office, that no living native had ever bought a farm in the 'Free' State from a white man—in short he accused us of telling lies. Fortunately Mr E. Dower, who remembered that some native landowners in both the Hoopstad and Thaba Ncho districts of the 'Free' State had acquired their properties from white people under the Republican regime, was present at the interview and he then bore out our statement: thus on May 15, 1914, the Prime Minister and Minister of Native Affairs heard for the first time in his life that there were some natives actually living in the 'Free' State who pay him quit-rent on farms which they had bought from white people under Republican rule.

The assertion that 'Free' State natives lost nothing by the enforcement of the Natives' Land Act is but one phase of the maze of ignorance through which the Union Government is groping in a hopeless attempt to discharge their trust to the native taxpayers.

The co-operation of intelligent and responsible native taxpayers, which could sweep away these administrative cobwebs of ignorance, is always at the disposal of the Government if they deigned to avail themselves of it; but they prefer, at enormous cost to the taxpayers (including native taxpayers), to purchase from the non-native section of the community armchair views based largely on hearsay evidence, which is often tainted by colour prejudice. Hence the shroud of ignorance which surrounds the native policy of the Union of South Africa.

150

15   The appeal for imperial protection

On arrival in London the native delegates were received by several friends, including Dr Chas. Garnett, M.A., of the Brotherhood League; Rev. Amos Burnet, of Transvaal, introduced them to the Wesleyan Missionary Committee in session at Bishopsgate; the Anti-Slavery and Aborigines Protection Society communicated with the Colonial Office regarding an interview. The Colonial Secretary agreed to see the deputation on condition that they were accompanied by no one from the Society.

When the native deputation reached England there were a number of South African missionaries on furlough in England who had taken part in church meetings in Africa, of protest against the Act. Some of these gentlemen had witnessed the cruel operations of the Act; but the decision to receive the native delegates by themselves meant that no such eye-witnesses as these could testify to what they had seen of the working of the Act.

In accordance with the time fixed for the interview, the deputation duly waited upon the Secretary of State, whose reply was more fully given in Parliament. At the interview he took notes on nothing, and asked no questions. On every point he had 'the assurance of General Botha' to the contrary.

No headway having been made with the Government, it was resolved upon that the delegates should appeal to the British Parliament and thence to the British public in terms of the native mandate.

Later on Messrs T. Buxton and J. H. Harris, the secretaries of the A.S. and A.P.S., arranged a meeting for the delegates to meet certain members of Parliament. The meeting took place in No. 11 committee room of the House of Commons. The British peerage was represented by Lords

Emmott and H. Cavendish Bentinck. After hearing the delegates and asking them questions, the members of Parliament intimated that their decision would be arrived at later in the absence of visitors. It must be mentioned here that besides the above secretaries of the A.S. and A.P.S. there were also present at this meeting a few sympathisers who were not members of Parliament. They included Miss S. Colenso of Amersham, and the Rev. Dr Howie of Stirling, and Mrs Howie, etc.

By the kindness of Mr and Mrs Buxton, Mr and Mrs Cobden Unwin (in conjunction with Mrs Saul Solomon), Lady Scott of Westminster, Mrs S. J. Colenso of Amersham, and Mr. H. E. Wood, J.P., of Camberwell (the latter being a prelude to a successful meeting of the delegates with the Baptist Council of England), Sir Albert Spicer, M.P., and Lady Spicer, and Mr and Mrs Harris of Dulwich, receptions—some of them attended by English and colonial guests—held at the residences of the friends named, were given in honour of the delegates.

IN THE HOUSE OF COMMONS

Mr P. Alden: I wish to bring to the notice of the right hon. Gentleman the question of the native lands in South Africa. I happen to have been responsible for a resolution passed unanimously in this House previous to the passing of the Act of Union, and in the discussion which took place on that occasion the Under-Secretary of State to the Colonies laid it down as one of the duties of the Imperial Parliament to protect in every possible way the interests of the natives in their land, and protect their rights and liberties in that respect. If we take away the land from the native we take away his liberty. In reference to the Natives' Land Act of 1913, I want to put two or three points before the right hon. Gentleman. In the Union of South Africa, blacks own about 4,500,000 morgen of land, and the whites own fourteen times as much land as the blacks, though, of course, they are very much smaller in number. The inequality is very noticeable in the Transvaal, where there are

300,000 whites holding 31,000,000 morgen of land, and the 1,000,000 natives only have 500,000 morgen of land which they can call their own.

It has been said over and over again in South Africa that this law applies equally to Europeans and whites as well as to the natives. There is, they say, no injustice. The European is estopped from this purchase of land, just as the native is estopped. All I can say in answer to that is that the fallacy is shown the moment you begin to ask what land the natives have to sell. The native areas are already overcrowded, and they positively have no land which they could sell. When once a native leaves his farm or is evicted, or has to quit for any reason whatever, the Act does not allow him to purchase, hire or to lease anywhere else for farming purposes except from natives, who have not the land to lease or to sell. He therefore must become a servant on the farm. There is absolutely nothing else for him to do but to become a servant. This Act has already produced very great hardships. It has produced hardships to the people who were under notice to quit at the time the Act was passed, to the people who have actually since then been evicted from their farms, to the natives who were in search of land and who are wandering about with their families and stock and have nowhere to settle, and to the natives who have had to leave their crops unreaped. There are many hundreds of such cases of hardship which have been inflicted under the Act which is being enforced on all sides. I do not wish to go into this question at very great length, because the right hon. Gentleman knows more about it than anybody in the House in all probability, and he knows the difficulties of the situation.

I want to put before him just one point with regard to what can be done. *We call ourselves the protectors of the rights of the natives,* and we claim that we have always, in season and out of season, insisted that those rights should not be infringed, and that no action should be taken against their liberties. The Imperial Government cannot, of course, intervene in the sense of asking the

Government of South Africa either to rescind an Act of Parliament or to amend an Act of Parliament, unless it is their own wish, but I must point out that Clauses 1, 4 and 5 do operate most harshly against the native, and it might be possible, on the representation of the right hon. Gentleman, for the Prime Minister of South Africa to mitigate the hardships.

Other sympathisers, including the Member for Woolwich, rose in different parts of the House to support the foregoing appeal, but the Colonial Secretary stopped them by delivering his reply.

The Rt. Hon. L. Harcourt: The hon. member for Tottenham (Mr Alden) and the hon. Baronet the Member for Hackney (Sir A. Spicer) have drawn attention to the South African Land Act. It is not a sudden inspiration of the Botha Government. It is the outcome and result of a Commission appointed by Lord Milner some years ago, presided over by Sir Godfrey Lagden. The Commission was appointed 'In view of the possible federation of the South African colonies to gather accurate information as to native affairs so as to arrive at a common understanding on questions of native policy.'

That commission sat for two years. It had upon it representatives of every colony and territory. It arrived at what I believe was a unanimous (sic) report,[1] and this Act is practically doing no more than carrying out its recommendations. The Act has already been in operation for twelve months. The Commission of Inquiry, which was to be instituted under the Act, is now sitting. It is bound by the terms of its appointment to report within two years, and will probably report by Christmas next.[2] The whole of this Act is a temporary measure until that Commission reports. A native deputation has

[1] Col. Stanford (the Cape Colony representative on the Lagden Commission) and Messrs Campbell and Samuelson (the Natal representatives) sent in two strongly-worded minority reports against such restrictions. *Vide* S.A. Native Affairs Commission, 1903-5, vol. I.

[2] After Christmas the Commissioners' 'terms of appointment' were altered from two years to three years.

come over and seen me, and I believe many other members. That deputation left Africa against the advice of General Botha, and against almost the entreaties of Lord Gladstone. They knew that the Act would not be disallowed, because it had been announced months before in South Africa. The day the deputation saw me the period of twelve months during which that Act could be disallowed on my recommendation had already expired, and it is now an act which can only be suspended by the Government and Parliament of the Union of South Africa.

Sir W. Byles: Does it forbid the holding of land by natives?

Mr Harcourt: Perhaps the hon. member will allow me to complete my statement as the time is short.[3] The suspension of the Act would be worse than useless at the present stage. It would suspend the Inquiry which is taking place at this moment in the interests of the natives themselves. I cannot believe that any further Commission is necessary, as the existing one seems to me both efficient and sufficient.

It is not clear why Mr Harcourt made this statement as the natives, in their petition to the King, never asked for a suspension of the whole Act. All that they wished was that the harshest clauses of the measure might be suspended, leaving the others in operation until the Commission rendered its report.

When Mr Harcourt's reference to the Commission was made known in South Africa the Commissioners, then sitting in Pretoria, were informed of the plight of evicted natives. The Commissioners replied that any grievance arising out of the operation of an Act of Parliament was beyond the scope of their inquiry, and that they could not consider such grievances. This was exactly what they had previously told the natives at King Williamstown and elsewhere. At Harrismith the Commission heard the complaint of a son of Chief Wietzie, who, during the Basuto wars, had always remained loyal to the 'Free' State Boers. The son

[3] Mr Harcourt would have shortened the time considerably, had he said 'Yes' or 'No', instead of replying in sixteen words.

had been evicted from the ground on which he and his fellow-tribesmen had resided for generations and he was forced live on an urban location where it is impossible to do any farming. The President (Sir William Beaumont) said he was sorry to hear that a son of Wietzie found himself homeless, but he regretted that the Comission could not help him. Mr Harcourt, therefore, must have been incorrectly informed regarding the functions of the Commission.

Yet another puzzle. After the appointment of this Commission in September 1913, there was a newspaper report to the effect that the Commission found the native difficulty most acute in the 'Free' State, and that it had decided on setting aside without delay a strip of territory in the western 'Free' State as a native settlement. Immediately after the appearance of this report in the press, angry meetings of the whites were held in Boshof and Hoopstad to protest against the proposals attributed to the Commission. In reply to these protests, Mr Theron, the Minister of Lands, evidently speaking on behalf of the South African Government, not only repudiated the report but he also added significantly that 'the Government had no intention of creating a native area in Hoopstad or anywhere else'. So, where do we stand? Can it be wondered that the natives are beginning to conclude that their position under the Union is hopeless?

But, to return to Mr Harcourt, the Colonial Secretary also gave the Imperial Parliament a fresh explanation of the Natives' Land Act. It is a pity that we cannot reproduce his explanation side by side with the four explanatory circulars issued by the Union Government in 1913. Such a reproduction would show the discrepancy between the five explanations. We wrote to South Africa but could only secure one of these circulars, which purports to be an explanation of a previous explanatory circular—an explanation of an explanation. However, the definition of the Act, as given by the other three circulars, leaves, as far as we can remember, the root principle of the Act unexplained. Moreover, the statements set forth in these circulars are not in harmony; they have only one point of agreement, namely, that when natives are driven out of their homes by the law, and are debarred by the same law from establishing other homes (the only provision made for them being that they should live as servants of the whites) the circumstances give them no ground for complaint.

Take for instance only two sentences in Mr Harcourt's explanation. In the first of these, he appears to approve of the system of forced labour established by the Act; in the second, he denies the evictions that took place in July when he spoke, and those that took place subsequently. He seems to flatly deny not only what is admitted by Lord Gladstone and General Botha, but he likewise contradicts the terms of the Act itself. Indeed, if we had not been there and heard him we should have felt, on reading this part of his speech, that he had been misreported in Hansard. Thus:

> If the natives are farm labourers there is no limit to the number who may reside on white property. If not, they are not dispossessed until Parliament acts upon the report of the Commissioners, and then only when suitable land is provided by addition to a native reserve.[4]

The Imperial explanation being as obscure as the colonial explanations which preceded it, the reader's remedy is to fall back on the plain English of the Act (Chapter 3), which alone has the force of law. Again Mr Harcourt:

> If General Botha breaks his word I have no power to enforce it. I cannot bind his successors. If the Government of South Africa is not to be trusted in this matter they are to be trusted in nothing; and we know perfectly well that they can be trusted in these matters. *Note what has been done with respect to the Indian Immigration Act. This was passed not from local desire, but from Imperial considerations. The provisions of that Act have been accepted by the Colonists and by the representatives of the Indians, who consider it the Magná Charta of the Indians in South Africa.* I think that that should be a sufficient guarantee as to the way in which General Botha proposes to act. General Botha, too, used *these words* in Parliament: 'He

---

[4] At Downing Street, Mr Harcourt informed the Deputation that he had the 'assurance of General Botha', that the natives have too much land already.

had told the deputation that he had given standing instructions to the magistrates throughout the country that if they found anyone in their districts ejecting natives from the farms, they had to go and make inquiries and report to him. He had in all those cases which had been brought to his notice used the influence of his Department.'

All we can say in regard to 'these words' is that the magistrates apparently ignored the 'standing instructions' alluded to, for they allowed the officials of the Department of Lands to scatter the native tenants from Government farms at Standerton, Colworth and elsewhere and sent them adrift over the country, well knowing that they could find no other shelter.

On the 31 of January 1914, the Magistrate of Ladysmith, presumably acting under instructions from one of General Botha's departments, issued the following notice to 79 native families in his district:

'To Vellem Sibisi, Kraal Head residing on one of the following farms, viz. Remainder of Brakfontein, Remainder of Weltevrede, etc.,

'Take notice in terms of Section 4 of Law 41 of 1884 that you are required to remove with your Kraal and inmates from whichever of the said farms you may be residing on, six months from this date, the afore-mentioned farms having all been purchased by Government for closer settlement purposes.'

The magistrate who so ruthlessly ejected these and other native families acted under the orders of the Government, who settled white people on the farms at the expense of a Treasury maintained also by native taxpayers. And it seems difficult to conceive how a Government which proved so indifferent regarding the fate of its own native tenants or of tenants on farms freshly acquired at the public expense, could be solicitous about the welfare of natives evicted by private landowners. The statement, on the face of it, is incongruous.

In his heroic efforts to defend South Africa's giant wrong, Mr Harcourt gave away his case when he referred approvingly to what he calls 'the Magna Charta of the

Indians in South Africa'. Now, what is that 'Magna Charta'? In 1913, when the South African Parliament was at the noontide of its 'mad career', it passed this iniquitous land law to repress the native race; and also a law imposing the most humiliating limitations on British Indians. Yet it must be added that the Indian law was the milder of the two, as it did not prohibit Indian residents in South Africa from living on the land. The Rt. Hon. A. Fischer, Union Minister of the Interior, who died two years ago, called these two laws of 1913, 'the Kaffir law and the Coolie law'.

As already stated, the London Committee of the Wesleyan Methodist Church asked to see Mr Harcourt and inform him how drastically the 'Kaffir law' was operating against their converts and other natives in South Africa, but Mr Harcourt discreetly refused to see the Committee.

As for the Indians, no one in South Africa paid any heed to their complaints against the 'Coolie law'; but their cry reached India and Lord Hardinge demanded the redress of their grievances. His lordship insisted so forcibly that (unlike the Wesleyan missionaries) he could not be ignored. The result was that the South African Parliament, 'not from local desire, but from Imperial considerations', was obliged in the next session (1914) to amend the 'Coolie law' with a 'Magna Charta of the Indians in South Africa', and Mr Harcourt's reference to this episode conveys the suggestion that what is sauce for the Indian goose, with Lord Hardinge at its back, can be by no means sauce for the native gander without the backing of a viceroy.

We cannot believe that to boast in one and the same speech about a 'Magna Charta of the Indians' and dismiss the native appeal against a vital wrong is true Imperialism. For if Imperialism stands for the protection of a few thousand Indians in South Africa because they are supported by a viceroy, and the neglect of the groans of five million natives because (unlike a viceroy) the missionaries who plead for them cannot enforce their claim with a political or diplomatic blow, then there would appear to be the suggestion of more fear than justice in imperialism.

Mr Harcourt further credits the Milner Commission, presided over by Sir Godfrey Lagden, with the origin of the

Natives' Land Act. We do not wish to defend the policy of these two former South African statesmen, as we feel certain that they can take care of themselves. But we must say at once that we read the recommendations of the Lagden Commission ten years ago, as carefully as we have since read the controversy of the Natives' Land Act; and with the knowledge thus gained, we can safely tell the reader that that Commission never recommended that:

1. 'Except with the permission of the Governor-General', Europeans must be debarred from buying land from natives (who have no land to sell), and natives must be debarred from buying land or leasing land from Europeans, who alone deal in land. (Section 1 Natives' Land Act.)

2. When evicted natives apply for the said 'permission of the Governor-General' they should be told that that permission 'will only be granted to a few exceptional applicants' and that it could under no circumstances be granted to natives in the colony in which the applicants resided. (The Government's reply to the 'Free' State wanderers.)

3. The Government should always take from three to six months to deliver this refusal, during which period applicants may have already become serfs or fled the country. (This has been the experience of all applicants within the writer's knowledge.)

4. There should be a fine of £100 or six months' hard labour on any farmer who provides the native with a shelter while he is waiting for this disappointing reply to his application. (Section 5 Natives' Land Act.)

5. Native tenants to be hounded out of the Government farms long before the segregation takes place and that white people, who are not debarred from buying or leasing land for themselves, be settled thereon at Government expense. (See magisterial notice above.)

If Mr Harcourt has been told by anyone that the Lagden Commission recommended any of these pitiless iniquities, then we are afraid that his informer is a romancer of the superlative degree. The Lagden report was never discussed in any South African legislature, much less adopted by any Parliament in South Africa; indeed, it is detested because it recommended a native franchise for South Africa like the Maori franchise of New Zealand.

One member of Parliament (Mr Joynson-Hicks) said South Africa was a home rule country and he wondered what would happen if after home rule had been granted to Ireland someone asked the Imperial Parliament to interfere with Irish legislation.

We wonder who could have told this hon. Member that there was home rule in South Africa! There used to be home rule in the Cape Colony alone, but this has been swamped by the Act of Union, which has since established an oligarchic Government throughout the country. And if by home rule to Ireland it is intended to give the franchise to a selfish, greedy and tyrannical few; and give *carte blanche* to this few, telling them thereby to do what they wish with the rest of the population of Ireland, and telling them further that they will be accountable to nobody for any good legislation that they might enact on the one hand, or any maladministration that they might perform on the other hand as is the case in South Africa—if that be what is meant by home rule for Ireland, then God have mercy on the Irish.

When the reply of Mr Harcourt was published in South Africa, supporters of this cruel law bubbled over with joy concerning it. One Dutch writer, after saying in a Dutch journal some very fine things about Mr Harcourt, wound up a high-sounding eulogy by congratulating South Africa on having such a good Colonial Secretary at Downing Street. 'Had Mr Harcourt's predecessors been like him,' said this writer to his readers, 'South Africa would have been saved many tears.' We doubt if Mr Harcourt, the object of this appreciation, would feel flattered by it if he knew that all the black victims of this cruel law, and all their European sympathisers, stood firmly by the Imperial Government and by the Colonial Government in the present struggle, while the gentleman at whose instance it was introduced in Parliament, as well as the Dutch editor of the journal alluded to, are at present (May 1915) committed for trial on charges of high treason; and the proprietor of another Dutch journal, in which we read similar vaunting adulations of Mr Harcourt, was fined £60 (so his paper says) for alleged com-

161

plicity in the recent rebellion. These facts should impel the Rt. Hon. the Colonial Secretary to stop, look round and inquire 'who's who' among his South African admirers.

Two members of the South African Parliament— Senator T.L. Schreiner and Mr Wilcocks, M.L.A.—the former an opponent and the latter a supporter of the Natives' Land Act, recently discussed the Act from separate points of view; and both came to the conclusion that the measure was designed to keep the blacks in subjection. This conclusion is in harmony with the bitter experiences of the native races since this Act was enforced. Yet in the face of this unanimous testimony of different observers, Mr Harcourt equivocates behind the irrelevant 'assurances of General Botha' about a possible segregation, which question is not now before the country. Assurances on segregation only serve to confound the issue. If the Beaumont Commission, or its successor, should ever report then the question of segregation may come before Parliament some time in 1926. The point before the country now is not segregation, but the Natives' Land Act of 1913, which is now scattering the natives about the country. That is the measure against which the native appeals for Imperial protection. Not the future segregation.

The only serious objection with which Mr Harcourt apparently was able to charge the native deputation, and one which the natives do not deny, is that they came to England against the 'entreaties of Lord Gladstone' (who previously had twice refused to see them), and against the 'advice of General Botha', by whose cabinet the measure was enacted and enforced.

It is a pity that Mr Harcourt did not at the same time tell the House of an authentic case where an aggrieved party ever sued for redress with the consent and advice of his oppressor. In this connexion, the scope of our reading being limited, our ignorance is possibly abysmal; but it must be confessed that we have never heard of such an interesting appellant and we are inclined to believe that there never has been one.

If General Botha wished to tell the whole truth, instead of making vague assurances to Mr Harcourt, he would say: 'I foresaw all the difficulties under which the natives are suffering; and when Mr Grobler proposed the summary stoppage of the sale and lease of land to natives before the areas are segregated, I warned the House against this trouble, but the Hertzogites being too much for me I had to give in.' General Botha could go further and say to Mr Harcourt:

If you will turn up page 579 of the South African Hansard (first column) reading from the top of the page, you will find my warning in these words: Unless they went slowly and carefully, there was a danger that they might take steps which would be unreasonable, unjust, and unfair on one section. For that reason, he regretted the amendment proposed by General Hertzog, because the amendment would have bad results if it were accepted. It would lead to an over-hasty measure of a most impracticable kind. This House would have to demarcate exactly and immediately those parts where the natives would have to live, and he asked them: was this House able to do so? (Cries of 'No'.) It was all very nice to talk and take a map and draw lines on it. On the map they might be able to beacon off parts, and say, 'This is for the natives,' but then, when they put their scheme into effect, they might find that the ground of many individuals had been taken away without any inquiries or any investigations having been made. (Laughter, and 'Hear hear'.) This House would expropriate the rights of many white people, and they would meet with the greatest opposition. Where were they going to put these people then? In the Transvaal, farmers certainly would not consent to this; he did not know the people of the Free State so well, but he doubted whether they would agree. (A Free State Member: 'No, they certainly will not.') Instead of taking any steps like this, they should be practical, and not land themselves into greater difficulties than they could help. Governments before them had done their best. He agreed that the squatting of natives should be put an end to as soon as possible, but they should not lose sight of the fact that many Governments before them had done their best to put an end to this squatting evil. He knew well how the Transvaal Government had, year after year, taken up this matter. But what did they find? Simply that when they had passed a Squatters Law they could only put it into operation in one small part of the country. (Hear, hear.) To introduce another bill like that would simply mean deceiving the country—(hear, hear)—and the natives. If they accepted the proposal of the Minister of Native Affairs to appoint a Commission to investigate the various conditions prevailing throughout the country, he thought they would be taking a step in the right direction. (Hear, hear.) However, care was essential, because they must prevent causing a sort of revolution through the country. What they wanted was a measure which would be acceptable to the white man as well as to the native. (Hear, hear.)

These were General Botha's views when the Land Act was first mooted, but in defiance of his solemn warning, the Bill, when gazetted, provided that the eviction of native tenants should precede the Commission's inquiry; harsher and still harsher clauses were inserted in the Bill until the Act finally embodied all the proposals brought forward by General Hertzog. The promise to refer the Bill to a Select Committee was also broken, presumably as a result of pressure from the caucus. The Government could not face a Select Committee after this complete change of front as they must have known that reason was absolutely against them.

It might be asked: 'How could a Minister turn round afterwards and give "assurances" concerning the benefits of a measure which he had opposed before?' To such a question we would hazard the following explanation: Our Prime Minister, on the one hand, is a British Privy Councillor and a General in the British Army; and, on the other hand, he is a simple Afrikander Boer, who only speaks Dutch in Parliament and addresses English audiences through an interpreter. And so in the eyes of General Botha, the British Crown Minister, if the natives be treated justly, as British subjects should be treated, it is right; and, again, in the eyes of General Botha, the Afrikander Boer, if the natives be treated harshly and barbarously, that too is right.

It is not unusual to find these two natures contending

against each other in one and the same person, whenever the Prime Minister deals with native questions; then more often than not the Boer view, being that of his own nature, dominates the British sentiment, which is a fresh acquisition.

Having given above a striking extract from a speech on native policy, by the Rt. Hon. Louis Botha, Premier of British South Africa, we will now proceed to give an extract from another declaration by General Louis Botha, the Transvaal Boer. The Union Premier was giving evidence before the Labour Commission in Johannesburg and this is what he then said:

11,302. **Sir George Farrar:** You said that you would recommend the breaking up of locations like Swaziland, Zululand and Basutoland and the putting of white settlers there? **General Botha:** I would suggest that these countries be given up to the white people to live in . . .

11,337. The general tenor of your remarks is that there is sufficient labour, and it only wants a little patience to wait for it, that is all? I have distinctly stated that there is a greater amount of labour than has at present been obtained. But there are farmers who have farms, and have no natives living on these farms. For these people it is difficult to obtain natives because the natives who are not living on the farms are in locations. If the locations were broken up the natives would be made to live on farms.

11,338. You suggest that we should break up such land as Basutoland, Swaziland and Zululand? Yes, I say that such places are a source of evil. It is building up a Kaffir kingdom in the midst of us which is not only bad for the Kaffirs themselves but is a danger in the future.[5]

11,339. But take Zululand, for instance; there is a quarter of a million people there. What would you do with them if you break up their territory? They would all live on the farms as the white people are doing now.

[5]One of the chiefs in these locations gave General Botha 200 bullocks to feed his troops engaged in crushing a rebellion of white men.

11,340. Oh, you want to cut up the land into farms, give it to the white people and retain the Kaffirs on the farms? Yes.

11,343. But what will the white people do with the Kaffirs, pay them wages or charge them rent for the ground? My opinion is that Kaffirs who now live in locations should work for the white people, and the land should be exploited. The white people would pay them for the work they did and this would civilise them.[6]

In the foregoing extract the reader has the root principle of the Natives' Land Act in a nutshell. Not from hearsay 'assurances' but from what fell from the Premier's own lips.

Mr Jacob de Villiers Roos, head of the Union Law Department (who knows more about South African law than outsiders who have to rely on 'assurances') says in his evidence given before the Select Committee on Public Accounts, February 25, 1914, incidentally or accidentally:

A circular was issued by our Department, at the instigation of the Native Affairs Department, asking that prosecutors under the Natives' Land Act, before commencing prosecutions, should refer to the Native Affairs Department as otherwise *it was feared that an upheaval might result*. The Transvaal Attorney-General drew our attention to this circular and said that it was an infringement of his powers . . . When Mr Beyers went away on leave Mr Greenlees was appointed Acting Attorney-General, and he first drew the attention of the Minister to it. The Minister took no action until Mr Beyers returned when the matter was again raised and then this circular was withdrawn.[7]

Now, what, in the name of common sense, does a supposedly civilised government want with a law that it knows will cause 'an upheaval'?

This Act should be abolished in the interest of the morality of the State and for the sake of the reputation of the Union Jack, because of the harm it does to the natives and because its promoters have rebelled against the Crown. The Act has benefited no one; it has driven the natives from the country

[6] *Transvaal Labour Commission,* pp. 717-726.
[7] S.C. 1914, pp. 136-137.

to the cities, and has also disappointed the white Labour Party, who supported it in the belief that by its clause forcing natives to work for white farmers it would keep the natives away from the industrial centres.

It should be abolished in the interests of the Boers, for it has aroused the bitterest enmity of the blacks against the Dutch section of His Majesty's subjects.

Further, the Act should be abolished because it has lowered the prestige of the Union Jack in the eyes of the coloured subjects of the King, who have suffered and are still suffering untold misery under it. Perhaps nothing illustrates more clearly this changed feeling of the natives than the present state of things in South Africa. Thus, if German South-West Africa had been annexed to the Cape before the Union, every native, south of the Zambesi, would have approved of the step, whereas today, as a result of the Natives' Land Act, there is a different feeling extant. For now the natives know that annexation to the Union will mean the elimination of the Imperial factor, and that as Cape Town, like Pretoria, has ceased to represent British ideas of fair play and justice, such a change would in the annexed territory establish 'Free' State ideals under the aegis of the Union Jack. The natives of the Union shudder at the possibility of the Damaras, who are now under the harsh rule of the Germans, being placed under a self-governing Dominion in which the German rule will be accentuated by the truculent 'Free' State ideas of ruling natives. And they think that in the existing state of circumstances, Portuguese or French rule would be infinitely better for the Damaras than a government which, although protected by the Union Jack, yet is inspired from Pretoria and Bloemfontein. And it is to be feared that the pernicious principles which Tommy Atkins is now fighting on the continent to suppress, are going to be rigorously applied in a South-West Africa under Burgher rule. The prosperity of no state can afford to alienate the sympathy of any considerable portion of its taxpayers. And so, as 5,000,000 blacks have been alienated in their sympathies to the Union by this oppressive law, and as the Union Government is unable or unwilling to amend it, in the interest of the Union Government, no less than the 5,000,000 blacks, outside intervention becomes a necessity.

During three separate white men's upheavals in the last two years—two bloody strikes and a civil war—white revolters made frantic efforts to embroil the Union in a native rising, but the natives very sensibly sided with the Government. The native leaders, in order to counteract this mischief-making, had to incur the expense of journeys by rail besides financing their own mission to reach the scene of the would-be native disturbance.

The time will come when these leaders will tire of spending their own money in paying fares to the government railways, to render free services to a government which taxes them to pay other people lavishly for similar work, while it does not even tender them so much as a word of thanks.

Instead of the smallest recognition for our voluntary services, the Union Government repays our loyalty by persecuting our widows and fatherless children with the cold-blooded provisions of the Natives' Land Act. These cruelties are euphemistically described as the first step towards the segregation of white and black, but they might more truthfully be styled the first steps towards the extermination of the blacks.

When the war broke out, the Government promptly suspended the inquiries of the Commission, whose report is naively alleged to be pregnant with the fruits of the millennium, but the cruel evictions under the same law of the rebel Grobler are pursuing their course while the war lasts and the Union Government remains unconcerned. It was only when a whole tribe was evicted during the war that the Government interceded on behalf of the victims, but then, the only extent of the intervention has been to secure exemption for the chief of the tribe alone, on the condition that *he forced the rest of his tribe to render every year three months' labour to the landowner*. Yet these people could live happily on some other farm did not the Government prohibit their happiness at the behest of a rebel who, at or about the time of this enthralling compromise, was conducting treasonable operations against the Government.

The sublime ingratitude of the Union Government is well-nigh unbearable!

16   The London Press and the Natives' Land Act

The native deputation (thanks to Mr H. Cornish, secretary of the Institute of Journalists) can truthfully assure their people, at the present critical state of their position, of the sympathy of the London press. It is hardly necessary to mention that religious papers, to which the object of the deputation was made known, published some very encouraging articles on the same, and bespoke the deputation a cordial reception and a sympathetic hearing throughout the United Kingdom; but the mission might have been somewhat monotonous had we friends only and no enemies in the London Press. And a weekly paper with a yellow cover, called *South Africa*, did its best to fill the rôle of an enemy.

It abused the Brotherhood Movement and the Aborigines Protection Society for taking up the cause of the deputation. The General Press Cutting Association, however, through whom we learnt of the attacks of *South Africa*, did not tell us whether this journal also abused our other friends represented by the London Press. Such has been our good fortune in this respect that friends frequently congratulated us on the unanimity of the press in our favour. In this we think they were right, as a cause with only one enemy could very well be depended on to take care of itself.

On one occasion some of our friends heard that the author was going to interview the fine-fingered editor of the *Westminster Gazette* by appointment, and they strongly advised us against doing so. 'Why not?' we asked. 'Oh,' said our friends, 'he edits the leading Government organ, and he is going to pump you of all information in order to use it against your cause and in favour of the Government.' But we went—firstly, because we refused to believe that the editor of that great organ of British thought was capable of taking such a mean advantage of us; and secondly, because we were confident of being able to take care of ourselves against any kind of pump; and we can now say with satisfaction that, on the part of the British public, there was such a demand for back numbers of the two editions of the *Westminster Gazette* which contained a report of our interview and a photograph of the deputation that in a fortnight both issues were sold out of-print. Further, it is safe to say that from the wide area from which inquirers wrote to us mentioning the *Daily News*, it would seem that either the journal has a very big circulation or its readers are mainly interested in South African affairs. And what, may be asked, are the qualifications of the newspaper *South Africa* which attempted to run counter to this overwhelming opinion in our favour?

Unlike some of its contemporaries, *South Africa* has not a single native contributor to its columns. Some London newspapers are in regular receipt of exchange copies from native newspapers published in South Africa, London papers which never claimed a monopoly over South African thought; yet here is a paper, South African in title and in pretensions, which cannot even boast of a South African native paper on its exchange list! What information, then, can the editors of such an exclusive London paper possess about an Act specifically enacted to operate against natives? Logically, they would know absolutely less than next to nothing about such a law or its fell work. That alone should dispose of the qualifications of this enemy of the deputation, and his authority to speak on the subject of its mission.

The *African World* is an Anglo-African weekly which has native newspaper exchanges and several African correspondents both white and black. Its editor-in-chief was born in South Africa and was a journalist there before he came to reside in England; and it must be admitted that a paper with such connexions is in a better position to discuss the subject from both points of view. And so the *African World* says:

THE SOUTH AFRICAN NATIVE DEPUTATION
It must be admitted that the South African Native Deputation now in this country have gone about their business with decorum. They have not pressed them-

selves forward unduly, and, so far, the publicity given to them has been moderate in its tone, and the expressions by the members of the deputation have been equally moderate. Of course, their best friends discountenanced this visit, as we have noted from the South African press, but it seems to be the general opinion that even though no appeal lies under the Union Constitution to the British Crown as regards native rights, an extraordinary anomaly seems to exist in this: That the natives of South Africa within the Union appear to have fewer rights than those outside the Union, especially so far as an appeal to London on various matters affecting their interests is concerned. We are aware that Mr Harcourt treated the deputation with the utmost discretion when he received them. We also know that Mr Harcourt and General Botha are on very friendly personal relations, and under these circumstances, without wishing to dictate any action in the matter to the powers that be on both sides of the water, we would like to join our contemporary *The Globe*.

And what did *The Globe* say?

THE NATIVE APPEAL

The complaint of the South African natives who have laid their grievances before certain members of Parliament amounts in effect to a complaint that Parliament is not Imperial. Their grievances are real and pressing, as anybody can discover who troubles to look up the recent proceedings of the Union Parliament, but they have no constitutional means of ventilating them. No native franchise exists in South Africa, and although certain members of the Union Senate are presumed to keep an eye on native questions their influence has proved ineffective. No appeal exists under the Union Constitution to the Crown as regards native rights, for although this omission was pointed out at the time the Act of Union was debated in the Imperial Parliament and was adversely commented on, no steps were taken by the Colonial Office to rectify the constitution in this

171

respect. We are, therefore, brought up against the extraordinary anomaly that natives of South Africa within the Union have fewer rights than those outside—for the Basutos, who remain under direct Imperial control, have successfully appealed to London on various matters affecting their interests—or even than the natives of Crown Colonies elsewhere, as the appeal of native landowners on the Gold Coast against recent legislation in that territory attests. In the latter case the appeal to the Colonial Office was successful in modifying the offending enactments; in the far more serious grievances of the South African natives the Colonial Office has no constitutional title whatever. Nevertheless the relations between Mr Harcourt and General Botha in other respects are notoriously so close and confidential that we may hope the Colonial Secretary will take the present occasion by the hand and urge upon the head of the South African Government the wisdom of dealing with native discontents in his own proper sphere before he prosecutes his claim for the inclusion of the Basutos and Rhodesia in the Union—a claim which both black natives and white colonists have repudiated with all the emphasis at their command. General Botha could scarcely fail to give heed to private advice from the Colonial Office. In the case of the Natal Indians, whose grievances he recently redressed, he proved himself a man capable of taking a broad and generous view of a difficult question. There is no reason to anticipate until the contrary is proved, that he will fall below his own level in the present not less difficult or dangerous case.

VIEWS OF THE *DAILY NEWS*

The South African National Congress, after resorting to every constitutional means of pressing their case against the Land Act on the Union Government, have sent five of their numbers to London in the firm conviction that the King of England, to whom they look as their natural defender and vindicator, will turn no deaf ear to their pleas. Two of the five—the Rev. J.L. Dube and Mr Saul Msane—are Zulus; Dr Rubusana is a Xosa; Mr Mapikela, a Fingo; and Mr Plaatje, the secretary of the National Congress, a Bechuana. All of them are men of obvious culture and with a striking command of the English language.

Having failed to make any impression on the Union Government ('If we had votes,' Dr Rubusana observed, 'we could fight our own battles') the deputation has come to England in the hope of influencing the Imperial Government through the Colonial Secretary.

What they ask for is:

First, a suspension of the operation of the Act pending the report of the Delimitation Commission:

Second, an inquiry into native grievances under the Act; and

Thirdly, an assurance that the Home Government will express its concurrence with certain promises made recently on behalf of General Botha, but obviously depending for their value on the continuance of his personal political supremacy.

FOUR BLACK TO ONE WHITE

In carving out estates for themselves in Africa the white races have shown little regard for the claims of the black man. They have appropriated his land, and in appropriating his land have taken away his economic freedom, and have left him in a worse case than they found him. How the native has been dispossessed may be illustrated by the facts in regard to the Union of South Africa. Here the blacks, as compared with the whites, are in the proportion of four to one; but they are in legal occupation of only one-fifteenth of the soil.

Under the self-governing' Land Act, which has brought the matter to a crisis, even the poor fragment of rights in the soil that remains seems doomed. For under the Act the native is denied the right—except with the quite illusory 'approval of the Governor-General' — to purchase, hire, or acquire any rights in land from a person other than a native. Under this provision, the native whose tenancy expires, or who is evicted from a farm, is legally denied any career

173

except that of a labourer. He cannot own, he cannot hire, he cannot live a free man.

A LEGAL SERF

In the language of Mr Dower, the Secretary for Native Affairs, he must 'sell his stock and go into service'. He must accept any conditions the white farmer chooses or the mine-owner gives, and an ingenious clause encourages the white farmer to exact unpaid service from the native tenants. In a word, the native is a legal serf in his own land.

As British subjects, the deputation of natives now in England have appealed to the Imperial Government for protection. They asked for its help to secure the suspension of the Act until the Land Commission report is before Parliament, and for machinery to inquire into and redress their grievances. They have got no satisfaction on these points.

It is time that Parliament gave some attention to its obligations in regard to the South African native. He has no vote and no friends—only his labour, which the white man wants on the cheapest terms. And the white man has got this by taking his land and imposing on him taxes that he cannot pay. In fact, the black man is 'rounded up' on every side, and if, as the deputation suggests may be the case, he is forced to acts of violence, it will not be possible to say that he has not had abundant provocation.

RIGHTS TO THE SOIL

There is only one principal that can be applied for his protection. It is the principle that he has rights in his native soil. Perhaps segregation is the only remedy now, but if so the reservations allocated to him in the Union area ought to have some relation to his needs. We cannot do much for him there, but we should do what we can.

Mr Advocate F.A. Silva wrote to the Daily News:

AN APPEAL FOR JUSTICE

Sir,

Will you please allow me space, while appreciating your editorial of this date, to bring to the kind notice of your readers the distinction between 'British justice as supposed to be' and 'British justice as it is' with regard to the subject races, especially the black men?

If even the 'hair' of a 'white' British subject were to be touched in China or Japan or Turkey or Russia, the whole of the political parties of England, with their usual patriotism, will rise to the occasion, and with one accord demand the use of physical force against that country.

But here in South Africa, on the day the 'Act' came into law, all agreements with regard to land were terminated, and thousands of the natives have found themselves ruined and homeless. From tenants they have become serfs.

If the Imperial Parliament looks with complacency on these tyrannical proceedings of a local Parliament, then the British public should not be surprised if the intelligent and thoughtful among the subject races of 'Britain' consider 'British justice' and 'Russian tyranny' to be synonymous terms.

Let us draw attention to one more letter, by an Anglo-African to the *Daily News*, which was typical of the rest:

THE BLACK MAN'S BURDEN

Sir,

Those of your readers who, like myself, have some first-hand knowledge of the natives of South Africa, know that this grievance voiced by the native deputation is a very real one. That such a deputation should have come to England to urge such a plea is humiliating enough to them and to us. That their plea should be urged in vain would be disastrous to the last degree.

If the Natives' Land Act is the best thing the Union Government can do in the discharge of its responsibilities to the native tribes placed under its care by the King, then many of us would have to revise our faith in self-government as a fit instrument of national evolution; and would, moreover, strenuously resist the ultimate incorporation of the northern territories within the Union as being infinitely worse for the black man then even government under Chartered Company control.

One hopes that it is not yet too late for both Boer and Briton in South Africa to see that this debasement of the whole idea of self-government is to affront and discourage all in Great Britain who saw in the grant of its own political freedom to that great country a healing for its many woes. In the meantime liberalism must back the native deputation at all costs, and it is well that *The Daily News and Leader* should lead the way.

VIEWS OF *'THE STAR'*

We have always realised that one of the gravest problems of self-government in South Africa is the native question. On the one hand, South African colonial opinion—by which is meant 'white' opinion—will bitterly resent any shadow of dictation from Downing Street; on the other hand, the conscience of the British people cannot remain indifferent to any flagrant oppression of or injustice to the native races under the British flag. A very difficult question of this kind is raised by the deputation of South African natives, which is now in this country, seeking to move the Colonial Office on the subject of the Natives' Land Act recently passed by General Botha. The ultimate object of General Botha's plan is the greatest exodus since the days of Moses; it is apparently to get rid of black landholders in areas in which the majority of the landowners are white, and to buy up tracts of land elsewhere from white landowners, in order to settle natives upon them. In this way the black and white races, so far as landholding is concerned, will be segregated into separate areas, with a reduction of possible cause of friction, and in some respects this is an excellent policy. But the trouble is that General Botha has passed the first part of his policy and has left the second part to the future. The Land Act provides that hereafter, 'except with the approval of the Governor- General'—which proviso is mere leather and prunella—a native shall not buy or hire any land from a person other than a native. The effect of this is that at the termination of any existing tenancy a native will have to relinquish his farm, and will not be able to hire or buy another from any white owner. If the Government had provided farms in the proposed native reserves for these men, their policy would be complete, but nothing has been done, and the fulfilment of that promise depends upon General Botha's continuance in office, and does not bind his successors. It is not surprising the South African natives regard this Act as a means of driving them into the labour market either at the mines or for white farmers. Mr Dower, the Secretary for Native Affairs, addressing a meeting of natives at Thaba Nchu, in the Free State, gave a strong hint of this when he said: 'My best advice to you is to sell your stock and go into service.' Here at home we hear a great deal about the 'magic of property' and the importance of giving the worker an interest in the soil he tills; but in South Africa they apparently agree with the Southerner in the *Biglow Papers* that:

> Libbaty's a kind o' thing
> Thet don't agree with niggers.

It is clear that it is the duty of the Colonial Office to guarantee, in conjunction with the South African Government, the carrying out of the full policy as outlined by General Botha, and we hope occasion will be taken to urge action on these lines.

CAN BRITAIN PREVENT SLAVERY

A question of great importance and a question which may easily strain the links that bind the various parts of the empire and the mother country, has arisen in South Africa owing to the operation of the Natives' Land Act passed last year by the Union Parliament. The native question is by far the greatest problem South Africa has to solve, and its difficulties are so great that nobody has been able to advance any feasible scheme for its settlement, though there may have been many suggestions as to the broad lines on which the matter may be settled. The Land Act is an attempt to establish modified segregation—i.e. confining the white man and the black to separate areas of the country. It is by no means a well thought-out nor a very practicable enactment, and unfortunately has had the effect of greatly irritating the natives throughout the Union. The natives do not think they are being treated fairly, and have used every legitimate means to obtain a hearing. These means, however, are exceedingly meagre, practically non-existant, since they have no one to represent them, and as they have no vote they can bring no pressure on Parliament. Having failed in South Africa, they have sent a deputation to Great Britain, since, as they are British subjects they consider that Government cannot interfere in the internal policy of a self-governing colony, and so are left with no means of obtaining redress. It is surely impossible to admit that Great Britain can do nothing for the mass of the native population, although at the moment it appears to them that though they are subjects of the King he cannot even hear their appeal, and will do nothing for them, and has abandoned them, a state of affairs which is quite incomprehensible to them and leads them to depend solely on themselves to obtain redress—and that way rebellion lies. Britain is in an awkward position as she still has obligations to secure justice to the natives. If South Africa were to enact slavery, would Britain still be able to do nothing to prevent it?

OUSTING THE NATIVE

Surely Mr Harcourt can suggest to the South African Government the necessity of appointing a Commission to inquire into the working of the Act, a Commission which would include natives as well as whites? That the natives have a material grievance is certain. The Act says that there shall be certain areas in which no native can own or lease land, and similarly areas in which no white can own or lease land. That within a certain period the natives owning land in the white area must sell out, and when their leases run out they shall not be renewed, similarly for the whites in the black area. Now at present no black area has been delimited, and the Commission performing this task will not report for a year or more; meanwhile the blacks are being turned off the land and have nowhere to go. The only course left to them is to hire themselves out as servants to the whites; and in fact, that is the real object of the Act. The farmers found that the natives were acquiring land rapidly, and working for themselves rather than for the white man. There was a shortage of labour, and farmers wished to force the natives to work for them rather than for themselves. This ejection with no other alternative is obviously most unfair, especially as there are indications that the native areas will not be delimited for a considerable time. The South Africans have always feared a combined action of all the native tribes, but surely by this Act they have chosen the simplest way of irritating every native in South Africa. This condition of affairs is exceedingly grave, and, though the results are suppressed at present there is no knowing what may happen if the British Government whom the natives regard as their final court of appeal shows itself powerless. We know that the native question in South Africa is terribly difficult, but it is an obvious course to be pursued in order to maintain good relations between the two races that grievances should be fairly heard and dealt with justly.

—*Review of Reviews.*

17   The P.S.A. and Brotherhoods

In a previous chapter we mentioned a yellow-covered newspaper which abused our English friends for supporting the appeal of the native deputation. It characterised the advocacy of the aims of the deputation by the Brotherhood as 'Rubbish—a commodity which can always be picked up, and quite a lot of people spend much of their time in collecting it.' 'Why,' exclaims this paper with indignation, 'we had imagined that the ''Brotherhood'' Movement was of a religious nature.'

Our answer to this taunt is, that just because the Brotherhood Movement opposes the Natives' Land Act it must be religious, for Anglican bishops in South Africa have denounced this law in their episcopal charges (*vide Church Chronicle*, 1913, October issues), and Anglican bishops in South Africa are nothing if they are not religious. Nonconformist ministers have condemned this law in their annual synods and conferences. Ex-Premier W. P. Schreiner, K.C., C.M.G., at present the London representative of the Union of South Africa, is the son of an old South African missionary. He was a member of the Union Parliament when this law was passed and was one of the few senators who had the pluck to vote against it after condemning it; and it is monstrous to suggest that these pious and learned men could conspire to denounce a law just for the pleasure of denouncing it. And to our untutored mind it seems that if it be true that all these good men are working for the spread of Christ's kingdom in South Africa, then we must be pardoned the inference that in the same country protagonists of this Act are working for the establishment of another kingdom. This inference grows into a belief when it is recalled that the men who are responsible for the recent commotion are the very men who forced this law upon the Government.

In the various reports of the South African church synods of 1915, the character of this 'Church closing' law stands out in bold relief, and it is there revealed as an opponent of Christ and his work. Let us refer to only one of them. 'The native work of the (Transvaal) District has been seriously hampered by the operation of the Natives' Land Act. As the result of evictions under the Act, some of the churches on farms have ceased to exist.'—Cape *Methodist Churchman*, Jan. 22, 1915.

The numerous South African opponents of this law had no share in the recent upheaval, and the Brotherhoods by lending their platforms to a campaign in opposition to a law that emanates from such a quarter show that their cause, in addition to religion, is on the side of law, order, and constitutional liberty. We know, of course, that no doctrine of liberty would be acceptable in South Africa that did not also imply 'liberty to ill-treat the blacks'. Hence the Brotherhood propaganda, being colour-blind, explains the fury of the London mouthpiece of 'lily-white' South Africa.

Early in July the deputation called at the Brotherhood headquarters in Norfolk Street, Strand, to explain to the National Brotherhood Council the object of their mission. Mr William Ward, the national secretary, received the deputation in person; Mr John McIntosh, secretary to the London Federation, Mr W. Mann and other officers being also present. They invited the deputation to the quarterly meeting of the London Federation at Bishopsgate on July 14, 1914, after which the deputation received invitations to address meetings in various parts. Some of these engagements still remain unfulfilled.

At the Bishopsgate gathering Mr Will Crooks, M.P., was the 'star turn'. He welcomed the deputation and regretted the cold reception accorded to it by the Colonial Secretary. He added, however, that if they proceeded along the same moderate lines followed by Dr Rubusana and Mr Msane (the two members of the deputation who spoke that evening) he felt certain that they would do more good for their cause in the country than they did at the Colonial Office.

The *Brotherhood Journal*, the newspaper organ of the

movement said:

BEAR YE ONE ANOTHER'S BURDENS

For Brotherhood men and women there can be only one response to their appeal. For Brotherhood is not only between man and man, but between nation and nation, and race and race.

In our movement, at any rate, there can be no colour bar to love and justice. If our Brotherhoods did not rise to a cause like this, we might well question the reality of their fraternal pretensions.

We are told that the problem has its difficulties. No doubt. But they can be overcome, if only our states-men will act in a spirit of courage and faith. Surely empire means not only privilege and power and glory, but also responsibility and obligations. If it means only commercial profit, and injustice is to be done with impunity under the Imperial flag,

OF WHAT WORTH IS SUCH AN EMPIRE?

This is a matter in which every one of our members should exert the force of opinion on the side of right. Let us open to our coloured brothers' cause our plat-forms and our hearts.

The five members of the deputation will be in this country for some months, and are prepared to address Brotherhoods and Sisterhoods, and to send informa-tion as to their case to any who wish it.

We doubt not that they will find in our midst not only a most sympathetic hearing, but active help in educating public opinion in this country, in order that a great wrong may be righted.

How unlike so many poor attempts at brotherhood, organ-ised in the name of Christianity, especially in our part of the globe, where 'they have made the welkin ring with the sorrowful tale of the unfortunate condition of the weak, but, like the rich man in the parable, they liked their Lazarus afar off,' and considered their fraternal pretensions satisfied if they sent their dogs to lick his wounds. No, the Brother-hood movement is no such parody. It is practical Christian-ity which knows no distinction of colour or boundaries between nations. Our nine months' association with Brother

Martin and Brother Timberlake, of the Shernhall Brother-hood, confirms this view; and our acquaintanceship with other members of this wonderful movement (which counts judges and members of Parliament as well as factory hands among its office-bearers) satisfied the writer that they are always ready to practise what they preach.

A noteworthy occasion in connexion with the campaign was our visit to the Southall Brotherhood on Sunday March 14. We can hardly forget the day; it was on Crocus Sunday when thousands of Londoners went to Hampton Court in crowds to see the crocus bulbs in bloom. It was a glorious day and we remember it as the second day in 1915 on which the European sun shone through a cloudless sky from sunrise to sunset. Thousands of people attended at Hyde Park to witness the church parade, and still more thousands took advantage of the glorious spring day after a strenuous winter to flock to Epping Forest and other popular resorts.

In the afternoon we took part in an Imperial indoor demonstration organised by the 'Southall Men's Own' at the Central Hall. Mr William Cross of Hanwell represented England; Mr T. Owens, F.C.I.S., represented Wales; Mr S. S. A. Cambridge, a black barrister, represented his home-land, British Guiana; Miss Ruth Bucknall, the celebrated lyric soprano, who artistically contributed the solos, repre-sented Australia; while Scotland and the Emerald Isle were also represented in the orchestra and elsewhere in the hall; Mr and Mrs Lionel Boote, of Auckland, New Zealand, represented 'the most English of the Colonies' (unfortunat-ely the Indian representative could not reach Southall in time), and the writer represented South Africa, the baby member of the British family.

Among such intellectual giants, one was inclined at the outset to feel somewhat out of place, but thanks to the encour-aging Brotherhood cheers which always accompany their reception of a speaker, the stripling soon finds himself at home, as is always the case on any Brotherhood platform, and that was how we felt that day.

Mr W. Cross said, in part, that one of the most striking proofs of the unity of the empire was shown in the splendid way that men had come forward to assist the mother country on the battlefields of Europe from all parts of our Dominions. The coloured men from India had come as free men and fellow-subjects to do their share. The empire was composed of territories and people—once separated by race and creed, now united under one flag. There was a great resemblance between Brotherhood and empire. In it all kinds of religion were represented, yet all were united in one great principle. It had been said the soul of Russia was pity, of France reason, and of Britain justice. No empire could be built to stand unless based on justice and freedom. The principle of freedom underlay empire as it underlay Brotherhood also. There was no limit to the empire that was founded upon unity, toleration, justice, and liberty; it surely had no end. Similarly there was no frontier to the kingdom of Brotherhood, and they looked for a kingdom out-spanning far beyond the roll of British drums—the kingdom of Brotherhood—the kingdom of Christ.

Referring to the limitations of colour in South Africa, Mr Cambridge said: 'Have you no cattle and sheep in South Africa? Are there no birds? Have you not observed that they are of different colours and yet are not restricted in their flight on that account; and are you going to run counter to the work of nature in regard to human beings? The British empire has a population of over 430,000,000, of which less than 100,000,000 are white, and there was a big problem to solve: "How to rule with justice and equity this great multitude of various races and creeds and consolidate them as fellow-subjects of one great and mighty Empire." The future of the British empire could be secured by following the high ideals of "Brotherhood" which were foreshadowed by Christ in the Bible, and by great writers such as Shakespeare and Addison. The fall of Rome was due to her failure to recognise the duty of welding her subjects together as brothers one and all under the Fatherhood of God. . . .'

It is a pity that the argument used by Mr Cambridge would not go down with the majority of the rulers in South Africa. If it did one would remind them that even South African ladies pay higher prices for black silks than they do for white silks; that the value of domestic animals does not as a whole appear to be influenced by their colour: thus, whereas the fleece of white sheep commands a higher price in the South African wool market than the fleece of black sheep, their mutton has about the same flavour. Again of horned cattle, which give the same quality of beef, irrespective of colour; farmers will tell you of them that coloured cattle are among the best for farming and other purposes, while white bullocks are subject to sore eyes, and white cows continually suffer from erythema of the nipples; yet we have not heard that this peculiarity had any influence on the quality of their beef or the quality of the milk they give. The springbuck, whence the best South African venison is obtained, has the colours of black, white and brown; and this blend has not prevented it from having the reputation of being the prettiest and most graceful antelope in the world. But argument in this respect is simply wasted on the ruling caste in South Africa: there, Mr Cross's views about 'freedom, liberty', etc., will simply be laughed out of court, unless he limits them to white men; so that one sometimes wonders whether Christ's metaphor about 'casting pearls before swine' does not find an application here. Look at the weighty arguments delivered inside and outside Parliament against the Natives' Land Act. Surely no legislature with a sense of responsibility could have passed that law after hearing arguments of such force and weight against it; but the South African legislature passed that Act and seems to glory in the wretched result of its operation.

Mr Boote expressed his pride in finding how shining was the native policy of New Zealand when contrasted with the native policy of South Africa. 'Why,' said Mrs Boote to us, with evident satisfaction, 'we have got Maori members of Parliament and our country is all the better for it.' She had every justification to look pleased at the comparison which reveals the justice of her country's rule, for we remember how the women of New Zealand got the vote. The white members of Parliament in New Zealand were equally divided on the Women's Enfranchisement Bill; but for the native members, there would have been a tie, as was the case in South Africa three years ago, when the white members of the South African Parliament, as seemed likely there, wheedled the Women's Suffrage Bill out of the House.

Happily for women's franchise in the Antipodes the Maori members voted solidly for the Bill and secured the passage of a reform which, judging by the satisfactory results in Australia and elsewhere, gave the lead to the rest of the empire.

It was at Hammersmith, where the chairman after hearing our story of the operation of the Natives' Land Act, in moving a resolution, in a sympathetic speech, asked: 'Why did we spend £240,000,000 and kill 10,000 men in the South African War if this is the result?' He asked the permission of the audience to change the last hymn on the programme and sing the Brotherhood Song of Liberty.

As the newspaper *South Africa* seems to insinuate that the Brotherhood movement by allying itself with our cause had deviated from its aims and objects, we would explain that the chairman did not run out of the meeting to borrow a book from somewhere containing that song. The song is No. 26 of the *Fellowship Hymnal*—the hymn-book of the P.S.A. and Brotherhoods.

At subsequent meetings it had often been our pleasure, after delivering the message from the South African natives, to sit down and hear the chairman give out that hymn, and the orchestra lead off with the tune of Costa's March of the Israelites. A pleasant variety was lent to it at the Victoria Brotherhood in Monmouthshire, which we visited on the first Sunday in 1915. There the chairman gave out the now familiar hymn, and the grand organ chimed the more familiar tune of 'Jesu, lover of my soul' (Hollingside's), and the variety lent extra freshness to the singing of the Brotherhood Song of Liberty, which is reproduced:

> Men whose boast it is that ye
> Come of fathers brave and free,
> If there breathe on earth a slave,
> Are ye truly free and brave?
> If ye do not feel the chain
> When it works a brother's pain,
> Are ye not base slaves indeed—
> Slaves unworthy to be freed?
>
> Is true freedom but to break
> Fetters for our own dear sake,

And with leathern hearts forget
That we owe mankind a debt?
No! true freedom is to share
All the chains our brothers wear,
And with heart and hand to be
Earnest to make others free.

They are slaves who fear to speak
For the fallen and the weak;
They are slaves who will not choose
Hatred, scoffing, and abuse,
Rather than in silence shrink
From the truth they needs must think:
They are slaves who dare not be
In the right with two or three.

F. R. Lowell

18 Armed natives in the South African War

THE GALLANT BAKHATLA TRIBE

When Bechuanaland was invaded by the Republican forces at the outbreak of the Boer War, the British police force in the Bechuanaland Protectorate, finding themselves hopelessly isolated in that far-away region, decided to evacuate Gaberones and effect a junction with Colonel Plumer's force which was then coming south from Rhodesia. The British Commissioner, before leaving Gaberones, advised the native chiefs of the southern protectorate to make the best terms possible with the invaders until the Transvaal Republic was conquered by the advancing British army.

Chief Lentsue of the Bakhatla, acting entirely on his own responsibility, sent his brother Segale with a message to the Dutch commandant, reminding him that the war was a white man's war, and asking him at the same time not to traverse his territory with armed Boers; he also added that any invasion of his territory would be resisted with all the means at his disposal. Naturally, this message was treated with the contempt that a Boer would habitually treat any frankness on the part of a 'Kaffir', and the Boers, in utter disregard of this warning, invaded Bakhatla territory. Chief Lentsue was not in a position to attack the Boers at the beginning of the invasion. He had the men but hardly enough ammunition to last for a whole day, so he had to bide his time, scheming the while to secure an arsenal. The Dutch contempt for Lentsue's threats advanced by 100 per cent when they overran his outer villages on two occasions and he failed to offer any resistance, but they had not calculated that his intelligence department and war office were hard at work in order that this threat to the Boers might not come to naught. Accordingly on a certain day a convoy of huge buck-wagons, each drawn by sixteen African bullocks, carrying ammunition to the Dutch troops in Bechuanaland, meandered its way slowly in the direction of the Marico River, escorted by a squadron of mounted Burghers. All of a sudden they were surprised and disconcerted by a fusil-lade of musketry, and the situation grew in gravity from the fact that whichever way the members of the convoy scam-pered, they appeared to be running from the frying-pan into the fire. The ruse was swift and successful, indeed so success-ful that the train of ammunition and provision wagons pro-ceeded on its way to Lentsue's town, Mochudi, but under a different escort.

What had happened was this: the sub-chief Segale, who has since been known as Lentsue's fighting general, had closely watched the movements of the Dutch and studied their plans till he was able to anticipate the coming of this convoy and to waylay it. He captured enough ammunition in this and succeeding attacks to enable the Chief Lentsue to arm his men. Thus they repulsed two invasions of the Boers, followed up the enemy into his territory, and came home with numbers of head of cattle, and Lentsue's territory was never again invaded by the Boers.

This isolated action of the Bakhatla chief and people in a remote corner of the Empire, on the boundaries of the late Boer Republic, had its moral and material value. The Boers, who virtually owned the whole of Bechuanaland to the south, except Mafeking town, found that it would pay them better to adopt a friendlier attitude towards the other Bechuana tribes. Thereby a Dutch field cornet pronounced all the Bechuana chiefs as the original Afrikanders—with the exception of Lentsue of the Bakhatla, and Montsioa of the Barolong in the Mafeking. These two chiefs, the field cornet said, were traitors to their country as they had joined the foreign Rooineks against their black and white fellow Afrikander. But the armed Burghers ceased to help them-selves to native property, and the Government's huge compensation bill at the end of the war became less formid-able in consequence. Furthermore, the task of that unack-nowledged hero—the native dispatch runner—became so

189

appreciably easier that an almost regular bi-weekly communication was maintained between headquarters at the Cape and the siege garrison at Mafeking, for the native runners after crawling through the lines of the investing Boers, under cover of the night, could move through the peasant villages with much less danger of detection by Boer patrols.

But it must be confessed that Chief Lentsue's defensive activities were wholly illegal, inasmuch as the Boers, although they had declared war against Lentsue's sovereign lady, Queen Victoria, were not at war with him. It was defined, by an uncanny white man's mode of reasoning, that the war was a white man's business in which the blacks should take no part beyond suffering its effects. The natives' retort to this declaration was in the words of a Bechuana proverb, viz., 'You cannot sever the jawbones from the head and expect to keep those parts alive separately.' It was this principle, we presume, that guided Lentsue's action. Still from the standpoint of white South Africa, the chief's operations were a purely filibustering adventure; and while it seemed difficult to indict Lentsue on any definite charge, some of his men were arrested for having taken part in a cattle-raiding expedition in Transvaal in the course of which they shot and killed a German subject of the Transvaal Republic. These men were tried at Pretoria after peace was declared, and three of them were sentenced to death. All through the trial the chief stood by his men, who pleaded justification. He accompanied them in the first instance to Pretoria, and afterwards paid for their defence at the trial, and it was evident that he took the verdict and sentence very much to heart.

If the verdict strained the loyalty of the Bakhatla, it had the effect of satisfying the Boers across the Bechuana border, in the Western Transvaal, who had to live down the sad memory of a victory gained by a black chief over their white army and of their purposes thereby. From a Dutch point of view nothing could be more humiliating than that black men should have gained such a signal success over them, and they are constantly crying out for the repression of Lentsue and his 'proud' Kaffirs. The Boers demand that the Union authorities should make the thraldom of the natives more effective, forgetting that the armed forces of the Boers when left to themselves during the temporary British evacuation of Bechuanaland were unable to do it. Notwithstandng this fact, the newspapers, especially the Rand Sunday press, seem always to have open spaces for rancorous appeals to colour prejudice, perhaps because such appeals, despite their inherent danger, suit the colonial taste. Preceding the introduction of the Natives' Land Act, the clamour of a section of the colonists and most of the Transvaal Boers for more restrictive measures towards the blacks was accompanied at one of its stages by alarming reports of 'native disaffection', 'Bakhatla insolence', and similar inflammatory headlines. One Sunday morning it was actually announced in the Sunday press of Johannesburg that the Bakhatla had actually opened fire on the Union police and were the first to draw blood. Our own inquiries proved that the British Protectorate, in and around Lentsue's territory, where the Bakhatla dwell, was abnormally quiet. All that had happened was that two Dutch policemen had unlawfully crossed into Bechuanaland with firearms; that the natives had disarmed them and taken them to their chief, who in turn turned them over to the British authorities at Gaberones, where they were tried and sentenced.

It is not suggested that Sunday papers in giving publicity to disturbing reports lend their space to what they know to be untrue; but the fact remains that, right or wrong, their editorials seem ever ready to fan the glowing embers of colour prejudice into a blaze; and after arousing in this manner a most acute race feeling, the editors, upon discovering their mistake, if such it was, did not even trouble to tell their readers that they had unwittingly published exaggerated accounts—since after a fair trial before the British tribunal at Gaberones, the offending Union police were fined £50. The fact is that while under the quasi-Republican laws of the Transvaal a native policeman dare not lay his 'black hands' on a 'lily-white' criminal, even if he caught him in the very act of breaking the law: in British Bechuanaland, 'there shall be no difference in the eye of the law between a man with a white skin and a man with a black skin, and the one shall be as much entitled to the protection of the law as the other', and so in spite of scaremongers' ravings to

191

the contrary, Chief Lentsue proved himself once more on the side of the law of his empire.

THE BAROLONG AND THE WAR

The Barolong and other native tribes near Mafeking were keenly interested in the negotiations that preceded the Boer War. The chiefs continually received information regarding the mobilisation of the Boer forces across the border. This was conveyed to the magistrate of Mafeking with requests for arms for purpose of defence. The magistrate replied each time with confident assurances that the Boers would never cross the boundary into British territory. The Transvaal boundary is only ten or twelve miles from the magistracy. The assurances of the magistrate made the natives rather restive; the result was that a deputation of Barolong chiefs had a dramatic interview with the magistrate, at which the writer acted as interpreter. The chiefs told the magistrate that they feared he knew very little about war if he thought that belligerents would respect one another's boundaries. He replied in true South African style, that it was a white man's war, and that if the enemy came, Her Majesty's white troops would do all the fighting and protect the territories of the chiefs. We remember how the chief Montsioa and his counsellor Joshua Molema went round the magistrate's chair and crouching behind him said: 'Let us say, for the sake of argument, that your assurances are genuine, and that when the trouble begins we hide behind your back like this, and, rifle in hand, you do all the fighting because you are white; let us say, further, that some Dutchmen appear on the scene and they outnumber and shoot you: what would be our course of action then? Are we to run home, put on skirts and hoist the white flag?'

Chief Motshegare pulled off his coat, undid his shirt front and baring his shoulder and showing an old bullet scar, received in the Boer-Barolong war prior to the British occupation of Bechuanaland, he said: 'Until you can satisfy me that Her Majesty's white troops are impervious to bullets, I am going to defend my own wife and children. I have got my rifle at home and all I want is ammunition.'

The magistrate duly communicated the proceedings to Cape Town, but the reply from headquarters was so mild and reassuring that one could almost think that it referred to an impending Parliamentary election rather than to a bloody war. But the subsequent rapid development of events showed that the natives of Mafeking were in advance and that those at headquarters were far behind the times. In a short time after the interview of the chiefs with the magistrate, the Boers, following the terms of their ultimatum, crossed the border between the Cape and Transvaal, cut the lines of communication north and south of Mafeking and, before any arms could reach this quarter, Mafeking (a little village on the banks of the Molopo) was surrounded, with Montsioastad, a town of 5,000 native inhabitants. The population of these places was largely increased by refugees, both white and black, from outside the town and also from the Transvaal.

At this time of the investment General Cronje sent verbal messages to the chief advising him not to mix himself and his people in a white man's quarrel. This view of General Cronje's was, at the beginning of the siege, in accord with local white sentiment. The European inhabitants of the besieged town had a repugnance to the idea of armed natives shooting at a white enemy but the business-like method of General Cronje in effecting the investment had a sobering effect upon the whole of the beleagured garrison; the Dutch hundred-pounder Creusot especially thundered some sense into them and completely altered their views.

The Barolong youth had his baptism of fire on October 25, 1899, when General Cronje tried to storm the garrison by effecting an entry through the native village. He poured a deafening hail of nickel into the native village. The natives who were concealed behind the outer walls of Montsioastad waited with their rifles in the loopholes, according to Captain Marsh's instructions, till the Boers were quite near to them, then returned the fire with satisfactory results. After this encounter the whites, for the first time, regretted that there were not any arms in the place with which to arm all the natives. As this attack was unmistakably severe and a Red Cross wagon moved around the Boer lines in the afternoon,

193

it was feared that the native casualties were heavy, and medical aid was offered by the white section of the garrison. But all were aggreeably surprised to find that beyond slight damage to the housetops their were no casualties among the Barolongs. The following was the only injury: a shell burst in front of Chief Lekoko as he was engaged in repelling the Boer attack, but no fragments of it touched him. One piece of shell, however, struck a rock and a splinter of the rock grazed his temple. At best only a few founds of ammunition could be handed out to those of the Barolongs, who used their own rifles, and it is doubtful if so little ammunition was ever more economically used, and used to greater advantage.

The investment of Mafeking was so effective that only certain natives could crawl through the Boer lines at night. Throughout the seven months of the siege, only one white man managed, under the guidance of two natives, to pass into the village. All the dispatches which came into and out of Mafeking were carried by Barolong runners. Before the Boers moved their stock into the far interior of the Transvaal, the Barolongs continually went out and raided Boer cattle and brough them into the besieged garrison. Often the raiders had to fight their way back, but sometimes as they returned with the cattle in the night the Dutch sentries preferred to leave them alone. The result was that General Snyman, who commanded the besiegers after General Cronje went south, issued a general order authorising the shooting dead of 'anyone coming in or out of Mafeking', armed or unharmed.

At his village called Modimola, ten miles outside the beleagured garrison, there lived Chief Saane, uncle of the Mafeking chief. Being apparently harmless he was not for some months molested by the Boers. Later, however, they rightly suspected him of supplying the garrison with information. They then took him and his followers to Rietfontein, where they placed him under surveillance, but Chief Saane proved even more useful in captivity than in liberty. He used the seemingly inoffensive young men of Rietfontein, to glean all first-hand information from the Boers, who still had command of the lines of communication. Then he sent the news in verbal messages to his nephew, the paramount chief in the siege, who in turn communicated to Her Majesty's officers in command. By means of this self-constituted intelligence bureau the garrison learnt of the surrender of Cronje — a happy consummation of the battle of Paardeberg—shortly after the good news reached their besiegers; and when official confirmation came from the Cape, more than a week later, Chief Saane's messengers were there again with fresh news of the surrender of Bloemfontein. This news, as might well be supposed, was glad tidings to the besieged people. They were in fact the truths that King Solomon thus sets forth: 'As cold water is to the weary soul, so is good news from a far country,' for, in those days, before the invention of aeroplanes and Marconigrams, no country in this wide world was further than a besieged garrison.

Among the first civilian bodies raised in Mafeking for purposes of garrison defence was the 'Cape Boy Contingent', a company of mixed classes in varying degrees of complexions. Sergeant-Major Taylor, a coloured bricklayer, who led the contingent and directed the crack snipers of that company, was killed during the fourth month of the siege, by a fragment of a huge shell in the outer trenches.

His funeral was attended by General Baden-Powell and other staff officers, and was probably the only funeral of a coloured person in the South African war that was accorded such distinguished military attendance.

The language of the Cape coloured or mixed people is the same as that of the Boers, viz., the Cape Dutch. At times during the siege our advance lines and those of the Boers used to be less than 100 yards apart, and when the wily snipers of both sides saw nothing to snipe at, they used to exchange pleasantries at the expense of one another, from the safety of their entrenchments. Sometimes these wordy compliments made the opponents decidedly 'chummy', to borrow a trench phrase. In that mood, they would now and again wax derisive or become amusing, be-speaking the fates of one another or the eventual outcome of the war. Whoever got the worst of the argument used to cut off communication with an unpleasant remark; but when it was mutually amusing, both sides enjoyed an advantage and each joined heartily in the resulting merriment. On more than one occasion a convial Dutchman momentarily forgot the martial aspect of the mutual hilarity and complied with an equally convivial coloured man's exclamation to 'kyk hier, jong' (look here, old fellow), and directly he 'kyked' the snipers did to him that which from the enemy's point of view would amount to 'devil's work'.

The reader of these reminiscences will perhaps permit us to pay a tribute to the Dutch Burghers who, under General Snyman, besieged Mafeking. Whatever we may say against them, in other ways, this much must be said in their favour, namely, that they left us entirely alone on Sundays. Such an opportunity gave the Mafeking people a chance to get about, to have a thorough wash-up, and to keep the Sabbath holy. Snipers put down their rifles on Sunday mornings, declared a day's peace among the contending forces between the opposing trenches, and pointed out to one another landmarks beyond which the opposing sentries might not cross, since to wander past these beacons might mean a sudden resumption of hostilities. But as the landmarks were religiously respected there seldom was any occasion to desecrate the Sabbath by the clash of arms. We had thus a whole day's recreation, when the trenchmen used to visit their families in the women's camp and make all-round preparations for another week's bombardment.

The 'Cape Boys' fought with distinction and maintained their reputation right up to the end of the siege. Visitors to Mafeking may now see near the obelisk in front of the pretty town hall of the famous siege town, a five-pounder gun 'captured by the Cape Police during the siege'. This gun was seized by the coloured Sergeant Bell and two other subalterns of the Cape Boys contingent; their contingent was then under the command of Lieutenant Currey of the Cape Police.

Besides the brave coloured men who fell during the defence of Mafeking, one painful effect of the siege, in connexion with this contingent, was that of Mr Swartz, who was blinded by an exploding Boer shell and has never been able to regain his eyesight.

Two other small companies who filled their posts without reproach were the Fingo contingent and the Black Watch, so-called, presumably from the jet-black colour of the members. The Black Watch included Mozambique and Zambesi boys, Shangaans and others from among the blackest races of South Africa. The greatest disaster sustained by this company was when a party of thirty-three of them dashed into the Boer lines on an ill-starred attempt to loot cattle from the enemy's herds. After their night's dash out of the garrison they got to a hiding place for the day, but they were followed there and were surrounded by a Boer commando, which peppered them with a maxim and a big gun. They fought up to the last cartridge, but were helplessly outnumbered and outranged by the Boers, who killed them to a man.

Cattle-raiding was a dangerous business in which the crafty Barolong, who belonged to the country, alone were well-versed. A subtle warrior among the Barolong, named Mathakgong, was a regular expert in this business. He led the occasional Barolong dashes into the Boer lines in search of beef and he invariably managed to rush his loot into Mafeking. He did this throughout the seven months' siege with the loss of only two men. The only misadventure of this intrepid looter was when he attempted to rush in an unusually large drove of cattle which Colonel Plumer had been buying and collecting at his Sefikile camp about four miles north of Mafeking for the besieged garrison. Dutchmen tell us that for days they had learnt that Colonel Plumer was arranging to send cattle into Mafeking. They even knew the exact number—a hundred head— and so they sent scouts to the north every day to watch the roads and warn the besiegers of the event. Hence, although they had left Mafeking unobserved, when Mathakgong's party approached Mafeking on the return trip with the cattle, a strong Dutch force was waylaying him and waiting to give him and Colonel Plumer's cattle a hot reception. They opened a rattling fusilade upon the cattle drivers, which could be heard from Mafeking. Over half of the cattle were killed in the ensuing fight, and the remainder, like the fat carcases of the dead bullocks, fell into the hands of the Boers. The drivers escaped with only two wounded out of the party of twelve.

They said that they owed their escape almost entirely to the carcases of dead cattle, which they used as ramparts.

When Mathakgong heard subsequently how the Boers had planned to annihilate him and his small party, he became very indignant at what he called 'the clumsy European method of always revealing their intentions to the enemy'.

Away out in Basutoland, 'the Switzerland of South Africa', the Paramount Chief Lerothodi offered to send an army on Bloemfontein while the 'Free' Staters were engaged in the British colonies of Natal and the Cape, which they had invaded. Lord Milner strongly forbade him from taking that step, and it was all that Sir Godfrey Lagden, the British Resident in Basutoland, could do to restrain the Basuto warriers from swooping down upon the Orange 'Free' State.

On one occasion, however, the Basuto mountaineers were quickly mobilised. Word reached Maseru that General De Wet, whose guerrilla career was then at the height of its fame, was seriously harassed by Imperial troops in the 'Free' State, and that it was feared he would escape through Basuto territory. In such a case it was ruled that the Basuto would be justified in opening fire upon the trespassing commandos, but not until the Boers actually set foot upon Basuto territory. Therefore the Basutos, in anticipation of this violation of their territory, under the leadership of Councillor Philip Modise, made a record turn-out in one night, in a mountainous country, without telegraphic communication, and where all the orders were conveyed by word of mouth by men mounted on the sure-footed Basuto ponies; so that at daybreak as the Boers at the frontier near Wepener awoke, they found the Basuto border to be one mass of black humanity. The Basutos made strong appeals to Maseru for permission to cross the border and rush the Boers, and again they were forbidden. At length General de Wet, amid a rain of British shells, withdrew his commandos and carried his operations elsewhere.

General De Wet, in his book on the South African War, admits that he was once hopelessly cornered and that then his only safe way of escape lay through the territory of the Basuto. He next proceeds to give his reasons for not violating Basuto territory: it is that the Basutos showed no hostility towards the Boers, and that he had no wish to provoke them. No mention is made that armed Basutos barred his way, but if General De Wet's restraint were voluntary it would be the first instance in history that a Boer general had shown any regard concerning the rights or feelings of the natives.

General Botha has on several occasions mentioned the loyal assistance rendered to the Transvaal burghers by the natives of the Transvaal. We may also mention the case of Chief Mokgothu, of the Western Transvaal, who with his headmen was detained at Mafeking after the siege. In fact that chief died in the Mafeking prison where he was interned with the Republican political prisoners for participating in the war on the side of the Republic.

On another occasion General Botha (obviously referring to natives other than those around Mafeking) unwittingly paid a tribute to the valour of British natives during the South African war. Speaking in the Nieuwe Kerk, at Middleburg, Holland, the General said:

> The Kaffirs turned against us and we not only had to fight against the English but against the natives as well . . . when the attacks of the Kaffirs increased, our cause became dark and black . . . All these facts taken collectively compelled us to discuss terms of peace.[1]

The southern defences of Montsioastad were maintained by the Barolong, under their own chief Lekoko, in their own way and with their own rations and rifles. These were only supplemented by supplies of ammunition, of which there was not too much in the garrison. And the only instructions which Major Godley and Captain Marsh gave the defenders was to 'sit tight and don't shoot until the enemy is quite close'.

The rest of the native population in the besieged town was under the fatherly care of Mr C.G.H. Bell, the civil magistrate. And the harmonious relation between white and black as a prevailing characteristic of the population of the garrison throughout the siege was largely due to the tactful management of Major Lord Edward Cecil, D.S.O., Colonel Baden-Powell's chief of staff. At the end of the siege, Lord Roberts sent General Sir Charles Parsons to thank the Barolong for the creditable manner in which they defended

[1] *'De Boerengeneraals in Zeeland'*, p.29.

their homes throughout the siege. The veteran soldier evidently thought that he had not done enough in the matter, so later on he sent Major the Hon. Hanbury Tracey from Pretoria with a framed address to the Barolong Chiefs, written in gilt letters.

Colonel C.B. Vyvyan, who was escorted to Montsioastad by a squadron of the 4th Bedfordshire Regiment, headed by their band playing patriotic airs, presented the address in the presence of a large gathering of Barolongs and European visitors. The ceremony was described by the *Mafeking Mail* as follows:

Within the square, seated on chairs and stools, were the Barolong men, whilst the women, attired in their brightest dresses, took up positions wherever they could get a view of the proceedings. On the arrival of the Base Commandant (Lieut-Colonel Vyvyan) and the Resident Magistrate (Mr C.G.H. Bell), a Union Jack was hoisted to the accompaniment of a general cheer. A large number of civilians and several military officers witnessed the ceremony, among them being the Mayor (Mr A.H. Friend), Mr W.H. Surmon (Acting Commissioner), Lieut-Colonel Newbury (Field Paymaster), Major the Hon. Hanbury Tracey (the officer who brought the address from Pretoria), and Major Panzera.

Mr Bell, addressing the assembled natives, said: Today is an historical one in the history of the Barolongs as represented by Montsioa's people. I am sure it must be most satisfactory to you all who have so bravely assisted in the defence of Mafeking to have this honour conferred upon you, which is unprecedented in the annals of the history of the native tribes in this country. The Field-Marshal commanding Her Majesty's troops in South Africa has expressed in the address which is about to be presented to you his thanks for the services you rendered during the siege—an honour which I am sure you will appreciate at its full value, and which I can assure you is fully recognised by the Europeans who took part with you in the defence of the town. On many occasions bravery was displayed by both Europeans and natives. We have fought and risked our lives together; we have undergone privations; we have eaten horses and various other animals of a like character; we have seen our friends fall, shattered by shells; and we have endured hardships and trials which very few men endure more than once in a lifetime. We have fought together for one common object. We have attained that object, and it is now impossible for us to do otherwise than experience a feeling of fellowship which is accentuated by the proceedings of today. You Barolongs at the commencement of the siege declared your determination to be loyal to the Queen, and when we had a meeting here shortly before war broke out you were assured by General Baden-Powell that if you did remain loyal services would not be forgotten, and the Field-Marshal has endeavoured today to convince you of the truth of that statement. There are certain names mentioned on the address; but I cannot help, while talking to you now, mentioning the names of other persons who were of great assistance to us during the siege. It was altogether impossible to include the names of everybody in the address, and some of you may think that your names are not there because you have been overlooked, but that is not so. I will just mention the names of a few which, had there been room, might have appeared. First, there is Saane, who remained outside and assisted our dispatch runners, and who when he heard news sent it to us. It is only those who suffered from news hunger at the time can understand the pleasure we experienced at the assistance continually rendered to us by Saane. Then there is Badirile, who so bravely commanded his young men on the western outposts, and who on many occasions went through determined encounters with the enemy. Then again there is Joshua Molema, Motshegare and Mathakgong, all of whom did good service. Then there was Dinku, who on the day Eloff came in and when the enemy was behind him, stuck to his little fort, and who during the attack was wounded by a shell, which has since caused his death. His memory will not fade away amongst you Barolongs, as he was known as a brave man.

Colonel Vyvyan then stepped forward and said: Chief Wessels and men of the Barolong nation, Lord Roberts, Commander-in-Chief of the British Army in South Africa, has sent a special officer from Pretoria to bring you his greeting and to deliver to you a mark of his approval and the approval which he expresses on behalf of the Queen. Gathered here today are subjects of the Queen from various parts of her wide dominions—men who have come overseas from England, from Australia, from Canada, and from India—and they are here this afternoon to meet her native subjects of the Barolong tribe; whilst we, the officers and soldiers of the Queen who fought in Mafeking, wish to show what we think of our friends and neighbours down here in the stadt. You have done your duty well. You will remember that some time ago an officer was sent by Lieut-General Baden-Powell to thank you for your services, and now the greatest General of all has sent you a special mark of his esteem in the form of this letter, which I shall read to you:

The Chief Wessels, Lekoko, and the Barolong of Mafeking, I, Frederick Sleigh Baron Roberts, K.P., G.C.S.I., G.C.I.E., V.C. of Kandahar and Waterford, hereby testify my approbation of the loyalty to H.M. Queen Victoria, and the good behaviour of the Barolongs under the leadership of Wessels, Lekoko, and the headmen Silas Molema and Paul Montsioa, throughout the long and trying investment of Mafeking by the Boers, from October 13, 1899, to May 17, 1900, and I desire to congratulate these leaders and their people on the successful issue of their courageous defence of their homes and property against the invasion of the enemy.

(Signed) ROBERTS,
Field-Marshal

Pretoria, July 1, 1900

Addressing Chief Wessels, and at the same time handing him the letter the Colonel concluded: I give you this on behalf of Lord Roberts and the Queen. You are to accept it on behalf of your nation. You are to keep it and show it to your children and tell them why it was given to you and that they are to be proud of it.

The Colonel held out his hand which Wessels gripped very cordially. The band played the National Anthem, and the Barolongs joined in one of their native cheers.

Wessels then rose, and taking off his white helmet, replied on behalf of his tribe.

Replying to the address and speeches Chief Wessels Montsioa asked the officers to convey to Lord Roberts the gratitude of the Barolong for the relief of Mafeking, adding: 'I have gone to extremes into which my forefathers scarcely ever went in defending their homes. I have eaten horseflesh, donkey and mule flesh, and had the relief column not come when it did, I was going to eat dog flesh, if by that means I would have been enabled to hold up my gun and keep the enemy out of doors, until Lord Roberts sent relief.'

Mr Chamberlain, who visited Mafeking two years later, inspected the old siege position and addressed the largest meetings we had ever seen in Mafeking. He said to the thousands of assembled Barolongs: 'You ask in your addresses that the conditions secured to you, when you were transferred from the Imperial Government to the Colonial Government should remain as they are. I do not think that Sir Gordon Sprigg or any one who may succeed him will alter them in any respect, and should any one attempt to alter these conditions, you will have your appeal to His Majesty's Government.' This was said in the presence of Sir Gordon Sprigg, the Cape Premier of the day, Mr Thomas L. Graham, the Cape Attorney-General (now Judge of the Supreme Court at Grahamstown), and Sir Walter F. Hely-Hutchinson, Governor of the Cape Colony. But what must be the feelings of these people, and what must be the effect of these assurances upon them now that it is decreed that their sons and daughters can no longer settle in the Union except as serfs; that they no longer have any claim to the country for which they bled, and that when they appeal to the Imperial authorities for redress of these grievances, they are told that there is no appeal?

A promise of a farm was made to the Fingo and Kaffir contingent, but that promise still remains unfulfilled.

When His Royal Highness the Duke of Connaught visited Mafeking in 1906, he was touched by the grateful references which Chief Lelolo made to the benign rule of His Royal Highness's late illustrious mother. And he assured the assembled natives, in the name of His late Majesty King Edward VII, that the death of their beloved Queen would 'not alter their status in any manner whatsoever as His Majesty took the same deep interest in the welfare of the native population as the late Queen did'. In view of this statement by His Royal Highness, Chief Lekoko congratulated his people on having had the honour of receiving 'assurances of Imperial protection, not from an Imperial official, but from the lips of His Majesty's own brother, and in the King's English.' The Barolong felt that they were reclining on a veritable rock of ages.

Since the inauguration and meeting of the first Union Parliament, laws have been enacted which threaten to annul all this. As far as the Barolongs are concerned, the colonial government is not the only aggressor.

In the early nineties a British boundary commission awarded the territory of Mokgomana to a northern tribe. The award caused great dissatisfaction amongst the Barolong; accordingly they sent a deputation to the High Commission about the award. It was only after they announced their unalterable intention to assert their claim to that territory by means of the sword, that the Imperial authorities, in the name of the Queen, reconsidered the former decision, and that Sir Hamilton Goold Adams restored that land to the Barolong, under date March 11, 1896. But the Colonial Office, completely ignoring Sir Hamilton Goold Adams's signature on behalf of the Queen, and without referring the matter to the native inhabitants in any way, lately confiscated that territory and declared it the property of the Crown. In consequence of this high-handed proceeding there is much bad blood among the Barolong.

It might be said in support of this act of the Colonial Office that strangers will not be settled in the territory, but Sir Garnet Wolseley once declared that 'as long as the sun shines in the heavens, Zululand shall remain the property of the Zulus'. The sun is still shining in the heavens, and right up to the time of the outbreak of the European War in 1914, the Union Government were very busy cutting up Zululand and parcelling it out to white settlers under the Land Settlement Act of the Union (for white men only), parcels of land to survey which black taxpayers are forced to pay, but which under the Natives' Land Act no black man can buy; and what is true in regard to Zululand, British Kaffraria, East Griqualand and other native territories, is equally so in regard to Bechuanaland.

19 The South African races and the European War

Africa is a land of prophets and prophetesses. In the course of our tour of observation on the ravages of the Land Act, we reached Vereeniging in August 1913, and found the little village astir because the local pastor, Rev S.H. Senamela, was returning from a certain funeral service. To many of the people of the place the event seemed to be a momentous one, affecting as it appeared more people than would be ordinarily the case. The person whose death and funeral caused all this stir was a black seeress of Vereeniging, of whom it was said that in her lifetime she prophesied the Anglo-Boer war and some such situation as that created by the Natives' Land Act. Before breathing her last, this interesting lady (whose sayings carried great weight among the surrounding native peasants and the Dutch neighbours on the farms of that neighbourhood) had, it was said, uttered her last prophecy. It was to the effect that a great war would take place in the near future, amongst the white peoples of the country, that there would be much bloodshed, but that the survivors would live very peacefully with the native population. We are sorry now that we did not care to listen to the whole story when it was related, and we very much wish that we had remained to interrogate the narrator as to whether the black population that would thus remain to share life with the white survivors in South Africa would be a contented one, or whether they would be living in chains, of which the thraldom of coming events appears to be casting its shadow before. But at the time it sounded parlous to think that anything could interrupt the calm of the tolerant British colonists and egg them against their Dutch rulers, who call them foreign adventurers. Nor could we conceive of any reason why the Boers, who have now more freedom than they ever dreamt of possessing under their own flag, including the right to partially enslave the blacks, should suddenly rise up against the English, whose money and brains are ever at the beck and call of the Dutch. Here, however, is the war, predicted by the native seeress, and evidently we have to make the best of it.

The writer was in London at the end of July, 1914, when there were many disquieting reports about the activities of suffragettes, and when there were still more serious reports about the unlawful mobilisation of volunteer armies in Ireland.

It was in this exciting period that attention was at once transferred from Ireland to the Continent of Europe. There it seemed that every moment was ticking to drive us towards the greatest war that the world ever saw. And though matters grew hourly more serious, it did not occur to the writer, a stranger then of only six weeks in London, that after seeing the capital of the empire under conditions of peace, he was soon to see it under a war cloud filled with all the horrors of the approaching war storm and all the signs of patriotic enthusiasm. We were about to see Mafeking over again, but through the biggest magnifying glass.

To walk along Oxford Street of an afternoon and see the multitudes of well-dressed women pouring into the streets from the underground stations (the 'Tube' and the 'Met', as they are called in the vernacular), round Charing Cross and Piccadilly, and see them walking up and down the thoroughfares and looking at the wares displayed in the dazzling shop windows; or to come down Bishopsgate of a morning and see the stupendous swarms of white men rushing to and fro along the pavements of Threadneedle Street, crowding the motor-buses round the Mansion House, St. Paul's and Ludgate Circus—yet all this throng so well regulated by the City Police that nobody seems to be in the other's way—the disproportion of men and women in the east and west respectively forming a partial segregation between the sexes: to see these myriads of humanity gave one the impression that if the Garden of Eden (whose whereabouts has not yet been defined) was not actually in London, then some very fertile human germ imported from the Garden must have been planted somewhere in the vicinity of Trafalgar Square, or the Elephant and Castle. These great masses of people when the war broke out were swept over, as already indicated, by a wave of patriotism, and sections of them reinforced by a regular inflow from the provinces, and foreign tourists—Americans, Scandinavians, orientals and colonials—rushing back from the danger zone on the Continent, stranded in London with their pockets bulging with useless credit notes, all those joined the buzzing groups in Fleet Street in scanning the latest telegrams posted at the windows of the newspaper offices, or, going to Hyde Park, they listened to the open-air speeches delivered there. In this gamut of personalities and nationalities there were, at first, faint murmurs by some of the English against their country joining the strife and in favour of her remaining neutral and leaving the Continentals to 'stew in their own juice'. But when German seamen laid mines in the English Channel, and capped their deeds by sinking the *Amphion* and the *Pathfinder,* with hundreds of officers and men, the 'protestants' found that their efforts were out of date and that their arguments could have held water in the good old days, before the declaration of war, but not after. For the silent determination of the London crowds, of both sexes and all colours, was so emphatic that one could almost read it in their thoughts, and see it, as it were, percolating through every fibre of their systems. If the weaker races of the world—and which race is weaker than the coloured?—are ever to enjoy rest, then the great powers must avenge the violation of the neutrality of Belgium.

Early in August, we left London to visit the Scottish capital, and as far as the swiftness of the North British Railway would allow a glimpse, the country towns and villages of the north appeared to be swarming with Territorials in khaki. A painful sight at some of the stations was the number of restive horses forced into the railway trucks by troopers—beautiful, well-fed animals whose sleek appearance showed that they were unaccustomed to the rough life to which the Tommies were leading them. Further, it was sad to think that these noble creatures by their size were to be rendered easy targets for the marksmen of the enemy's forces, and that they would in addition be subjected to the severity of inclement weather conditions, to which they likewise were unaccustomed.

At Edinburgh, the Cameron Highlanders marched along some of the streets in their battalions, flinging the Highland kilt like the plaited reeds of so many thousands of Bojale[1] girls. Handsome young Scotsmen, all of them, and it was shocking to think that these fine young fellows in the flower of their youth were going to be fired at with a set purpose to kill them as if they were a flock of springbuck on a South African veld. Surely it is time that civilisation evolved a less brutal and less savage form of warfare! On Sunday evening we attended divine service at St. Giles's Cathedral, and the critical political situation permeated the entire service. This feeling was not lessened by the announcement that one of the gallant boys who sank with the *Amphion* was a son of one of the sidesmen of St. Giles's. It was a war as unmistakable as it was grim.

After the declaration of war between Great Britain and Germany, the Irish tension at once died away. The self-constituted opposing armies of Dublin and Belfast, or rather Ireland and Ulster, came forward and offered themselves and their arms to the Imperial authorities. They were anxious to proceed at once to the Continent and assert British prestige on the battlefield; the suffragettes likewise at the outbreak of the war declared a truce and offered their humble services to the empire. 'More power to their hatpins!' But how about South Africa, the baby member of the British family? Where does she come in?

Within a week after the outbreak, Mr Harcourt sent the following dispatch to the Governors-General of Canada, Australia and New Zealand:

Please communicate to your Ministers the following message from His Majesty and publish: 'I desire to express to my people of the overseas Dominions with what appreciation and pride I have received the messages from their respective Governments during the past few days. The spontaneous assurance of their fullest support recalls to me the generous self- sacrificing help

[1] Bechuana circumcision rites

209

given by them in the past to the Mother Country. I shall be strengthened in the discharge of the great responsibilities which rest upon me by the confident belief that in this time of trial my Empire will stand united, calm, resolute, trusting in God—George R.I.

More offers of men and money came from the Dominions; and when such well-deserved royal encomiums are showered on the already laurelled heads of other Dominions, a self-respecting South African like ourselves walked the streets with a drooping head. And when our kinsmen in West Africa under the leadership of British officers, annexed German Togoland rather early in the campaign, we found these questions reverting in our thoughts: What is our Government doing? When is it going to move? Surely our Prime Minister, who is also Minister of Native Affairs, should now postpone the constant pampering of the back-velders, hang colour prejudice for a more peaceful time, call out the loyal legions—British, Boer, and Black—and annex German South West Africa without delay! As a British General and Minister of Native Affairs, he should himself lead the black contingents and leave the whites to be led by their regular officers.

At the beginning of August, a special meeting of the South African Native Congress was called at Bloemfontein, first to express its disappointment at the cold reception given to the native deputation by the Imperial Government; and secondly, to express its thanks to the British public for the kind reception given to the deputation; and thirdly, to devise ways and means for the deputation to tour the United Kingdom on a mission, revealing to the British people the manner in which the colonial government discharges its trust to the coloured people.

Many of the delegates to the Congress had travelled long distances by rail and road, but on their arrival at Bloemfontein it was only to learn that war had broken out between Great Britian and Germany. Hence the Native Congress, in view of the situation, resolving itself at once into a patriotic demonstration, decided to hang up native grievances against the South African Parliament till a better time and to tender the authorities every assistance.

Mr Dube, the president of the Congress, who had just returned from England in time for the conference, proceeded direct to Pretoria with the executive, to lay at the feet of the Government this offer of service made by the Native Congress. Offers of service poured into the administrative capital from native chiefs and people in all parts of the country. Magistrates who held meetings in their districts on the instructions of the Government to explain the situation to the natives received similar offers. And besides all these, offers of service also came from the Zulu chiefs and headmen, from Chief Dalindyebo of the Tembus, Marelana of the Pondos, and from Griffiths of Basutoland. In Bechuanaland, the veteran Chief Khama and other Bechuana chiefs offered the services of native warriors as scouts in German South-West Africa, and the Swazi princes offered a Swazi impi, besides undertaking to help in any other manner, as they did in the campaign against Sekukuni in the seventies. The members of the native deputation in England were longing to catch the first steamer back to South Africa to join their countrymen and proceed to the front. But while all these offers were gratefully acknowledged, none were definitely accepted. Surely there must be something wrong. Is it that the wretched South African colour prejudice is exerting itself even in these critical times?

At Pretoria, Captain W. Allan King, the popular Native Commissioner of the Pretoria District, held a meeting of Transvaal natives, which amongst others was attended by His Worship the Mayor of the Union capital; and there again native offers of service were tendered. Mr Makgatho, the chairman, in his denial of the report that appeared in the newspapers to the effect that 'South Africa could not take the field as she had a native menace to watch', voiced the prevailing feeling of the natives. Captain King, however, assured the natives that no such slanders were uttered by the Government. He further reminded them the Imperial Government was face to face with the biggest struggle that ever took place since the foundation of the world; and that there would be fighting on land, in the air, on the water and under the water. He urged the natives to go to work as usual and see to it that there was no slackening of industries. He also made a plea for the abiding respect of the natives to the German missionaries of the Transvaal, having regard to what those good men had done in bygone years for the evangelisation of the natives of that province. How little did any one dream at the time that he was thus pleading for others, that Captain King would be among the victims of the war and that he would fall, not from a German bullet, but from one fired by one of the Dutch traitors, in a brisk fight to quell the Boer rebellion.

White men wrote to the newspapers that as France, our great ally, was using native African troops, there could be no objection against England doing the same—as if England had rejected the assistance of her coloured subjects pending a decision by France. A well-known Natal campaigner wrote to the authorities offering to raise a crack Zulu regiment composed of men who had formerly fought for the old flag against their own people. He said he felt certain that those Zulus could give as good an account of themselves against any regiment in the field as any force yet mobilised; but there was no definite acceptance of these offers by the Government. The native uncertainty that arose from this attitude of the South African Government went on until October, when our colleagues of the native deputation returned home from England and threw themselves into the vortex of the martial enthusiasm that was then sweeping through the country, and as no offers were accepted by the Government, Dr Rubusana made to it the following further offer:

The Right Hon. the Minister of Native Affairs, Pretoria, Transvaal.
Sir,

Coming as I do so near from the scene of operations in Europe, I feel that something more practical than mere lip-loyalty is required from those who boast of the fact that they are British subjects, and are loyal to the British Crown, more especially during this present crisis. That being so, I am prepared to raise, if you deem it necessary, a native levy of 5,000 able-bodied men to proceed to German South-West Africa, provided the Government is prepared to fully equip this force for the front. I should, of course, be prepared to accompany them.

I have the honour to be, Sir,
Your obedient servant,
W.B. Rubsuana

REPLY
Union of South Africa,
Department of Defence,
Pretoria.
November 2, 1914

Sir,

With reference to your letter of the 20th ultimo, I am directed to state that the Union Government greatly appreciates the loyal sentiments which are being expressed by the native citizens of the Union.

I am, however, to refer you to the provisions of Section 7 of the South Africa Defence Act, 1912, and to state that the Government does not desire to avail itself of the services, in a combatant capacity, of citizens not of European descent in the present hostilities. Apart from other considerations the present war is one which has its origin among the white people of Europe and the Government are anxious to avoid the employment of its native citizens in a warfare against whites.

I have the honour to be, Sir,
Your obedient servant,
H.B.M. Bourne,
Secretary for Defence

Dr W.B. Rubusana,
East London, C.P.

General Botha was once confronted with a definite request to reconcile two conflicting declarations of policies enunciated by two members of his Cabinet, and in reply to that request he gave the following highly diplomatic explanation: 'The one Minister had said things which should not have been said, and the other Minister had said things which should have been said in a different way.'

If there is one document which contains things that should

not have been penned, or that should have been differently worded, surely it is the document we have just quoted. Fancy refusing native assistance in the present world war on the ground of colour! For weeks before Dr Rubusana sailed from Europe the Turcos and Algerian and Moroccan troops had been doing wondrous deeds on the continent for the cause of the allies. These coloured troops also included a regiment of wealthy natives from North Africa who had come to fight for France entirely at their own expense—a striking evidence of what the empire is losing through the South African policy of restricting native wages to one shilling a day, in a country where the cost of living is about the highest in the world. The Union Government rejected the native offer a week after Lord Roberts laid down his life, having delivered the appreciation of a grateful empire to the gallant Indian regiments who with distinction were participating in the same war; and a month after the first German General Freise was captured in the course of a daring charge by North African natives from the French colonies; ten days after the Germans at Tsiengtau had surrendered to the British and Japanese forces; and nearly three weeks after the Germans had successfully involved Turkey in the strife; and while the Canadian troops on Salisbury Plain included Red Indians. Where then, is the wisdom of telling Dr Rubusana, who knows all these facts, that the Government's rejection of the native offer is due to the fact that the present struggle is an all-white one? The truth of the matter is that the South African Government worships an idol, which was best described by Sir Gordon Sprigg as 'the demon of ignorance and prejudice', and the claims of this fetish in South Africa precede those of the empire.

Under the old Republics we had a law which since the Union has become the unwritten law of South Africa. In this law it is laid down that a coloured policeman shall not lay his black hands on a white man even if he found him red-handed in the commitment of a crime. The duty of a coloured policeman in such circumstances would be to look around for a white constable and report the misdemeanour to him. Rather than suffer the humiliation of a black official taking a white criminal into custody white South Africa would prefer to have the country overrun with white criminals, *ergo*, if the safety of the Crown is at stake and it could be saved only by employing black men, we would much rather let the Crown go than suffer the humiliation of seeing black warriors resisting a white enemy. If there is one point upon which white South Africa is agreed, it is that the claims of South Africa come first and those of the empire afterwards. The 'bitter-enders' go further: they say that 'the empire comes handy only in so far as it is useful to us, but when we have sucked it dry, like an orange, it must be thrown away.'[2] It may be that the blacks have their reasons for objecting to these creeds: they would prefer Imperial lines all the time, for Imperial lines are benevolent while South African lines are cruel; consisting largely of repression and slavery.

There is talk in South Africa, which unhappily is not confined to Dutch-speaking South Africans. It advocates the elimination of the Imperial factor, because that factor is said to interfere with colonial liberties, among which is the right to 'correct' a native in a manner that a colonial deems fit. Thus, under the inconvenience of the epistilential 'Imperial factor', a colonial magistrate was forced to fine General De Wet the sum of 5s on his pleading guilty to having horse-whipped a native. Under German rule, which threatened the Union, the liberty of chastising the native according to colonial ideas would be extended, for the German method is that of the old 'Free' State, where a native used to be tied to a wagon-wheel and whipped. If he dies in consequence of the beating, his death was but a nominal offence. This state of things explains the determination of the native races to fight for the retention of the Imperial factor, or for what vestige of it still remains in the country.

A native clergyman sends us the following letter. We are not quite certain if the reverend gentlemen desired to enlist as a private or as a chaplain; anyway, this is what he says:

> Can it be really true that we, too, belong to the British empire? This war is growing in such dimensions that it is even affecting the King's household. The Prince of Wales has gone to the front, and His Majesty the

[2] General Botha's reply to General Hertzog on the ministerial crisis of 1912.

King has also gone, yet we are told that we are not worthy on account of our colour to fight for our King and empire. White men only must defend the King's dominions while we remain behind with the women and children. Surely it cannot be the wish of the loyal Boers that we must not defend our empire; it is only the wish of the rebels, and it seems that our Government will continue to study their feelings even while they are engaged in shooting down loyal people.

It would seem that the South African Government is so deeply in love with the natives that they are scrupulously careful lest the natives should singe so much as a hair in the present struggle and that white men alone may shoot and kill one another. But, in point of fact, black men *are* required by the Union Government to proceed to the front as Government wagon-drivers, driving provisions and ammunition wagons, and acting as orderlies to the white burghers. In these capacities they are exposed to all the risks and horrors of the war, yet even if they are shot, they must not, under any circumstances, be mentioned in the casualty lists, nor must they carry arms lest their behaviour should merit recognition; their heroic deeds and acts of valour must, on account of their colour, not be recorded. These native drivers are classed with the transport mules, with this difference, that while the owner of a mule receives monetary compensation for each animal that falls on the battlefield, or is captured by the enemy, the Government's interest in the black driver ceases when he is killed.

Suppose the services of these muleteers were recognised in a combatant capacity, someone might get it into his head to ask: 'Why should loyal fighting taxpayers be debarred from the rights of the franchise that are liberally bestowed on white rebels and their relations, some of whom are said to contribute nothing towards the upkeep of the state?' So then to refuse these natives the right to carry arms in defence of the empire, and to send them to the front without arms is to deprive such inquirers of this and similar arguments.

On St. Patrick's Day, the *Westminster Gazette* appeared with a leading article, from which we make the following extract:

It will be impossible, when we have had the assistance

of the Indian Army in Europe, to restrict the promotion of its officers in the manner laid down hitherto. It will also be impossible to restrict natives of India *who have proved their ability and experience by long service* in their own country *to positions in which they are subordinate to the rawest new arrival from the covenanted service.* All these discriminations which rest simply on race and are justified by no natural disability will have to be swept away, and new and more generous conditions laid down for the whole Indian public service.

Surely what is true in regard to the Indian public service is equally so in regard to that infallible South African taxing machine, the adjunct of the Union Civil Service, which is officially called the Native Affairs Department. There, raw recruits serve their apprenticeship while lording it over natives who have proved their ability and experience by a quarter of a century's service in their own country. It is to prevent the application to South Africa of broadminded views like those expressed by the *Westminster Gazette* that native Africans must not serve against the Germans. Therefore it seems to have occurred to the authorities that the best course is to engage the natives in a capacity in which their participation will demand no recognition. These statements are not mere empty phrases, for the writer recently caused inquiries to be made through the Department of Native Affairs in South Africa as to whether there were any coloured people who had been killed or wounded while on active service at the front. And the result was a long list of killed, wounded, and captured up to the end of October, 1914, among natives and coloured people who had not been mentioned in the casualty lists.[3]

This deference to South African prejudice would at least seem reasonable if the King's enemies also had colour scruples. But so far from that being the case, natives living far away from defended centres are always the first to suffer when a white man's war breaks out. In fact they are always subjected to indignities from which they would be immune

[3] When the enemy airmen attacked the British camp at Garub (G.S.W.A.), on March 27, 1915, and dropped bombs on General Botha's guns, Reuter says, 'only one native was slightly wounded'.

if they had arms. One of the first steps taken by the 'Free' State rebels under General De Wet during the recent rebellion was to dash for the nearest native owner of horses and annex their mounts. The unarmed proprietor's recourse in that case was to take to his heels and leave the rebels to plunder his stock. Any hesitation to run away has involved some unfortunate native in the danger of being horsewhipped into the service of the King's enemies, and if he took the first opportunity to escape from the rebel commando, a detection of his act would positively have meant a bullet behind his neck. The late Dean Green of Natal, writing years ago, said:

> Every chief should have his own militia and police. Our common human nature tells us that it is the duty of everyone capable of bearing arms to fit himself to be able to defend his country and Government. Were the Government to refuse permission to the chief to enrol his young men, it would inflict a wrong on them, against which their manliness would revolt. Our Government however, is not established to alienate from us the native races, but to attach them to us by giving them full freedom to exercise under restraints of Christianity all those instincts and desires which are proper to their manhood.
>
> The Houssas and Soudanese on the north, the negro tribes on the west, form part of the Imperial forces, and have shown themselves true, brave and useful troops. On no possible ground of justice can the loyal Bantu tribes be placed under a ban, and refused to serve in the ranks for the defence of the empire. A youth debarred from the legitimate opportunities of exercising his manly energies will become riotous and unruly, and addict himself, for the sake of excitement, to sheep-stealing, etc.

The *Christian Express,* which has always acted as the mediator between the overbearing section of colonial opinion on the one hand and the subject races on the other, tried to allay the disappointment of our people with the excuse that the Government refused the native offer on the ground that it desired to use men from the more advanced races who were capable of being more easily trained.[4] In the face of historical records, however, this argument will not hold a drop of water. British archives are overloaded with instances of the valour and tractability of the aboriginal races of South Africa and no less than those of their nephews, the Cape coloured people. Not having enough space to enumerate them at length we may only refer to two instances of recent date.

During the South African war, the writer was asked by the military authorities to recruit twelve young natives to act as scouts in the Western Transvaal. The young fellows were handed to Sergeant Clemens of the Cape Police for training. Three days after they were enrolled we met the Sergeant who was highly pleased with his 'raw recruits'. He told us with evident satisfaction that, after he had given them oral instructions in the handling and use of firearms, he took them to the range to try them at shooting; and all but two of them hit the bull's eye with the first attempt. This is but one isolated instance which is typical of the rest.

It is doubtful if any white man is a greater authority on the character of the Zulus than Mr R.C. Samuelson of Natal. Writing on the outbreak of the European war and the advisability of raising native levies, he said:

During the late rebellion I was captain and adjutant of 350 men composed of men, half of whom were Christians and the other half heathens of the Amang-wane, a section of the Ambabomyu tribe, who at the beginning of the rebellion were raw recruits, but who, after three months drill and manoeuvring, were as expert in their drill and use of the rifle and riding as any corps in the field. In all my dealings with all these men and many more, I found them most attentive, most orderly, most careful about their arms, most alert on duty, perfectly reliable, and in and out loyal to the Government and those they were under. Having been a volunteer for many years, and a cadet at college in the Cape, I can safely say that I never found our people as a body so easy to manage and train in the military

---

[4] The *Express* is now advocating the raising of an army of 100,000 natives.

art, and so orderly and attentive as these natives were.
                    Izwe Lakiti, August 12, 1914

The writer has received several letters expressing the native resentment of the idea that they should fold their arms and cogitate while other British subjects, irrespective of colour, are sacrificing their lives for the defence of the empire in this, the darkest period of His Majesty's reign. Our reply to each of these letters was that the natives should subscribe, according to their small means, to the several war funds; and our latest information is that they are subscribing to the Prince of Wales' Fund, the Governor-General's and the Belgian Relief Fund. When we last heard from home the Basutos had given £2,700 to the National Relief Fund, the list being headed by Chief Griffiths with a donation of £100. Chief Khama of Bechuanaland gave £800, Chief Lewanika of Barotseland £200, Chief Lekoko and two other chiefs, each £30, while the Zulus, Tembus and Pondos were still collecting. At Kimberley the natives gave concerts for the benefit of the Mayor's Relief Fund. At their Beaconsfield concert the Kimberley Band under Herr Carl Rybnikar, known as the best volunteer band in South Africa, attended and gave selections; and Chief Molala of the Batlhaping gave General Botha 200 bullocks to feed the Union troops.

In April 1915 the Minister of Native Affairs gave the following testimony of native loyalty and co-operation. Speaking from his place in Parliament Mr Malan said 'he thought it his duty to say that the attitude of the large number of the natives entrusted to their care, all through the troubles, had been most examplary and most patriotic.[9] There was one exception to which he would refer,[5] but from the commencement, from all parts of the Union resolutions came to Government of expressions of loyalty on the part of the natives, and of their support in the measures Government was taking in connexion with the war. They (the natives) gave oxen and supported liberally, according to their means, the different patriotic funds which had been established, and generally gave the Government every assistance. The

[5] The 'one exception' referred to by Mr Malan was the Hlubis of Matatiele District, who forcibly resisted the cattle dipping regulations because, they said, the frequent dipping killed their cattle.

Government had been able to enrol between 23,000 and 24,000 natives for service in German S.W. Africa, in building railways and in transport work. The chief of the Tembus has volunteered to send his own son to German S.W. Africa for the purpose of superintending the members of his tribe, a large number of whom had volunteered for the front. All that spoke well for the natives and he would be neglecting his duty if he did not testify to that.'

In opening the Rhodesian Legislative Council, on April 28, Mr Administrator Chaplin concluded by saying that the behaviour and attitude of the native population since the outbreak of the war left nothing to be desired. All information available showed that any attempts by emissaries of the enemy to stir up trouble would fail to meet with support. 'Numerous expressions of loyalty to His Majesty have come from leading chiefs, taxes are readily paid, and perfect order has been maintained.'

What a happy land in which to live South Africa would be if, instead of the present god of colour prejudice, we had some such confidence as is reposed in the blacks by the British authorities in East Africa and elsewhere. The naughty white piccaninnies who always insult inoffensive black passers-by would be taught that the native is a useful neighbour whose strong right arm may be depended upon in times of trouble, instead of being taught, as they are taught in Transvaal, that every man Jack of them is a black peril monster who must not only be discriminated against, but who must be indiscriminately insulted and repressed.

20   Coloured people's help rejected

The African Political Organisation was early in the field. Dr Abdurahman, its president, during the first week of the war, had a force of 3,000 coloured men at Cape Town ready to take the field against the Germans. These men included those who had fought for the British flag, side by side with the British troops in the Matabele wars and other South African campaigns in various capacities. In a few days the number of this force rose to 5,000 able-bodied men ready to go to the front. A definite offer of the service of this force was communicated to the Union Government, who replied that the offer was under consideration.

Mr William Hosken, the famous Johannesburg politician, member of the Transvaal Parliament before the unification of South Africa—a gentleman whose legislative talents are now unfortunately in abeyance, because his liberal views on colour are too advanced for the palates of the lily-white voters of his state—offered to pay the cost of recruiting such a coloured force. Application forms were scattered through-out the country, asking volunteers to send in their names and addresses to the A.P.O. headquarters signifying their intention to serve as units of the Hosken Division. Our old friend Mr N. R. Veldsman, a coloured political organiser of considerable ability, who had been in retirement for the past year or two, came forward, took his place among the coloured leaders, and addressed patriotic meetings at Saron and other Cape districts on behalf of the recruiting movement.

At Johannesburg, Mr Koopman presided over a crowded meeting of the Rand branches of the Coloured Organisation, which unanimously endorsed the proposal to raise the corps. Similar meetings, under the respective chairmanship of Mr Keiler, Mr Samuels, and Mr I. Joshua, were held by the Pretoria town and country branches and at Kimberley. At Pretoria, Rev. G. Weavind and Mr Hanford, both missionaries, also spoke offering to associate themselves with the coloured people in any benevolent efforts undertaken to alleviate the distress that might follow the outbreak of the war. Port Elizabeth and other district branches also moved in the same direction. Cape Town, the headquarters of the Organisation, was the centre of these activities, and a number of coloured women wrote to the A.P.O. secretary offering their services as nurses to accompany the coloured volunteer force to German South-West Africa, so that the coloured people, as the A.P.O. newspaper puts it, 'have closed their book with its ugly record against the Botha Government, and offered the Prime Minister their loyal support during the war'.

But while these things were in progress, the Union Defence Force, which had mobilised near the German frontier under Colonel Maritz, rebelled against the Crown, and with their arms and ammunition they joined the Germans. This act of rebellion occasioned the greatest alarm among the coloured population near the boundaries of German South-West Africa. And they appealed to the Government for arms to protect their homes and properties. They remembered what happened during the Boer War, when the Dutch inhabitants of those districts joined their kinsmen from across the Vaal, and how that natives who were armed always remained free from molestation. That their present fear was not groundless the following declaration shows:

I herewith declare that my brother and I were on a visit to the farm Groen Doorn, Cape Province, on the morning of September 16, 1914.

When we got opposite the police camp, we were surprised to see the camp invaded by Germans. The Germans then beckoned us to come up, and told us that we were prisoners, and that we must go with them to the station of Ukamas. My brother on hearing that turned his horse and galloped back. The Germans called on him to halt at once, but he did not stop. Then they fired at him and shot him dead.

223

My brother was left lying where he fell. After he was shot I asked if I could go to him, but the Germans would not allow me. Afterwards I was taken to the German camp, where I found all the coloured people of Groen Doorn that were captured by the Germans. Two old women who were too weak to walk all the way were left half-way without either food or water; one of the two was a cripple, and the other an old woman between sixty and seventy years of age.

I stayed at the German camp at Nakob till the first German patrol went back to Groen Doorn to guard. Then that same evening I ran away from the German camp, and fortunately got safe home to my house at Nudab.

I again declare that this story is an exact reproduction of what I have seen with my own eyes.

(X his mark)
Jacobus Bezuidenhout

Witness: T. Kotzee.

Signed at Keimoes this 6th day of October, 1914.

This statement was conveyed to the Union Government by Mr M. J. Fredericks, secretary of the African Political Organisation. With it there was a request by a meeting of coloured people at Calvinia and adjacent districts near the German frontier asking for arms. General Smuts replied, regretting the situation in which the coloured residents of the districts of Calvinia, Kenhardt, Keimoes, and Upington found themselves; and said that he hoped the Union forces would ere long remove the cause of their anxiety. He added that the question of arming coloured citizens had been carefully considered by the Government, but that, for reasons already published, their request for arms could not be complied with.

Finally General Smuts expressed regret at the shooting of the brother of Jacobus Bezuidenhout. 'Apparently the deceased had been shot because he attempted to escape, and in the circumstances,' added the General, 'the Germans were clearly justified in shooting him.'

If General Smuts is right in his concluding remarks, then the Germans are quite justified in pillaging Belgium, as the reason they ravaged that country was because the Belgians refused to comply with a plain request to allow German troops to proceed through Belgium to France. But whatever the view of the South African Government might be on these subjects, we would like to point out that it is against a coloured man's grain to obey the orders of a man, no matter who, if he is at war with the coloured man's chief. It would be nothing unusual for a German to order a coloured man about in times of peace, but once war was declared, it became an outrage upon the traditions of the blacks to obey Germans who were now the enemies of their country.

General Smuts will no doubt remember his own operations in 1901, before he became a British subject. How he then invaded Cape Colony, and got a number of recruits from among the Dutch inhabitants of certain Cape districts. How eventually, when he came to the district of Calvinia, his burghers, reinforced by rebels, found a coloured blacksmith there, by the name of Abraham Ezau. How the burghers demanded certain information from this man, and he refused to supply enemies and rebels of the crown with any information. That the man was severely ill-treated and tortured, but that he would not disclose anything. And how that a gang of Boers dragged this coloured man out of the town and shot him down; that they also looted Abraham Ezau's shop and took away the murdered man's tools, which his widow never recovered, and for which the writer has been informed she never received any compensation. The Cape Government, prior to the Union, erected a tombstone over the grave of this man, who sacrificed his life for it rather than betray his country. And the sight of that memorial stone was no doubt a grim reminder to the inhabitants of Calvinia of what would happen if the rebels invaded Calvinia once more.

The natives and the Cape coloured Afrikanders were not alone in tendering loyal offers of service to the Government. The Indians of Natal and other coloured residents likewise offered their services to the Government, besides subscribing liberally according to their means to the various war funds. The St. Helenians of Cape Town passed the following resolutions, which Mr S. Reagon, the secretary, forwarded to the Government:

(1) That this meeting of St. Helenians expresses its unswerving and devoted loyalty to His Majesty King George and His Governments.

(2) That it expresses its full confidence in the Union Government in the present crisis through which the empire and Union are passing, and congratulates General Botha, and expresses its deep appreciation of his practical patriotism in having taken command of the Union Forces in the field.

(3) That the services of the Association and its members be hereby offered to the Union Government in whatever manner they may be of assistance to ensure the triumph of the empire and for the maintenance of law and order.

Shortly after the outbreak of the present war, Dr Abdurahman offered the Government the services of the 5,000 coloured warriors recruited through the A.P.O., and General Smuts replied that the offer was under consideration. Meanwhile the A.P.O. recruiting agency had been continuing its work, and no fewer than 13,000 coloured men had sent in their names and addresses and signified their intention to take the field. So Mr Fredericks, the secretary of the A.P.O., wrote once more to General Smuts, on October 23, offering the services of these men in the name of the Coloured People's Organisation. This offer brought forth the following definite reply, which is couched in identical terms to the one sent on the same date to Dr Rubusana, who wrote offering the services of 5,000 natives:

Department of Defence,
Pretoria,
November 6, 1914.

Sir, With reference to your letter of the 23rd ult., I beg to inform you that the Union Government greatly appreciates the offer of service of the Cape coloured people.

I am, however, to refer you to the provisions of Section 7 of the South African Defence Act, 1912, and to state that the Government does not desire to avail itself of the services in a combatant capacity of citizens not of European descent in the present hostilities. Apart from other considerations, the present war is one which has its origin among the white peoples of Europe, and the Government is anxious to avoid the employment of coloured citizens in a warfare against whites.

No doubt the Government of British South Africa was actuated by the loftiest motives in rejecting voluntary offers of service from citizens of non-European descent; but it is clear that such a reply at such a time ought not to please many people in Great Britain who had to offer the cream of British manhood to defend their portion of the empire, and then to offer in addition more men to lay down their lives for the safety of the colonies, including South Africa, a land with thousands of able-bodied and experienced warriors who are willing to defend their own country. For the same reason this decision ought not to please our French allies, who, besides sacrificing men and money on the battle-fields of continental Europe, must provide more men and money to guard their colonial possessions in different parts of the globe. This decision ought not also to cheer anyone in Belgium, where fathers and mothers and their children are separated and starving, a nation living practically in exile, or in bondage, its brave monarch sojourning in foreign terri-tory. On the other hand, if there is any one place where this decision of the Government of British South Africa would be hailed with the liveliest satisfaction, it is certainly Berlin, and that particularly after the bitter experiences of German troops in encounters with native African troops, both in conti-nental Europe and in East and West Africa.

Similarly this decision of the South African Government ought not to please the Boers themselves, inasmuch as, finding the request for volunteers amongst the whites failed to secure sufficient men, the Union Government had perforce to resort to coercion, in that some 300 Boers who refused to enlist for service in the expedition to German South West Africa were fined or imprisoned. This course, which is practically conscription, would have been unnecessary had the Union Government accepted the offered service of the 18,000 and more volunteers whom it curtly rejected.

The coloured people, judging by the letters that many of

them have sent to the Press, felt humiliated to find that during the empire's darkest hour a Government to which they pay taxation is publishing decisions that ought to wound the feelings of the Allies' sympathisers and give satisfaction to the enemy.

It is just possible that the Government refused the offer of the coloured people in deference to the wishes of a section of the white people of the Union; but judging from the African Press, that section, although somewhat noisy, was an infinitesimal one. This section, as is shown from the extract below, also discussed the voyage of the Indian troops to Europe. The *East Rand Express*, a paper published in one of the most important suburbs of Johannesburg, said:

COLOURED TROOPS AND THE WAR

The news that Great Britain intends to employ Indian native troops against the Germans has come as a shock to many South Africans. We can but hope the news is incorrect. In our opinion it would be a fatal mistake to use coloured troops against the whites, more especially as plenty of whites are available. From the English standpoint there is probably nothing offensive in the suggestion. Most Home people do not seem to see anything repugnant in black boxers fighting whites, but they have not had to live in the midst of a black population. If the Indians are used against the Germans it means that they will return to India disabused of the respect they should bear for the white race. The empire must uphold the principle that a coloured man must not raise his hand against a white man if there is to be any law or order in either India, Africa, or any part of the empire where the white man rules over a large concourse of coloured people. In South Africa it will mean that the natives will secure pictures of whites being chased by coloured men, and who knows what harm such pictures may do? That France is employing coloured troops is no excuse. Two blacks in any sense do not make a white. The employment of native troops against Germany will be a hard blow on the prestige of the white man.

These emotionalists urge the Imperialists against the use of black warriors for the simple reason that it would give them (the emotionalists) 'a shock'. So that the agony of British troops and the anxiety of British wives and mothers is not to be lessened, nor the perils of non-combatants greatly minimised, or the war hastened by a decisive concentration of the empire's forces on the battlefield, because of the 'shock' it would give the emotionalists for black to fight against white. The common-sense view would show the advantage in permitting all subjects, including the coloured races of South Africa, to take part in the struggle and thus enable the authorities to place more men on the Continent, instead of sending drafts of Imperial troops to take the places of men at the outposts of the empire, who are disqualified solely by their colour.

Last New Year the author received a letter from a well-known British mother conveying her well-wishes besides the following moving particulars:

We are almost beside ourselves with grief over this awful war. My young nephew has been home on a nine days' holiday at Christmas and he has now returned to the front. He has been awarded the D.S.O. for blowing up a bridge and so delaying the Germans in their march upon Paris. My cousin, Mrs —, has lost her two only sons—both killed on the same day, December 21. Besides other English friends and relatives fighting on the British side, I have also a young German cousin fighting on the other side. He has been so badly wounded in his throat that the vocal chords have received such an injury as to lead to the loss of his voice, and his career as a barrister is probably at an end. His poor mother is a widow and has only one other son, who is very delicate.

The writer has during the past six months come across instances of the loss of an only son, but all these agonies count as nothing to your colourphobic emotionalists, who must, at any price, be spared their 'shock' regardless of the sufferings of others. Now ask these men what they would offer the empire as a substitute for the coloured troops whose employment against the enemy gives them 'the shock', and you will find that they have nothing to offer, but their colour prejudice.

What, for instance, could the leader-writer of the *East Rand Express* offer to the empire in place of the generous help rendered to it by the Maharajah of Mysore, a lad of only eighteen years of age, who besides the services of his men gave the 'trifle' of £330,000, or in place of the present of the Nizam of Hyderabad, who contributed £396,000 towards the cost of the Hyderabad contingent; or the Maharajah Scindia of Gwalior, who handed to King George, as a Christmas present for the troops, a 'tiny fleet' of forty-one motor-ambulances, four motor-cars for officers, five motor-lorries and repair wagons, and ten motor-cycles; or to come nearer home, and to deal with a more modest gift, the two hundred bullocks which Chief Molala Mankuroane, near Kimberley, gave General Botha to feed the Union troops?

And when these liberal sacrifices are made by black men for the safety of the empire, *including British South Africa*, one is constrained to ask: Where are those loud-mouthed pen-men who, possessed of more pretension than foresight, wrote bombastic articles in the Transvaal Press before the war, threatening that 'South Africa will cut the painter', and 'paddle her own canoe', if men and women in Europe made themselves a nuisance by advocating ideas of justice in favour of the blacks? General Botha confessed last September that the South African Government tried to, but could not, borrow more than £2,000,000; that the Imperial Government had come to the rescue and 'helped the Union out of its embarrassment with a loan of £7,000,000' of British money. When from his seat in the Union House of Assembly the Prime Minister announced this failure, why did not these secessionists come forward and display their 'paddling' capacity? What has suddenly become of them?

Is it not about time that the empire recognised the unprofit-ableness, and even the ruinous policy, of these gentlemen, and that it ceased paying so much attention to those whose views are distorted by colour prejudice, whose object is to inflict unnecessary harm on the minds, bodies and spirits of loyal subjects of the Crown? One cannot help saying that if their career in this respect is not checked, their evil policy will land the empire in a tangle of difficulties from which its rescue will require the highest statesmanship, much expenditure of treasure, if not also the shedding of blood.

We have already stated that coloured men *are* serving the empire at the front, but mainly in capacities that do not involve their recognition. We have recently read of the trial of two coloured men at Willowmore, in the Cape Province. They were said to have expressed the view that if coloured persons are not fit to fight for the empire 'in a war originating entirely among Europeans', they could not be considered fit to drive military wagons in the same war. Recruiting of military drivers was in progress at the time, so they were charged under martial law, and sentenced to nine months, with hard labour, for obstructing the recruiting work. In this case our difficulty is that, not being a lawyer, we are not able to draw the fine distinctions between legal phrases. But to our untutored lay mind it seems that if to give expression to such logic (whereby ten drivers may think twice before enlisting) is a crime under martial law, then it should be over ten times more criminal, under the same law, for a Government to refuse the offer of service, in the same war, of 18,000 warriors and thereby barring the enlistment of a possible 80,000.

One of the best replies to colour sentimentalists which we have ever read on this subject is quoted from the *New York World* by the *Crisis* (Professor Du Bois's paper) of the same city. Says the *New York World*:

The German Ambassador has announced to the United States that he is 'unconditionally opposed' to the use of coloured troops. This is a curious prejudice on the part of the diplomatic representative of a Government that is seeking to bring Turkey into the conflict and trying to persuade the Turk to instigate a 'holy war' in Egypt and India against all non-Mohammedans.

When Germany went to war with the British empire she must have expected to fight the British empire, and not merely a selected part of the population, the colour of whose skin happened to meet the approval of Berlin.

It is natural enough that Great Britain should bring up her Indian troops, who, by the way, are as completely identified with the Aryan race as the Prussians. But

231

no matter what their race may be, they are part of the empire and part of Great Britain's regular military power.

If Germany were at war with the United States her troops would have to meet our negro cavalry, than whom there are no better soldiers in uniform.

German denunciation of the Indian troops is as futile as German denunciation of the Japanese as 'yellow-bellies'. It is too late to draw the colour line in war. That line was erased more than fifty years ago by Abraham Lincoln in that noble letter to the Springfield Convention: 'And there will be some black men who can remember that, with silent tongue and clenched teeth and steady eye and well-poised bayonet, they have helped mankind on to this great consummation.'

One South African writer to the press had humanitarian reasons against the employment on the continent of coloured troops from India. He said that 70,000 of them will be like a morning meal to the trained soldiers of Germany. This sympathetic view does not appear to be shared by German writers to the *Berliner Tageblatt*, who have a high regard for the ferocity of 'these Eastern devils'. Apparently this is the only German view which is in harmony with the dispatches of Generals French and Joffre. His Majesty the King has since been to the front, where, in the presence of H.R.H. the Prince of Wales, Sir Pertabh Singh and other high Imperial officers, His Majesty personally decorated Havildar Darwan Sing Negi (an Indian) of the 39th Garhwal Rifles, with the Victoria Cross, and we need hardly add that V.C.'s are not awarded for fun.

On the first Saturday in March 1915, King George went to Aldershot and acted as starter in the big military race in which over 500 soldiers competed. Her Majesty the Queen was also present and graciously distributed the prizes. The race was won by Private Stewart, a black trooper from Jamaica. Even the Coldstream Guards have their coloured private in training for the front; but South Africans inform you that the heavens will fall if coloured troops are sent against the white Germans, who, from the beginning, never scrupled to send black warriors against the British.

In regard to the award of the V.C. to Indians, many writers sent letters to the press claiming that it was unprecedented for coloured warriors to wear the V.C. Whitaker and similar publications might have told them that a native African sergeant of the West Indian Regiment wears the V.C. won on the Gambia River as long ago as 1892.

21   Epilogue

After partaking of hot cross buns at the family table of a dear old English family the day before yesterday (Good Friday), I went to Walthamstow, and there heard a moving discourse delivered by the Rev. James Ellis on the sufferings and death of Christ for the redemption of mankind.

At my abode this morning, after receiving such tokens of friendship as Easter eggs and artistic picture cards, I attended an Easter service at the London University Hall and heard the little choir of four voices rendering mellifluous anthems to the glory of God. At the invitation of the Rev. R. P. Campbell this afternoon I went to Lloyds Park to tell the P.S.A. there about a South African Easter and to deliver at the same time the native message to the British public.

In the evening I went to the City Temple, where I listened to an intellectual Easter sermon, by the Rev. R. J. Campbell, on the triumph of Christianity, and heard the uniformed choir artistically sing doxologies to the risen Christ.

As I recall these services, I am transported in thought to St. Martin's Church in the heart of the 'Free' State 6,000 miles way, where thirty-seven years ago, as an unconscious babe in my godmother's arms, I went through my first religious sacrament, performed by an aged missionary who made the sign of the cross on my forehead and on my breast. I think also of another church on the banks of the Vaal River where, over twenty years ago, another missionary laid his white hands on my curly head and received my vow to forsake the devil and all his works. I know that in these two places, as well as in all other native churches and chapels throughout South Africa, native congregations have this day been singing in their respective houses of worship and in a variety of tongues about the risen Christ. But thinking also of the lofty spires of the Dutch Reformed churches in the South African towns and dorps, I am forced to remember that coloured worshippers are excluded from them. Still, in these churches as well, Dutch men and Dutch women have this day been singing of the triumphs of the risen Christ. Yet tomorrow some of these white worshippers, in the workshops and in the parks, will be expressing an opposite sentiment to that conveyed in their songs of praise, namely, 'Down with the *verdoemde schepsels*' (damned black creatures)—the natives—for whom also, these white worshippers say, Christ died.

The infant Christ, when King Herod sought to murder Him, found an asylum in Africa.

The Messiah, having been scourged, mocked, and forced to bear his cross up to Golgotha, and sinking under its weight, an African, by name Simon of Cyrene, relieved him of the load.

Today British troops are suffering untold agony in the trenches in a giant struggle of freedom. In this stupendous task they are assisted by sable Africans from the British, French, and Belgian colonies of the Dark Continent, thus fulfilling the Biblical prophecy, 'From Africa (Egypt) I have called my son.' But other Africans, again, are debarred by the South African constitution on account of their colour from doing their share in this war of redemption. This prohibition surely carries the conviction that the native complaint against the South African constitution is something more than a mere sentimental grievance.

The newspapers are telling us of 'a growing spirit of justice in South Africa'; but in the face of what is happening today, the natives are wondering if the word *justice*, in this newspaper allegation, is not a misprint for *hatred*, for up till as late as 1914 whole congregations have been arrested on leaving some of their farm chapels on 'Free' State and Transvaal farms. They had their passes in their pockets, but the police contended that they had no special permits, signed by the landowners on whose farms the chapels are situated, to attend divine service at the particular places of worship on that particular day, and the courts upheld this contention. Up to five years ago no such sacrilegious proceedings interfered with the Sunday attendances of native worshippers in the same country, so that there is no mistake as to the kind of spirit that is 'growing in South Africa'.

When a man comes to you with stories about a 'growing spirit of justice in South Africa', ask him if he knows that in 1884 there was a great debate in the Cape Parliament as to whether natives should be permitted to exercise the franchise, and that the ayes had it. Ask him, further, if he thinks that such a proposal could ever be entertained today by any South African Parliament. If he is honest, he will be bound to say 'no'. Then ask him, 'Where is your growing spirit of justice?'

In 1909 a South African Governor made a great speech in which he declaimed against the South African policy of pinpricking the blacks.

In 1911, another South African Governor authorised the publication of regulations in which, by prohibiting the employment of coloured artisans on the South African mines, the pinpricks were accentuated.

In 1913, a South African Governor signed the Natives' Land Act which made the natives homeless in South Africa. Whereas the Government have announced their intention not to disfranchise the South African rebels, judging from the present legislative tendency we fear that, unless the Imperial Government can be induced to interfere, it is not improbable that should the rebels return to power after the general election in 1916, there will be horrible enactments in store for the blacks.

In 1906, His Majesty's Government gave the Transvaal Colony self-government under a constitution which included a clause placing the voteless native taxpayers under the special protection of the Crown.

In 1907, His Majesty's Government likewise gave the Orange River Colony (now Orange 'Free' State) self-government under a constitution which contained a similar provision. At this time the Governor of Natal, as representing the King, was Supreme Chief of the Zulus in that Colony. The natives lived happily under these protecting reservations, and the white people had no complaint against the just restraint of the Imperial suzerainty.

236

In 1909, His Majesty's Government passed the Union constitution, sweeping away all these safeguards. In that Act they practically told South Africa to do what she liked with the natives in these three colonies and South Africa is doing it. Where, then, is this 'growing spirit'?

During the South African War in 1901, the Imperial Government informed the Federal (Dutch) Government that no peace terms could be considered which did not extend to the native races the same privileges—the rights to the franchise—which are enjoyed by the natives of the Cape Colony.

In 1902, the British Imperial and Dutch representatives signed the peace terms at Vereeniging. In these, the rights of the coloured citizens were postponed till after the old Republics had responsible Government. Responsible government has since been granted, and has in turn been succeeded by the Union.

But when the Imperial Parliament, in 1909, considered the Act of Union, English and Dutch South Africans came over and represented to the Imperial authorities that there would be a striking demonstration (or words to that effect) against the federation, and even against South Africa's relation to the mother country if native rights were as much as mentioned in the constitution; and the South African native franchise has now receded as far off as the Greek calends. So where is that 'growing spirit of justice'?

When you speak of converting Mohammedans, let the question be asked: 'What must Mohammedans think of those whose religion having said "In the sweat of thy brow shalt thou eat bread", they nevertheless uphold the policy of rulers who pass regulations debarring one section of the community from following an honest occupation in their native land? And what impression must be created in the minds of black converts who are subjected to discriminations, including prohibitions that were not in existence five years ago?'

And if in spite of beautiful voices that I have heard this Easter Sunday singing anthems concerning the triumph of the kingdom of love the British flag continues to defend the policy of repression and colour hatred in South Africa, then I fear that the black victims of this policy, many of them converted to Christianity through your efforts, might very well class your Easter anthems and their great teaching with the newspaper canard relative to a 'growing spirit of justice in South Africa'; for our bitter experience proves that spirit to be at best but a dwindling one.

Two years ago I was alarmed by the impious utterances of a coloured man whose friendship I valued. He being influential among our people, I gently remonstrated with him lest through his action many of our people become unsettled in their faith. This was his explanation: He was going along an East Rand suburb at eleven o'clock one Sunday morning when the bells were ringing. He saw a number of people entering a Dutch church, and as he was far from home he mingled with them, intending to spend the hour at worship instead of continuing his walk. But no sooner was he inside than the usher jostled him out of the church, hailed a policeman and handed him in charge, so that he spent the next hour in the charge office instead of at chapel. On the Monday morning he was convicted by the East Rand magistrate and fined £1 for trespassing on a private place, to wit, a church. And that was a Dutch Reformed church, the state church of South Africa. Others had reproached him before me for such utterances, he said, but he will have 'no more of our religious mockery with its theoretical "Come unto Me" and its practical "£1 or a month with hard labour".'

John Ruskin, writing on *State Intervention*, says:

When a peasant mother sees one of her careless children fall into a ditch, her first proceeding is to pull him out; her second, to box his ears; her third, ordinarily, to lead him carefully a little way by the hand, or send him home for the rest of the day. The child usually cries, and very often would clearly prefer remaining in the ditch; and if he understood any of the terms of politics, would certainly express resentment at the interference with his individual liberty: but the mother has done her duty.

Ruskin goes further and depicts the calamities of a mother nation which, like a foxhunter, complies with the request of its daughter nations 'to be left in muddy independence'[1]

Let us appeal to you, in conclusion, to remember that the victorious Christ 'has gathered your people into a great nation, and sent them to sow beside all waters and multiply sure dwellings on the earth . . .

'Let not the crown of your pride be as a fading flower. But be equal to your high trust: reverent in the use of freedom, just in the exercise of power, and generous in the protection of the weak.'

This has been the most strenuous winter that the writer has ever experienced: a dark, dreary winter of almost continuous rains, snowflakes, cold, mud and slush. Reading of the severity of English winters at a distance, I never could have realised that the life I have lived in England during the past four months was possible. An existence from which the sun's rays are almost always obliterated by the inclement weather, by snow and by fog. I cannot describe the sensations caused by the dismal gloom of the sunless days—a most depressing life—especially in December, when it would suddenly turn dark, compelling one to work by gaslight when the clocks indicated that it was high noon. Not till then did I realise why some people are said to worship the sun. I find that I have unlearned my acquaintance with the larger planets and heavenly bodies (a knowledge acquired since boyhood) because the winter fog and clouds have continually hidden the moon and stars from view.

But now that the country is throwing off its winter cloak and dressing itself in its green, gorgeous array; now that King Day shines in all his glory through the mist by day, and the moon and stars appear in their brilliancy in the evenings; now that, as if in harmony with the artistic rendering of Easter anthems by your choirs, the thrush and the blackbird twitter forth the disappearance of the foggy winter with its snow, sleet and wet; now that the flocks of fleecy sheep, which for the past four months have been in hiding and conspicuous by their absence, come forward again and spread triumphantly over the green as if in celebration of the dawn of the new spring; now that the violet and the daffodil, the marguerite and the hyacinth, the snowdrop and the blue-

[1] *Political Economy of Art:* Addenda (J. E., Section 127).

bell, glorious in appearance, also announce, each in its own way, the advent of sunny spring, we are encouraged to hope that 'when peace again reigns over Europe', when white men cease warring against white men, when the warriors put away the torpedoes and the bayonets and take up less dangerous implements, you will in the interest of your flag, for the safety of your coloured subjects, the glory of your empire, and the purity of your religion, grapple with this dark blot on the Imperial emblem, the South African anomaly that comprises the justice of British rule and seems almost to belie the beauty, the sublimity and the sincerity of Christianity.

Shall we appeal to you in vain? *I hope not.*

22 Report of the Lands Commission: an analysis

During the past two years while the empire was involved in one of the mightiest struggles that ever shook the foundations of the earth, South Africa was wasting time and money in a useless and unprecedented attempt at territorial segregation betwixt white and black. Judging by the recently published Report of the Lands Commission, however, she has failed ignominiously in the task.

Whenever, on behalf of the natives, the hardships disclosed in this book were mentioned, the South African authorities invariably replied that these hardships would cease as soon as the Commission submits its Report. This has now been done. General Botha laid the Report on the table of the house on May 3, 1916, and intimated as he did so that 'the Government propose to take no immediate action upon the recommendations, but will give the country twelve months to consider the Report and the evidence'. Meanwhile the eviction of natives from farms continues in all parts of the country, and the Act debars them from settling anywhere, not even in Natal, although Natal witnesses (like the Chairman of the Commission) have definitely claimed the exemption of their colony from this form of Union tyranny.

It is a Report of many parts. A good deal of it is instructive and much of it is absurd. Most of the Commissioners and many of the witnesses have expressed themselves with a candid disregard for the rights of other people.

Government publications, at least, should be beyond question; thus, old Government archives give correct histories of native tribes for 500 years back, because their compilers invariably sought and obtained reliable evidence from natives about themselves. But this Commission's Report (to mention but one instance among several inaccuracies) tells us, on page

27 of U.G. 25, 1916, of 'the original inhabitants of Moroka ward who have lived in Bechuanaland under the Paramount Chief Montsioa [*sic*]. Their original chief was Sebuclare'!

No Barolong tribe ever had a chief by this name. The fact is, that Governments of today frequently publish unreliable native records, for they are mainly based on information obtained from self-styled experts, who, in South Africa, should always be white.

Again, it is not explained why the Commission publishes, in a permanent record, particulars of encumbrances on native farms such as we find on page 29 of the same volume. Is it to damage the credit of the native farmers? Supposing some of the hypothecations given in the 'list of mortgaged native-owned farms in the Thaba Ncho district' were wiped off before the Report was issued, will it be fair to the native owners to read, say in 1999, that their farms are mortgaged for those amounts?

In the published evidence given before other Commissions questions put to the witnesses are usually printed along with the answers. This has not been done in the present instance, and consequently some of these replies are so clumsily put that the reader cannot even guess what the witness was answering. If the questions had also been printed, the whole Report might have been illuminating. It is interesting, for instance, to read what was apparently a lively dispute between the Commissioners and one witness—Mr J. G. Keyter, M.L.A., the arch-enemy of the blacks and one of the promoters of the whole trouble—as to what is, or is not, the meaning of the Natives' Land Act. Indeed the various definitions and explanations of the Act, given by the Commissioners and some of the witnesses, contradict those previously given by the Union Government and Mr Harcourt. And while the ruling whites, on the one hand, content themselves with giving contradictory definitions of their cruelty the native sufferers, on the other hand, give no definitions of legislative phrases nor explanations of definitions. All that they give expression to is their bitter suffering under the operation of what their experience has proved to be the most ruthless law that ever disgraced the white man's rule in British South Africa.

The Report and the evidence at any rate bear out the statement set forth in this book, namely, that the main object in view is not segregation, but the reduction of all the black subjects of the King from their former state of semi-independence to one of complete serfdom.

THE COMMISSION'S AWARDS

The population of South Africa is very commonly overestimated. As a matter of fact there are in South Africa about one and a quarter million whites and four and a half million blacks. According to the census of 1911, the exact figure is a million less than the population of London—viz., 5,973,394—scattered over an area of 143,000,000 morgen—nearly ten times the size of England. A morgen is about 2⅑ English acres.

But if we are to understand what is proposed, we would have to consider the position in the subcontinent under different heads:

I. English or Urban areas, inhabited by 660,000 whites and 800,000 blacks: 1¾ quarter million morgen; and
II. The remaining 141¼ million morgen, which the Commission would divide as follows:
   (a) Native Areas, for the Bantu and such other coloured races as are classed along with them numbering just about 4,000,000 souls: 18¼ million morgen.
   (b) European Areas, or nearly the whole of rural South Africa, for the occupation of 660,000 rural whites (mainly Boers). 123,000,000 morgen.

The English Areas (I) are not affected by the troubles which form the subject of this book. None but the four million blacks will be allowed to buy land in the Native Area II(a); while all the blacks who hitherto lived in the Boer Areas II(b) must clear out. They would only be allowed to come back to Union territory as servants to the white farming population.

That, in a nutshell, is the Report of the Segregation Commission.

THE CHAIRMAN DISSENTS

On the whole these drastic findings are against the weight of evidence. The Report, moreover, shows that the decisions were not carried through without some difference of opinion. It would seem that Sir William Beaumont, the Chairman of the Commission, a retired Judge of the Supreme Court (whose legal training and experience were assuredly entitled to more respect than they received) gave a saner interpretation of the Natives' Land Act. He evidently wished to treat the amount of land awarded to natives as an instalment to which additions might be made in the future. This, he said, was quite within the power of the Commission to recommend. But his colleagues presumably preferred, not the legal, but their own interpretation, namely, that this same interpretation was 'contrary to the intention of the legislature'. The Chairman's well-weighed judicial verdict appears on page 42 of volume one of the Report:

> In my opinion, neither the Natives' Land Act, nor the terms of its reference, require the Commission to delimit the whole extent of the Union into European and Native Areas respectively . . . and I think it is quite competent for this Commission, where this cannot be conveniently done, to leave undefined areas which would be open alike to white and black for the acquisition of land. But this opinion is not shared by my fellow-commissioners, who regard it as contrary to the intentions of the legislature and the terms of the Act.

Sir William Beaumont's rejected opinion is supported by the evidence of Senator T. L. Schreiner, who said:

> When the Bill was before the House, I brought to its notice the fact that there were areas in the country which it was impossible to declare native areas or non-native areas. The late Minister said it was not the intention to divide the whole country of the Union; therefore I thought that the difficulty was covered (vol. 2, p. 224).

But as in Parliament so also in the Commission it would appear that the steamroller was set in motion; and it operated in each instance in favour of repressing the black races.

These four Commissioners presumably thinking that Imperial attention would be too much engrossed with the war to notice such insignificant affairs as the throttling of the South African blacks, seem to have decided that now or never was the opportune moment for degrading the aborigines into helots; therefore, the Chairman, finding that he could not persuade his colleagues to adopt his view of things, indited the following minority report respecting his own province of Natal and Zululand (vol. 1. p. 41):

The conditions in Natal are, and have been, totally different to those in the other provinces. There has been no demand in Natal for the enforcement of a Squatters Act or for any further segregation of the natives. Indeed, the opinion of Natal, as expressed in the evidence given before the Commission by those best qualified to know, is against the application of the Natives' Land Act to Natal.

In Natal, since it became a British possession, the natives have always had, and largely exercised, the right to purchase land outside their defined locations, and they regard any infringement of this right as a breach of the terms of the Proclamation issued by Her late Majesty Queen Victoria at the time the country was annexed by Great Britain. (See the petitions presented to the Commission.) The natives in Natal now privately own about 359,000 acres, on which are residing some 37,000 natives. These lands are, in certain areas, so intermixed with lands owned by Europeans that any line of demarcation can only be arbitrarily made, and may result in serious hardship or injustice to both European and native owners.

The area set aside for native occupation (including mission reserves) and preserved for their use by Royal Letters Patent and by the South Africa Act, amount to nearly two and a half million acres, or about 15 per cent of the whole of Natal. These areas are, according to the native mode of occupation, almost all fully occupied, and do not afford more than a very limited opportunity for the introduction of natives from outside.

A further point which has to be considered, and it

is one on which the natives lay great stress, is that it seems unjust to debar the native from purchasing land in areas where the Indian, who is alien to the country, is free to do so.

ZULULAND

As regards Zululand, it is sufficient here to point out that Zululand was delimited into native reserves and Crown lands by the Zululand Delimitation Commission of 1902-1904, the Crown lands being made available for disposal by the Natal Government, to which the country was annexed. It was not, however, intended, nor did the Zulus understand, that they were to be deprived of their right to acquire any portion of the reserved Crown lands by purchase.

The delimitation was made after a very thorough inquiry by persons well acquainted with the Zulus and their country; but, even so, we find that whole tribes or large portions of tribes who had long been in occupation of their lands—some of which were not acquired by conquest but by voluntary surrender— were not provided for, and were left on the reserved Crown lands. There are today some 24,328 Zulus and Amatonga occupying these lands, and they are asking today for their lands to be restored to them. The delimitation was acquiesced in by the Zulus only because they had no alternative, and the inevitable had to be accepted. Since the delimitation they have remained loyal and peaceful and the bitterness of the losses suffered is past.

The Delimitation Commission in its report expressed the hope that the delimitation would be 'as final a settlement as it is possible to effect, and that no further changes will be initiated in the near future . . .'; but if the question is now re-opened and European and native areas are defined anew, I think endless trouble is likely to ensue. If any alterations may be found necessary in the future, either in the interests of black or white, the machinery exists whereby such alteration can be effected with little or no disturbance of the natives.

COLONEL STANFORD REVERSES HIS VIEWS

One redeeming feature in a Report which otherwise is melancholy reading is to be found in the consistency of the statesmen of Natal, which is admirable in comparison with the fast degenerating land policy of Cape statesmen. Ten years ago the Native Affairs Commission reported on the question of land tenure in South Africa. Messrs Marshall Campbell and S. O. Samuelson, Natal representatives on that Commission—ably supported by Colonel Stanford, the Cape representative—expressed themselves unambiguously against this limitation of native progress. History was about to repeat itself in favour of justice in the latest Commission but for the manner in which Colonel Stanford completely reversed his former attitude. He is the only member of this Commission who had a seat on the first Commission, and in 1905 he was reported thus:

Col. Stanford dissented from the view of the majority on the question of restricting to certain areas only the right of the individual native to purchase land. He holds that the acquisition by the more advanced natives of vested individual interests in the land is a powerful incentive to loyalty. In his opinion sufficient cause has not been shown for the curtailment of privileges enjoyed for many years in the British Colony . . .

The contention that the safety of European races must be guarded by such restrictions as have been under discussion he does not hold to be sound. The church, professions, commerce, trade and labour are open to the ambition and energy of the natives, and with so many avenues open to their advance the danger of their swamping Europeans, if a real one, is not avoided by denying them the right individually to buy land.

He can see no decadence of the vigour, the enterprise and the courage which, since the occupation of the Cape Peninsula by the early Dutch settlers, have resulted in the extension of European control and occupation to the limits now reached. Moreover, artificial restrictions of the occupation of land in the late Dutch Republics resulted in the evasion of the law by various forms of contract whereby native occupation of farms was effected, while at the same time advantage was taken of the opportunities thus afforded of fraudulent practices on the part of Europeans employed as agents or so-called trustees . . .

If the design be to allow purchase by natives in localities regarded as unsuitable for Europeans, sight is lost of the fact that usually the native who desires to become a landed proprietor belongs to the civilised class, and such localities offer to him no attraction.

Europeans are more and more entering into occupation of land regarded as set aside for natives. Missionaries, traders and others are permitted to establish themselves and carry on the duties of their respective callings. Townships spring up at the various seats of magistracy and census returns clearly show that such influx is steadily increasing in volume. It is thus demonstrated that the idea of separate occupation of land by natives, even in their own Reserves, is not maintained at the present time, nor can it be in the future.[1]

But now we must conclude that the gallant Colonel has fallen a victim to the new reactionary spirit, for he has deserted Sir W. Beaumont, the Natal Commissioner, and taken up with the northerners, a position diametrically opposed to the noble sentiments he then laid down.

THE CAPE LAND POLICY

The pronounced inconsistency of the Cape representative on these Commissions is in harmony with the reaction which has set in as regards the land policy of the Cape. It is true that the Cape, so far, has been more liberal in the matter of the Franchise. And the very fact that some of the Cape

[1] *Colonies and British Possessions—Africa (Session* 1905), vol. 55, pp. 102-103.

voters' lists included some native names has had a restraining influence on the utterances of certain Cape members of Parliament who would otherwise have given expression to reactionary sentiments. But it is no less true that in later years the same native franchise has been hypocritically used as a cloak to cover a multitude of political sins, such, for instance, as free trade in liquor among the natives and the systematic robbery of native lands. To my own personal knowledge, the Cape Government have on several occasions, arbitrarily, on the slightest pretext, or none whatever, confiscated lands that were awarded to native tribes by Imperial representatives, in the name of Queen Victoria, and parcelled them out to Europeans.

A striking instance of such rapacity on the part of successive Cape administrations appears on page 30 of the Minute by Sir William Beaumont, Chairman of the Lands Commission. Sir William shows how loyal black taxpayers in Griqualand West had been systematically robbed of Queen Victoria's gifts and driven from pillar to post. Commission after commission had been sent out to them at intervals of ten years, systematic spoliation and pillage following the visit of each commission. It has been my sorrow to be among those who witnessed the coming and going of some of these decennial commissions and the truculent attitude of the Cape Government, who, trading on the people's ignorance, treated Queen Victoria's awards like so many scraps of paper, drove these taxpayers from their homes, and invited white men to occupy their territories.

This is what Sir William writes about the Commission of the last decade:

The case of these natives calls for special consideration. They were promised that they would never be removed so long as they remained loyal, and in the end they were burnt out. There is a very strong feeling amongst them that there has been a want of faith towards them.

The subject was specially reported on by Mr P. Dreyer, Civil Commissioner of Kimberley, on August 27, 1909. He made specific recommendations, which appear to be quite sound, but do not appear to have been adopted.

Now, this is only with reference to Griqualand West. But similar acts of violence have marked the landgrabbing propensity of the Cape in Bechuanaland, in Peddie and the Transkei, even during my lifetime.

THE SO-CALLED NATIVE AREAS

Turning to the evidence, we find that if we omit the depositions of Natal whites, of missionaries and of natives, the remaining witnesses—a minority of the whole—emphatically declared that the aborigines were not entitled to a square yard of their ancestral lands and that they should be tolerated only as servants. Those, at any rate, who thought that we were entitled to some breathing space, were willing to concede certain little 'reserves' in the centre of groups of white men's farms, into which black men and women could be herded like so many heads of cattle, rearing their offspring as best they could and preparing them for a life of serfdom on the surrounding farm properties. They held it to be the duty of the parent serfs to hand over their children, as soon as they were fit, to the farmers who would work them out; and when age and infirmity had rendered them unfit for further service, they could be hustled back to the reserved pens, there to spend the evening of their lives in raising more young serfs for the rising white generation. The Commission's findings seem to have been influenced largely by the latter type of white witness, for all that they award us, in our ancestral South Africa, might be called human incubators considering the amount of space.

A contemplation of the circumstances attending these selfish recommendations leads one to wonder whether the Commissioners suffered from the lack of a sense of humour or an undue excess of it. In North and South America, for instance, we read that the slave-pens were erected and maintained by the farmers at their own cost. That 'the interest of the master demanded that he should direct the general social and moral life of the slave, and should provide especially for his physical well-being'; but the pens proposed by the South African Land Commission, on the other hand, are to be maintained entirely by the slaves, at their own cost, the farmer's only trouble being to come to the gate and whistle for labourers.

It is lawful in certain parts of South Africa for natives to dispose of or 'sell' their daughters to men, the purchase price being sometimes fixed by the Government. It is thus that white magistrates have at times condemned unfortunate black girls to cohabit with men they hated, provided the latter have paid the price; and having regard to the object for which the proposed native pens are to be set aside, the reader can picture to himself the coming commercial traffic in black girls within the enclosures of the said 'native areas'.

Several of the witnesses have made the statement that natives are not making economic use of the land. As far as we have read, not one of such witnesses supported his point with figures. But most of those who expressed the contrary view— the native lands are shockingly overcrowded—have backed their statements with figures. Prominent among them, there was Mr Adamson, the Natal magistrate. In answer to further questions by Commissioner Wessels— questions which this Report does not disclose—the same witness also said: 'I say the location is crowded because there are too many natives for the ground, which is very poor and precipitous. It is only down towards the valley where they can do a little cultivation. The population is 12,368.'

Other magistrates and farmers gave similar evidence regarding their districts. They included Mr J. S. Smit, the Klerksdorp magistrate, who incidentally exploded the stale old falsehood about natives living on the labour of their wives. The Rev. J. L. Dube said *inter alia*: 'It is a fact that none can deny that the white man has got the best land. In the Free State you can go for miles without seeing anything; but if it had been native land there would have been an outcry, ''Look at this beautiful land, and the Kaffirs not cultivating it.'' Going to Johannesburg by the mail from here any day one can see waste land belonging to white people.'

Mr E. T. Stubbs, Commissioner of Louis Trichardt, said: 'The density of the native population on reserves is 106 to 177 per square mile; on white farms only 28, and on Crown land 3 to the square mile.' Yet in the face of these similar official figures, the Commission reiterates the unsupported allegation of prejudiced witnesses that 'Natives are not making economic use of their land'. But on turning to the census figures one sees at once how unfounded is the repeated charge. Take only one of the provinces—Cape Colony—in which it is said that natives hold (and therefore 'waste') the most land.

PROVINCE OF THE CAPE OF GOOD HOPE

Cape Colony is about 83¾ million morgen in extent. It is usually referred to as:

(a) The Colony Proper: 78,800,000 morgen, feeding 560,000 whites and 1,090,000 blacks, with their 1,603,625 cattle, 240,000 horses and 20 million sheep and goats; and

(b) The Transkeian Native Territories: 5,000,000 morgen, feeding 20,000 whites and 900,000 blacks, with their 1,111,700 cattle, 90,000 horses, 3½ million sheep and goats, and more poultry and pigs than in the Colony proper.

Surely, no further mathematical demonstration is needed to show on which side of the Kei there is a waste of land, if any. But it is a maxim in South Africa that, except as mechanical contrivances, natives do not count, and cattle in their possession are not livestock; thus the districts in which they eke out an existence are so much derelict land. The Commission, therefore, proposes the following alterations. The 20,000 whites in the Transkei must not be disturbed. A million morgen in the Transkei is set aside for them, and it shall be unlawful for the blacks to live there except as servants. On the other hand the million odd natives in the Colony proper must betake themselves to the remainder of the Transkei, with their cattle and other belongings. A million morgen of Kalahari sand-dunes, worthless for farming purposes, and the small tribal communes near Queenstown and King Williamstown, are also set aside as native areas. And then the whole of Cape Colony (supposing the Commission's extraordinary recommendations be enforced) will balance itself as follows:

(a) European Areas: 76,392,503 morgen, feeding 560,000

     whites, their 1,030,000 cattle, 180,300 horses and 15
     million sheep and goats.

(*b*) Native Areas: 7,356,590 morgen, feeding 1,500,000
     blacks, with their 1,580,000 head of cattle, 154,630
     horses and 8 million sheep and goats.

At first sight it would appear that these awards allotted
say 288 acres per white and 7 acres per black person; but,
as the bulk of the English (a quarter of a million) live in towns
and are not affected by this trouble, we may deduce the urban
districts and their white and black populations. Then the
Commission's allotments really work out at about 589.31
acres per Boer (man, woman or child) and only 10.3 acres
per native. And even then, this would be by no means the
limit of the disproportion. Appendix VIII (Annexure I) of
the same Report recommends future inroads by whites upon
those attenuated native reservations, but, to the blacks, there
is to be no territorial compensation from the Colony, which
an adoption of all these recommendations would practically
depopulate.

As things are at present, the black population of these areas
is as much as 70 to 90 persons to the square mile. In density
of population, some of these 'rural' native districts are second
only to Cape Town, Durban, and Johannesburg—South
Africa's most populous centres. Not one of the other South
African 'cities' can show a population of more than 20 to
30 persons to the square mile. So that every individual
inhabitant of a city occupies a larger space than some of these
natives farmers can have for themselves, their livestock and
agricultural pursuits. So says the Census Report (U.G. 32,
1912), which is fully borne out by the writer's own
observations in a travelling experience of more than ten
years.

The average density of the rural population in white areas
is about five to eight persons per square mile. In native areas
the average is ten times that number, while the black belt
along the Indian Ocean contains from 100 to 140 natives
per square mile (see Schedule F. and Tables XIII-XVI, of
the Census Report). Yet the Commission would saddle these
congested native areas with additional populations from the
colony proper and raise the density to something over 200

souls per square mile.

The density of cattle to the square mile in Cape Colony is 6,39 in white areas, and 61,15 in native areas (see U.G. 32h, 1912. pp. 1227-1228). Adopt the Commission's Report and you will have in white areas 0,24 and in native areas 163,26 cattle per square mile.

Is it fair or reasonable that the indigenes of an open country who pay taxation for the benefit of their rulers and not of themselves, should be forced to live the overcrowded lives of the Belgians without Belgium's sanitary arrangements, or the precautionary hygiene measures necessary in other thickly populated areas?

Is it natural that their cattle should be subjected to this starvation process, while the grassy tracks of their God-given territories are mainly untenanted and preserved as breeding grounds for venomous snakes and scorpions?

Has it come to this that the standard of our unfortunate country has sunk so low that dog-in-the-manger stories are now read in Parliamentary publications?

It is clear that under the proposed arrangement native cattle must starve and their owners with them. For it has come out in evidence that even now (while many Europeans hold large tracts of idle land) some of the blacks have not enough grazing for their stock. But that little difficulty the Commission solves by proposing that natives should be taught to give up cattle breeding, which alone stands between them and the required serfdom!

An African home without its flock and herd is like an English home without its breadwinner.

Von Franzius considers Africa the home of the house cattle and the Negro the original tamer . . . Among the great Bantu tribes extending from the Soudan toward the South, cattle are evidence of wealth; one tribe, for instance, having so many oxen that each village had ten or twelve thousand head. Lenz (1884), Bouet-Williaumez (1848), Hecquard (1854), Bosman (1805), and Baker (1868) all bear witness to this, and Schweinfurth (1878) tells us of great cattle parks with two to three thousand head, and of numerous agricultural and cattle-raising tribes . . . while Livingstone

describes the busy cattle raising of the Bantu and Kaffirs.[2]
But the Commission would force us to give up our agrarian occupation when we are debarred by Acts of Parliament from following other profitable industries in our own country. This is equivalent to saying that Englishmen must be taught to close down their shops, stop their shipping industry and give up their maritime trade.

The Orange 'Free' State

The provincial difficulties I have endeavoured to point out become more serious when we regard the conditions in the so-called 'Free' State. There the native position is rendered exceptionally desperate by a number of rigorous class enactments. Formerly these discriminating laws were eased by the action of the State Presidents who were in the habit of issuing exemption certificates to natives who wished to buy land, either from other natives or from Europeans; but now, these harsh laws, besides being rigidly enforced against all natives, were made more acute in 1913, while there is no one in the position once occupied by the President, who might be able or inclined to grant any relief.

Whenever by force of character or sheer doggedness one native has tried to break through the South African shackles of colour prejudice, the colour bar, inserted in the South African constitution in 1909, instantly hurled him back to the lowest wrung of the ladder and held him there. Let me mention only one such case.

About ten years ago Mr J. M. Nyokong, of the farm Maseru, in the Thaba Nchu District, invested about £1,000 in agricultural machinery and got a white man to instruct his nephews in its use. I have seen his nephews go forth with a steam-sheller, after garnering his crops every year, to reap and thresh the grain of the native peasants on the farms in his district. But giving evidence before the Lands Commission two years ago, this industrious black landowner stated that he had received orders from the Government not to use his machinery except under the supervision of a white

[2] *The Negro* (Du Bois), pp. 108-109.

engineer. This order, he says, completely stopped his work. The machinery is used only at harvesting time; no white man would come and work for him for two months only in the year, and as he cannot afford to pay one for doing nothing in the remaining ten months, his costly machinery is reduced to so much scrap iron. This is the kind of discouragement and attrition to which natives who seek to better their position are subjected in their own country.

THE NATIVE AFFAIRS DEPARTMENT

Perhaps the greatest puzzle in this ocean of native difficulties, to which one can but slightly refer in this chapter, is the attitude of some of the gentlemen in charge of the Native Affairs Department—the only branch of the South African administration run exclusively on native taxes. It is perhaps as well to cite one instance illustrative of their methods of administering native affairs. The Rev. J. L. Dube, President of the Native Congress, gave evidence before the Lands Commission and produced letters addressed to him by certain Natal firms, from which I extract the following passages:

> If you are prepared to purchase this land my Company would be prepared to do business with you . . . In view of the fact that you and Cele have already purchased portion of the Company's property adjoining the land now offered for sale, we think there would be no objection on the part of the Governor-General in giving his consent to the transfer.[3]

Another extract runs:

> We have a piece of land at the edge of our estate cutting right into land owned by various natives, and we are willing to dispose of this land to Cele for this reason. We understood that the Department of Native Affairs raised no objection, but we were astonished when everything was 'cut and dried' to find them refusing the application.[4]

How then can the native be expected to survive this organised opposition, on the part of the authorities, and also of these

[3] U.G. 22, p. 557.
[4] Ibid.

256

official beneficiaries and prospective pensioners of native taxes? Will it be believed that these gentlemen of the Native Affairs Department, whose salaries are actually paid by us, should have sent messengers at our expense to convene a meeting of their colleagues, at which letters were dictated prohibiting the sale of this land to Zulus—the stationery, the typewriter and the typist's labour, to say nothing of the cigarettes smoked by those present, being paid for out of native money?

Is it surprising if we feel that their adverse interference in matters which so vitally affect us has long since become intolerable?

It may be asked what useful purpose is served by the Native Affairs Department as it now stands? This would be my answer: The Department is responsible for the gathering in of all native taxes throughout the Union. And after paying the salaries of the staff, it pays over annually a huge surplus to the Union exchequer for the benefit of 'a white South Africa'. Further, the Transvaal natives believe that they would get along much better with the white population, and with officials of other Departments of State, were not 'the Native Affairs Department continually stirring them up against us'. The justice of this complaint is well exemplified at Johannesburg, where the autocrats of this department are armed with, and liberally exercise, the peculiar and exceptional powers of locking up natives without warrants, without any charge, and without a trial—powers which even the Judges of the Supreme Court do not possess.

GENERAL HERTZOG'S SCHEME

It may interest the reader to know that General Hertzog is the father of the segregation controversy. The writer and other natives interviewed him before Christmas, 1912, at the Palace of Justice, Pretoria, when he was still in the ministry. We had a two hours' discussion, in the course of which the General gave us a forecast of what he then regarded as possible native areas, and drew rings on a large wall-map of the Union to indicate their locality. Included in these rings were several magistracies which he said would solve a knotty problem. He told us that white people objected to black men in Government offices and magistrates in those areas would have no difficulty in employing them.

General Hertzog was dismissed shortly after, and it has been said that in order to placate his angry admirers the Ministry passed the Natives' Land Act of which this Report is the outcome. Judging by the vigour with which the Union administration has been weeding natives out of the public service and replacing them with Boers without waiting for the Commission's Report, it is clear that they did not share General Hertzog's intention as regards these magistracies. I cannot recall all the magistracies which General Hertzog mentioned as likely to fall in native areas; but I distinctly remember that Pietersburg and Thaba Nchu were among them; while Alice and Peddie (and possibly a neighbouring district) were to be included in a southern reserve into which the natives round East London and Grahamstown would have to move, the land vacated by them to be gradually occupied by the white settlers now scattered over the would-be native block. He went on to forecast a vast dependency of the Union in which the energies and aspirations of black professional men would find their outlet with no danger of competition with Europeans; where a new educational and representative system could be evolved for natives to live their own lives, and work out their salvation in a separate sphere. But the Lands Commission's Report places this plausible scheme beyond the region of possibility, for no native area, recommended by this Commission, includes any of the magistracies mentioned.

General Hertzog's plan at least offered a fair ground for discussion, but the Commission's Report is a travesty of his scheme. It intensifies every native difficulty and goes much further than the wild demands of the 'Free' State extremists. Thus even if it be thrown out, as it deserves to be, future exploiters will always cite it as an excuse for measures subversive of native well-being. In fact, that such legislation should be mooted is nothing short of a national calamity.

HOW THEY 'DOUBLED' A NATIVE AREA

Near the northern boundaries of Transvaal there lies a stretch of malarial country in which nothing can live unless born there. Men and beasts from other parts visit it only in winter and leave it again before the rains begin, when the atmosphere becomes almost too poisonous to inhale. Even the unfailing tax-gatherers of the Native Affairs Department go there only in the winter every year and hurry back again with the money bags before the malarial period sets in. A Boer general describes how when harrassed by the Imperial forces during the South African war, he was once compelled to march through it; and how his men and horses—many of them natives of the Transvaal—contracted enough malaria during the march to cause the illness of many and the death of several Burghers and animals. Of the native inhabitants of this delectable area the Dutch General says: 'Their diminutive deformed stature was another proof of the miserable climate obtaining there.'[5]

When the Lands Commissioners contemplated this 'salu-brious' region, their hearts must have melted with genero-sity, for whereas in our own healthy part of South Africa they have indicated possible native areas by little dots or microscopical rings (as in Thaba Nchu for instance), here, in this malarial area, they marked off a reserve almost as wide as that described by General Hertzog himself at our Pretoria interview. It is possibly in this way, and in such impossible places, that the Commission is alleged to have 'doubled' the native areas. In the rest of the country they ask Parliament to confiscate our birthright to the soil of our ancestry in favour of 600,000 Boers and aliens whose lan-guage can show no synonym for HOME—the English equivalent of our *Ikaya* and *Legae*!

The Britishers' vocabulary includes that sacred word: and that, perhaps, is the reason why their colonising schemes have always allowed some tracts of country for native family life, with reasonable opportunities for their future existence and progress, in the vast South African expanses which God in his providence had created for his children of the sun.

[5] *My Reminiscences of the Anglo-Boer War* (General Ben Viljoen), p. 222.

The Englishman, moreover, found us speaking the word *Legae*, and taught us how to write it. In 1910, much against our will, the British Government surrendered its immediate sovereignty over our land to colonials and cosmopolitan aliens who know little about a home, because their dictionaries contain no such loving term; and the recommendations of this Commission would seem to express their limited conception of the word and its beautiful signifiance.

NATIVES HAVE NO INFORMATION ABOUT THE COMING SERVITUDE

All too little (if anything at all) is known of the services rendered to the common weal by the native leaders in South Africa. In every crisis of the past four years—and the one-sided policy of the Union has produced many of these —the native leaders have taken upon themselves the thank-less and expensive task of restraining the natives from resorting to violence. The seeming lack of appreciation with which the Government has met their success in that direction has been the cause of some comment among natives. On more than one occasion they have asked whether the authorities were disappointed because, by their successful avoidance of bloodshed, the native leaders had forestalled the machine-guns. But, be the reason what it may, this apparent ingratitude has not cooled their ardour in the cause of peace.

Today the Native Affairs Department has handed over £7,000 from native taxes to defray the cost of the Land Commission, consisting of five white Commissioners, their white clerks and secretaries—the printing alone swallowed up nearly £1,000 with further payments to white translators for a Dutch edition of the Report. But not a penny could be spared for the enlightenment of the natives at whose expense the inquiry has been carried through. They have been officially told and had every reason to believe that the Commission was going about to mark out reservations for them to occupy and live emancipated from the prejudicial conditions that would spring from contiguity with the white race. For any information as to the real character of the contents of the Dutch and English Report of this Commission, they would have to depend on what they could gather from the unsalaried efforts of the native leaders, who, owing to the vastness of the subcontinent, the lack of travelling facilities and their own limited resources, can only reach a few localities and groups.

It may be said with some reason that English leaders of thought in South Africa have had a task of like difficulty: that they worked just as hard to get the English colonists to co-operate loyally with a vanquished foe in whose hands the Union constitution has placed the destiny of South Africa. It could also be said with equal justice that the Boer leaders' task has been not less difficult, that it required their greatest tact to get the Boer majority—now in power —to deal justly with the English who had been responsible for the elimination of the two Boer flags from among the emblems of the family of nations. But the difficulty of their task is not comparable to that of the native leaders. English and Dutch colonial leaders are members of Parliament, each in receipt of £400 a year, with a free first-class ticket over all systems of the South African Railways. They enjoy, besides, the co-operation of an army of well-paid white civil servants, without whom they could scarcely have managed their own people. The native leader, on the other hand, in addition to other impediments, has to contend with the difficulty of financing his own tours in a country whose settled policy is to see that natives do not make any money. His position in his own country approximates to that of an Englishman, grappling single-handed with complicated problems, on foreign soil, without the aid of a British consul.

BULLYRAGGING THE NATIVES

For upwards of three years the Government of the Union of South Africa has harrassed and maltreated the rural native taxpayers as no heathen monarch, since the time of the Zulu King Chaka, ever ill-used a tributary people. For the greater part of our period of suffering the empire was engaged in a titanic struggle, which, for ghastliness is without precedent. I can think of no people in the Eastern Hemisphere who are absolutely unaffected by it; but the members of the empire can find consolation in the fact that almost all creation is in sympathy with them. Constant disturbance has brought in a realisation to the entire universe that nature, like the times, is out of joint. The birds of the air and the fishes, like other denizens of the deep, are frequently drawn into the whirlpool of misery; and a mutual suffering has identified them as it were with some of the vicissitudes of an empire at war. And they too have in their peculiar way felt impelled to offer their condolence to the dependants of those who have fallen in the combat on land, in the air, on sea, and under the sea. And while all creation stands aghast beside the gaping graves, by rivers of blood, mourning with us the loss of some of the greatest Englishmen that ever lived, South Africa, having constituted herself the only vandal State, possesses sufficient incompassion to celebrate the protection conferred on her by the British fleet and devote her God-given security to an orgy of tyranny over those hapless coloured subjects of the King, whom the Union constitution has placed in the hollow of her hands.

Is there nobody left on earth who is just enough to call on South Africa to put an end to this cowardly abuse of power?

We appeal to the colonists of Natal, who have declared themselves against the persecution of their natives; and would draw their attention to the fact that in spite of their disapproval, expressed to the Lands Commission, the Union Government, at the behest of a prisoner, is still tyrannising over the Zulus.

We appeal to the Churches. We would remind them that in the past the Christian voice has been our only shield against legislative excesses of the kind now in full swing in the Union. But in the new ascendency of self and pelf over justice and tolerance, that voice will be altogether ignored, unless strongly reinforced by the Christian world at large. We appeal for deliverance from the operation of a cunningly conceived and a most draconian law whose administration has been marked by the closing down of native churches and chapels in rural South Africa.

We appeal to the Jews, God's chosen people, who know

what suffering means. We would remind them that if after 1913 there was no repetition of a Russian pogrom it was largely because the native leaders (including the author) have spared neither pains nor pence in visiting the scattered tribes and exhorting them to obey all the demands of the South African Government under the Grobler law pending a peaceful intercession from the outside world. But for this self-imposed duty on the part of the native leaders, I am satisfied that numbers of the native peasantry would have been mown down early in 1914, and humanity would have been told that they were justly punished for disobedience to constituted authority.

We appeal to the leaders of the empire—that empire for which my own relatives have sacrificed life and property in order to aid its extension along the Cape to Cairo route, entirely out of love for her late Majesty Queen Victoria and with no expectation of material reward. We ask these leaders to honour the plighted word of their noble predecessors who collectively and severally assured us a future of peace and happiness as our membership privilege in the empire for which we bled. They were among the noblest Englishmen that ever left the native shores to create a prestige for their nation abroad. They included heroes and empire-builders too many to mention, who all told us that they spoke in the name of Queen Victoria and on behalf of her heirs and successors. What has suddenly become of the Briton's word—his bond—that solemn obligations of such Imperialists should cease to count? And if it is decided that the Victorian Englishman and the twentieth century Englishman are creatures of different clay (and that with the latter honour is binding only when both parties to the undertaking are white), surely this could hardly be the moment to inaugurate a change the reaction of which cannot fail to desecrate the memories of your just and upright forebears.

We would draw the attention of the British people to the fact that the most painful part of the present ordeal to the loyal black millions, who are now doing all they can, or are allowed to do, to help the empire to win the war, is that they suffer this consummate oppression at the bidding of a gentleman now serving his term for participating in a rebellion during this war. We feel that it must be a source of intense satisfaction to Mr Piet Grobler in his cell, that the most loyal section of the King's South African subjects are suffering persecution under his law—a fact which looked at from whatever standpoint, is equal to an official justification of the ideals for which he rose in rebellion. And if there is to be a return to the contented South Africa of other days, both the Natives' Land Act—his law—and the Report of the Lands Commission, its climax—should be torn up.

COURTING RETRIBUTION

For three years and more the South African Government have persecuted my kinsmen and kinswomen for no other crime than that they have meekly paid their taxes. I had come to the conclusion, after meeting colonials from all quarters of the globe and weighing the information obtained from them, that in no colony are the native inhabitants treated with greater injustice than in South Africa.[6] Yet in spite of all I had seen and heard, I must say that, until this Report reached me, I never would have believed my white fellow-countrymen capable of conceiving the all but diabolical schemes propounded between the covers of Volume I of the Report of the South African Lands Commission, 1916, and clothing them in such plausible form as to mislead even sincere and well-informed friends of the natives. There are pages upon pages of columns of figures running into four, five or six noughts. They will dazzle the eye until the reader imagines himself witnessing the redistribution of the whole subcontinent and its transfer to the native tribes. But two things he will never find in that mass of figures; these are (a) the grand total of the land so 'awarded' to natives; and (b) how much is left for other people. To arrive at these he has to do his own additions and subtractions, and call in the

[6] Some white South Africans in recent years have migrated to the Katanga Region in the Belgian Congo. I have read in the South African daily papers, correspondence from some of them complaining of their inability to make money. They attributed this difficulty to the fact that the Belgian officials will not permit them to exploit the labour of the Congolese as freely as white men are accustomed to make use of the natives in British South Africa.

aid of statistics such as the census figures, the annual Blue
Books, etc., before the truth begins to dawn on him. They
talk of having 'doubled' the native areas. They found us in
occupation of 143 million morgen and propose to squeeze
us into 18 million. If this means doubling it, then our teachers
must have taught us the wrong arithmetic. Is it any wonder
that it is becoming increasingly difficult for us to continue
to love and respect the great white race as we truly loved
it at the beginning of this century?

We would submit a few problems in this Report for the
British people and their Parliamentary representatives to
solve:

Firstly: Who are to become the occupants of the lands from
which the Commission recommends the removal of the native
proletariat?

Secondly: In view of certain upheavals which we have seen
not very long ago, and others which might take place in the
future, it is pertinent to ask, concerning the 'very small
minority of the inhabitants'—the whites—alluded to by Mr
Schreiner at the head of this chapter, (a) what proportion
is in full sympathy with the ideals of the British empire; (b)
what proportion remains indifferent; and (c) what proportion
may be termed hostile?

Thirdly: Does the autonomy granted to this 'small
minority' amount to complete independence, or does it not?

Fourthly: Would it not be advisable also to inquire of 'the
vast majority of the inhabitants' the King's black subjects,
doomed by this Report to forfeit their homes and all they
value in their own country, (a) how many of these are loyal,
and (b) how many are not?

Finally and solemnly we would put it to all concerned for
the honour and perpetuity of British dominion in South
Africa, can the empire afford to tamper with and alienate
their affections?

As stated already, this 'very vast majority of the inhabitants' of South Africa has been strafed by the 'very small
minority' for over three years. And when the burden loaded
on our bent backs becomes absolutely unbearable we are at
times inclined to blame ourselves; for, when some of us
fought hard—and often against British diplomacy—to extend

the sphere of British influence, it never occurred to us that the spread of British dominion in South Africa would culminate in consigning us to our present intolerable position, namely, a helotage under a Boer oligarchy. But when an official Commission asks Parliament to herd us into concentration camps, with the additional recommendation that besides breeding slaves for our masters, we should be made to pay for the upkeep of the camps: in other words, that we should turn the colonials into slave raiders and slave-drivers (but save them the expense of buying the slaves), the only thing that stands between us and despair is the thought that Heaven has never yet failed us. We remember how African women have at times shed tears under similar injustices; and how when they have been made to leave their fields with their hoes on their shoulders, their tears on evaporation have drawn fire and brimstone from the skies. But such blind retribution has a way of punishing the innocent alike with the guilty, and it is in the interests of both that we plead for some outside intervention to assist South Africa in recovering her lost senses.

The ready sympathy expressed by those British people among whom I have lived and laboured during the past two years inspires the confidence that a consensus of British opinion will, in the Union's interest, stay the hand of the South African Government, veto this iniquity and avert the nemesis that would surely follow its perpetration.

Her mind must have been riveted on South Africa when, quite recently, Ida Luckie sang:

> Alas, my country! Thou wilt have no need
> Of enemy to bring thee to thy doom . . .
> For not alone by war a nation falls.
> Though she be fair, serene as radiant morn,
> Though girt by seas, secure in armament,
> Let her but spurn the vision of the Cross;
> Tread with contemptuous feet on its command
> Of Mercy, Love and Human Brotherhood,
> And she, some fateful day, shall have no need
> Of enemy to bring her to the dust.

Some day, though distant it may be—with God

A thousand years are but as yesterday—
The germs of hate, injustice, violence,
Like an insidious canker in the blood,
Shall eat the nation's vitals. She shall see
Break forth the blood-red tide of anarchy,
Sweeping her plains, laying her cities low,
And bearing on its seething, crimson flood
The wreck of Government, of home, and all
The nation's pride, its splendour and its power.
On with relentless flow, into the seas
Of God's eternal vengeance wide and deep.
But, for God's grace! Oh may it hold thee fast,
My Country, until justice shall prevail
O'er wrong and o'er oppression's cruel power,
And all that makes humanity to mourn.

Also in Longman African Classics

Fools and other stories

Njabulo Ndebele

Winner of the Noma Award 1983

'And when victims spit upon victims should they not be called fools?
Fools of darkness.'

A taut, lyrical and compelling collection of stories, vividly bringing
to life the black urban locations of apartheid South Africa.

These are rich and enchanting stories told with the warmth of
childhood memory: of the adulation of a child for his trumpet-
playing uncle; a teenager's trial of endurance to prove himself
worthy of his street-gang; a child's rebellion against his parents
snobbish aspirations.

And the title story, *Fools*, tells with painful intensity of events sparked
by a meeting between a disgraced teacher, haunted by the impotence
of his present life, and a student activitist railing against those who
do not share his sense of urgency.

The author believes 'we have given away too much of our real and
imaginative lives to the opressor'. These beautiful award-winning
stories of township life in all its complexity are his answer.

'Njabulo Ndebele's first book represents the kind of beginning in
fiction that will prove to have altered the contours of our literature
... His storytelling is full-fleshed and elegant ... of thrilling
significance'.

Lionel Abrahams Sesame

'Brings with it an exhilerating current of fresh air ... solid, vibrant
prose'.

E'skia Mphahlele The Sowetan

ISBN 0 582 78621 5

Hungry Flames and other Black South African Short Stories

Edited by Mbulelo Mzamane

From the bare concrete of the crowded prisons to the carpeted drawing rooms of the new African middle class, these fifteen short stories by South Africa's finest Black writers paint an urgent and vital picture of contemporary South Africa.

These stories rank with those of Steinbeck and Hemingway in their honest portraits of working men and women in all their strengths and in all their weaknesses — all of them living in the shadow of the apartheid state.

Ove fifty years of Black South African writing in English is represented in this collection. A critical introduction describes the evolution of writing from the pioneers, such as R.R.R. Dhlomo and Sol Plaatje, through the urban 'jazz' style of the fifties to the more politicised Black Consciousness writers of the Sharpeville and Soweto eras.

The editor, Mbulelo Mzamane, is himself a distinguished writer of short stories and is the author of *My Cousin Comes to Jo'burg* (1982) and of *The Children of Soweto* (1982). He now teaches in the Department of English, Ahmadu Bello University, Zaria in Nigeria.

ISBN 0 582 78590 1

Scarlet Song

Mariama Ba

Translated by Dorothy S. Blair

Mariama Ba's first novel So Long a Letter was the winner of the Noma Award in 1980. In this her second and, tragically, last novel she displays all the same virtues of warmth and crusading zeal for women's rights that won her so many admirers for her earlier work.

Mireille, daughter of a French diplomat and Ousmane, son of a poor Muslim family in Senegal, are two childhood sweethearts forced to share their love in secret. Their marriage shocks and dismays both sets of parents, but it soon becomes clear that their youthful optimism and love offer a poor defence against the pressures of society. As Ousmane is lured back to his roots, Mireille is left humiliated, isolated and alone.

The tyranny of tradition and chauvinism is brilliantly exposed in this passionate plea for human understanding. The author's sympathetic insights into the condition of women deserve recognition throughout the world.

ISBN 0 582 78595 2